FOR GOD
AND
COUNTRY

FOR GOD AND COUNTRY

Memorable Stories from the Lives of Mormon Chaplains

Richard Maher

Horizon Publishers

INTERNATIONAL STANDARD BOOK NUMBER
0-88290-064-1

LIBRARY OF CONGRESS CATALOG CARD NUMBER
76-29307

Printed in the
United States of America
by

HORIZON
PUBLISHERS
Post Office Box 490
55 East 300 South
Bountiful, Utah 84010
292-1959

Introduction

Approximately 12,000 chaplains served in the armed forces during World War II. The Church of Jesus Christ of Latter-day Saints (Mormon) provided the United States military forces with forty-five.[1] Thirty-seven served in the army (including the Army Air Corps) and eight in the navy. Latter-day Saint (LDS) chaplains saw duty in all major theaters of war, and served at the side of their men at such famous battles as Salerno, Attu, the Battle of the Bulge, Guadalcanal, Iwo Jima, Biak, Leyte, and Okinawa. Two of them, Theodore E. Curtis and Reed G. Probst, received the Silver Star for bravery. Four others, Rueben E. Curtis, Gerald L. Ericksen, L. Marsden Durham, and Grant E. Mann, were awarded the Bronze Star for outstanding performances as United States chaplains. In addition to receiving the Bronze Star, L. Marsden Durham was also seriously wounded during the battle for Okinawa and awarded the Purple Heart; he later died in an accident while recuperating from his wounds in Hawaii.

The forty-five members of the Mormon Church chosen by the army and navy to serve as chaplains during the Second World War were a select group of men. They performed their duties in an exemplary manner. According to a 1945 report, the Chief of Army Chaplains, General Miller, and his assistant, General Rixey,..."both praised our chaplains very highly. They especially pointed out the activities of Chaplains Curtis and Probst. They said their work was outstanding."[2] Another typical commendation came from the commanding officer at Fort Lewis, Washington. He was quoted as saying of another LDS chaplain, "Chaplain Neslen is the best post chaplain I have ever served with."[3] A similar report came from the Philippines. When Roy M. Darley asked why he had been transferred

---

1. Their dates of appointment and branch of military service are contained in Appendix I.

2. J. Willard Marriott to the LDS First Presidency, June 19, 1945, "Chaplains Commission Papers," located in the Special Collection Section of the Harold B. Lee Library at Brigham Young University, Provo, Utah.

3. *Church News*, 5 August 1944.

to what seemed a tough assignment, the X Corps chaplain replied, "...over a period of several years I have seen the Curtis boys and Chaplain Probst in action, and I have decided that if you need a nasty job done, assign a Mormon chaplain."[4]

These men, in addition to being successful chaplains, attained high positions in the profession of their choice, after the conclusion of the war. This book, for the most part, is not about the achievements of these men as chaplains, but consists of interesting, spiritual, and humorous experiences that they encountered during their military service. Historical data, however, is used throughout the book to better acquaint the reader with the background to the particular experience.

For God and Country: Memorable Experiences from the Lives of Mormon Chaplains also involves related experiences during periods other than World War II. For example, several World War II chaplains served in Korea and received additional experiences that the author felt appropriate to include in this book. Further, two of the chaplain's wives, Doris (Warren) Bowers-Irons of Nephi, Utah, and Irene (Hailes) Ricks of Provo, Utah, contributed some outstanding stories when interviewed regarding their experiences with military life. An early chapter deals with the experiences of the first Mormon Chaplains, those who served in World War I.

The research for this work came mostly from the extensive use of oral history. The author first became involved with the oral history method of research during the summer of 1973 when Brigham Young University offered a seminar course on the subject. Dr. Gary Shumway, one of the nation's most prominent scholars on the subject from California State College at Fullerton, taught the course as a visiting professor. My thesis chairman, Dr. Thomas G. Alexander, advised me to take the course, and while doing so, Dr. Shumway encouraged me to interview World War II chaplains. Several worked on the campus of Brigham Young University, and I found interviewing them so delightful that I sought out other chaplains to interview. Because of my apparent interest in the subject, Dr. Alexander suggested that I continue interviewing World War II Mormon chaplains and write my master's thesis on the subject.

---

4. Interview of Roy M. Darley by Richard Maher, December 2, 1974, Charles Redd Center for Western Studies, Oral History Project: World War II LDS Chaplains. Copies of the tape and bound transcript of this and all other interviews are available in the manuscript section of the Harold B. Lee Library at Brigham Young University.

Oral history is a fascinating method of obtaining historical material. The author, however, recognizes the limitation of oral history interviews inasmuch as individual recall of events happening many years prior cannot always be relied upon to be completely accurate. Therefore, some minor errors regarding names, dates, and places might exist in some of the accounts.

A second source of information employed was the chaplain's personal files. Still another major source of material was the Chaplain Commission Papers found in the Special Collections Section of the Harold B. Lee Library at Brigham Young University. This data was donated by Dr. Ernest L. Wilkinson who, during World War II, served as a member of the Chaplain Commission in Washington, D.C. representing the Mormon Church. Additional major sources of information include material obtained from the *Improvement Era; The Deseret News, Church Edition; The Church News, L.D.S. Service Men's Edition;* and various books and articles pertaining to the subject of chaplains during the period of the study.

It is a pleasure to express my thanks to the many people who helped in the preparation of this book. I am grateful to all the chaplains for their cooperation in being interviewed, for their efforts to provide me with dates and other data, and for reading and correcting the stories pertinent to their specific experience. In some cases, they rewrote the specific experience in a manner to which displayed their personal style.

My special thanks to the Charles Redd Center for Western Studies for its help by furnishing the necessary tapes and typed transcripts used. I am extremely grateful to Dr. Thomas G. Alexander and John Bluth of the Charles Redd Center for their encouragement in doing oral histories with the many World War II chaplains. In addition, I would like to thank Dr. Dean Garrett. I worked with Brother Garrett at Bountiful High Seminary during the 1974-75 school year, and it was he who suggested that I compile the stories accumulated during the oral histories into a book for publication.

To Duane Crowther of Horizon Publishers, my thanks for suggesting I include stories of a patriotic nature and for editing the book.

Further, I would like to thank the following who were not among World War II Chaplains for facilitating the use of their stories in this book: Bishop A. C. Gonzales, Jr., of El Paso, Texas; Samuel W. Taylor of Redwood City, California; Castle H. Murphy, Orem, Utah; and Ben F. Mortensen, Provo, Utah. Appreciation is expressed to the late Doyle Green, formerly of the *Improvement Era*, for permission to use "Sergeant Stewart" by Ben F. Mortensen;

Bookcraft Publishers for permission to use "Faith, A First Principle of the Restoration" by Wendell O. Rich; and J. Malan Heslop for permission to use several stories previously published in the *Church News*.

Finally, I would like to express my gratitude to Diane and Brent John of Layton, Utah, and Tina and Craig Harrison of Clearfield, Utah, for reading the stories and making recommendations regarding the book.

It is hoped that the true accounts contained within this work will inspire the reader to attain higher goals in life because of the examples of a choice group of Latter-day Saint men who served their country, their men, and their God during World War II.

Contents

I
The First Mormon Chaplains

During World War I, the Mormon Church provided the U. S. Army with three chaplains. This was the first time in the history of the Church that it was afforded the opportunity to have chaplains serving with the U. S. military. The U. S. Army permitted the Mormon Church to choose any three men it wished. The three men selected were Brigham H. Roberts, Calvin F. Smith, and Herbert B. Maw.[1]

Brigham H. Roberts, the dean of Mormon chaplains, was also a General Authority of The Church of Jesus Christ of Latter-day Saints, serving then as a member of the First Council of Seventy. He was 61 years of age in 1918 when he received his appointment as chaplain of the 145th Utah Artillery. Because of his age, he had to obtain special permission to receive his appointment. In addition, when the 145th Artillery was assigned overseas, he was granted special permission by Secretary of War Newton D. Baker to go with his unit. He served honorably, and after the war, he returned to Salt Lake City to resume his ecclesiastical duties.

Calvin F. Smith, son of LDS Church President Joseph F. Smith, became the second chaplain. He was appointed as a chaplain at large and was assigned to the 91st Division at Fort Lewis, Washington. Many Utah draftees served with the 91st Division, thus enabling Chaplain Smith to work with LDS men. While overseas, Chaplain Smith served with the 362nd Infantry, 3rd Battalion and was wounded. He remained in Europe after the conclusion of the war and attended school in England. He later became an outstanding educator in the state of Utah, serving as the superintendant of the Granite School District of Salt Lake County.

Herbert B. Maw was the third World War I chaplain selected by the Mormon Church. He was appointed chaplain at large with the 89th division and was assigned to the 342nd Artillery which consisted of men mostly from Arkansas and western Missouri including many members of the Reorganized Church of Jesus Christ of Latter Day Saints. Maw served overseas and fought in a number

---

1. *Church News*, March 22, 1941.

of battles including the battle of the Argonne Forest. At the conclusion of the war, he served with the occupation troops, and in July 1919, returned to the United States.

He has had three successful professional careers during his lifetime. He began as a teacher at the LDS High school in 1916. In 1923 he was appointed as an instructor at the University of Utah where he taught Speech and Political Science. Later, he became involved with politics and served in the Utah Senate and, in 1941, became the governor of Utah. His third vocational choice was law, and although in his eighties, Mr. Maw presently practices law in Salt Lake City.[1] The stories used in this chapter are some of the experiences related to two of those chaplains, B. H. Roberts and Herbert Maw.

Brigham H. Roberts:
Inspiration was the Key to the Thanksgiving Psalm

The following story appeared in the Church News *November 22, 1975. Brother A. C. Gonzales Jr., of El Paso, Texas, related the account after an interesting search to document its authenticity. His tenacious endeavors eventually led him to Floyde G. Eyre, who stated that B. H. Roberts told him the story while driving him to a Church meeting.*

When the Utah National Guard was mustered into the regular Army shortly after the United States entered World War I, Elder B. H. Roberts, a member of the First Council of the Seventy, was also serving on reserve duty as chaplain of the 145 Field Artillery (1st Utah Battalion).

Having passed his 60th birthday, Elder Roberts was worried whether or not his physical condition would keep him from serving on active duty.

Seventeen years earlier, the U. S. Congress had denied him his seat as U. S. representative from the State of Utah, which refusal withheld from him the opportunity to serve his country.

Elder Roberts was a patriotic man and the congressional refusal had been a painful experience. He was now determined to do everything possible to avoid a second denial.

---

1. Interview of Herbert B. Maw by Richard Maher, November 9, 1974, Charles Redd center for Western Studies. Oral History Project: World War II LDS Chaplains.

Consequently, he spent many hours conditioning his body in order to pass the physical examination. Happily, he passed, and when his unit was called to active duty in August 1917, he became the first member of the Church to serve in the Chaplain's Corps of the U. S. Armed Forces.

The bitter anti-Mormon feeling of the preceding century had not completely died out during the early 1900s. Ministers of other denominations had been ardent in their antagonism to, and their denunciation of the Mormons.

This resentment became very apparent in France during the Thanksgiving season of 1918.

The last Thursday in November fell shortly after Nov. 11, 1918, the signing of the Armistice. Everyone was grateful for the ending of hostilities and Thanksgiving Day found the American "doughboys" gathered in one grand Thanksgiving service.

The large attendance included high-ranking military officers. The services were conducted by the chaplains, who were seated on the grandstand.

Elder Roberts was relegated to one of the rear seats. He had not been asked in advance to participate on the program, therefore, it was with great surprise that he heard the chaplain in charge announce: "Elder Roberts, the Mormon chaplain from Utah, will now step up and read the Thanksgiving Psalm."

Elder Roberts had never heard of the term "Thanksgiving Psalm" but, hiding his personal embarrassment and possible impending embarrassment to the Church, he arose and walked to the podium, not knowing what he should say.

Years later he testified that, during the long walk to the front, he distinctly heard an audible voice announce: "The 100th Psalm." It was as clear as though another person had spoken at his side.

Elder Roberts faced the crowd, paused, then opened his Bible and read Psalm 100:

> Make a joyful voice unto the Lord, all ye lands. Serve the Lord with gladness: come before his presence with singing. Know ye that the Lord he is God: it is he that hath made us, and not we ourselves; we are his people, and the sheep of his pasture.
>
> Enter into his gates with thanksgiving, and into his courts with praise: be thankful unto him, and bless his name. For the Lord is good; his mercy is everlasting; and his truth endureth to all generations.

After Brother Roberts had closed his Bible and was returning to his seat, he noticed that his fellow chaplains refused to look at him; their eyes were immovably fixed on the floor.

It was then he realized that his part on the program had been a deliberate attempt to embarrass him, and to embarrass the Church and the priesthood. He acknowledged the help which he had received from the Lord in his moment of need and, when he returned to his tent that night, he reread the Book of Psalms, observing that the 100th Psalm contained the most pertinent and appropriate sentiments on Thanksgiving.

Herbert B. Maw:
A Call From the First Presidency

With a Church membership in the millions, it is obvious that the First Presidency of the Mormon Church would not know every individual member of the Church. Nevertheless, Church leaders, to the surprise of many, are well informed regarding the activities and devotion of many Church members. Their awareness surprises and even shocks some when one answers his telephone and the party on the other end says, "This is the First Presidency calling." Just such an experience happened to Herbert B. Maw.

For the United States, World War I began in April 1917. Herbert Maw enlisted in the army shortly thereafter, and after passing an assortment of tests, went to Kelly Field, Texas, to train as an air cadet. He enjoyed flying even though it was hazardous. At that time, flying airplanes was a dangerous occupation. Aircraft had few if any instruments, and pilots often flew without parachutes. Nevertheless, he looked forward to getting his wings, but a telephone call changed his plans.

One afternoon Maw was told to report to headquarters as he had an urgent telephone call waiting for him. Arriving at headquarters, he picked up the phone and said, "Hello, this is Herbert Maw."

The voice on the other end startled him, "This is Charles W. Penrose of the First Presidency of the Mormon Church."

For an instant he thought, what had I done. Why would a member of the First Presidency be calling me? He was completely flabbergasted that a member of the First Presidency had even heard of Herbert Maw let alone make a call to him. He thought it must be some sort of joke and replied, "Are you kidding?"

"Indeed I am not."

Indeed he wasn't. It was no joke. A member of the First Presidency was on the other end of the telephone. "What can I do for you?" he asked.

"Herbert, the United States government has, for the first time in the history of the Church, allowed us to provide the army with Mormon chaplains. They have allowed us to choose three men, any three we wish. We have chosen Brigham H. Roberts of the First Council of Seventy, Calvin F. Smith, the son of President Joseph F. Smith, and you. Herbert B. Maw, you are the third man we have selected."

It must have been both shocking and exhilarating for Maw to learn that out of all the qualified and worthy Latter-day Saints, he was one of the three men selected by the First Presidency to represent the Mormon Church.

He replied, "Thank you for your confidence."

"Good, we will see you in Salt Lake City before you report for your new assignment."

President Penrose hung up and the conversation ended. Herbert Maw must have felt like walking on air. After all, not eveyone gets a call from the First Presidency.

Herbert B. Maw:
A Blessing From the First Presidency

Often priesthood bearers are called upon to bless members of the Church of Jesus Christ for a variety of reasons—health, precaution, protection and healing are examples. Any worthy member holding the Holy Melchizedek Priesthood is authorized under God's law to administer certain blessings. Not often, however, does one receive a blessing under the hands of the three High Priests of the First Presidency. During the First World War, Chaplain Herbert Maw received such a blessing. He feels that that blessing afforded him inspiration that saved his life many times during the war.

While in Salt Lake City for a short leave before reporting for his first assignment as an army chaplain at Camp Funson, Kansas, Chaplain Maw took the opportunity to visit with the First Presidency. He wanted to see if they had any special instructions for him. President Joseph F. Smith instructed him to "...live as you have always lived and be an example to LDS manhood..." Maw thanked him for the confidence that he had in him and for this counsel. As he started to leave his office, President Smith said, "Chaplain Maw, would you like to have a blessing?"

He never expected such an honor, but he thought, "How many times in one's life does one receive an offer to get blessed by the First Presidency?" He replied, "I would love one."

He sat in the center of the room, and President Smith called upon Anthon Lund to pronounce the blessing. Chaplain Maw hoped that he would guarantee his return safely from the war. President Lund didn't grant his wish, but did say, and he will always remember those words, "...we bless you with every protection, guidance and inspiration that a representative of The Church of Jesus Christ of Latter-day Saints should have in a war...." The blessing lasted only a few moments, but for Herbert Maw it was a moment to cherish always. He thanked them for the blessing and left, feeling assured that if he lived worthily, he would return home safely.

As it turned out, those few words were all inclusive. Often in combat the chaplain felt that he was protected from death or injury because of his blessing. He survived many close calls because the spirit prompted him to move from place to place. He seemed to have had a special sense which helped him recognize when he was safe and when he was in danger. At one time, his unit was under fire for 65 consecutive days, and while located in a building in a small French town, he received a feeling that he had to move. The army had issued orders that all army personnel were to stay put. The enemy was using aircraft and balloons to observe their positions, and the army didn't want any unnecessary movement that might give away their position. He thought, "Should I move and disobey a direct order from military authorities, or should I move and obey the promptings of the spirit?

He faced a real dilemma, but for some unknown reason a thought entered his mind that gave him the answer. He thought of Wilford Woodruff and how he had tied his horse under a large tree for the night, and while he slept, he had a dream that lightning hit the tree and it fell, killing his horse. Wilford Woodruff awoke in the middle of the night, and obeyed the prompting of the spirit which he considered a warning to take action. He moved his horse. That night, lightning did hit the tree, and it fell on the spot where his horse had been tied.

That did it. Elder Maw had received the answer to his predicament. He moved immediately, even though it meant disobeying a military order. He moved down the street and hadn't gone half a block when a shell hit the very room that he had just left. Every soldier in that room died or was wounded. He credits the prompting of the spirit for saving his life because of the blessing he received from President Anthon Lund.

Herbert B. Maw:
An Unanticipated Parachute Jump

*Often the young seek danger and excitement with no more
thought than "It's fun to try something new." During the First
World War, the "baloney balloonist" had a very hazardous job.
Without any protection, he very often faced a determined enemy
trying to shoot him and his balloon down. The following story
tells of Chaplain Maw's harrowing experience 2,000 feet above the
ground in a "baloney balloon."*

During World War I, military forces on both sides used aircraft and "baloney balloons" to observe the activities of one
another. "Baloney balloons" received their name because they
were shaped like a tube of baloney. The balloons were attached to
cables and raised to about 2,000 feet altitude so that an observer
could watch the activities of the enemy and relate the information
to those on the ground. The balloonist had no protection, and was
at the mercy of enemy planes. When in danger, his only chance to
survive was to parachute out.

Chaplain Maw had a friend who happened to be a balloonist.
One day his friend asked if he'd like to go up with him to see the
view. "Chaplain, how would you like to go up in a balloon? I'm
going up soon, and I'm quite sure I can get permission for you to
go with me, because it's been quiet up there lately."

Being young enough to try anything once, Chaplain Maw
replied, "I think I'd like that fine."

The balloonist received permission from his commanding
officer to take Maw with him. They entered the balloon and got
into harnesses, a rope that ran from the back of their necks to a
folded parachute in a bag on the side of the basket. As they as-
cended, the balloonist pointed to the parachutes and said, "If an
enemy plane comes, we use these." Neither thought it would be
necessary.

As the balloon rose, the figures on the ground grew smaller
and smaller. In contrast, the expanse of the countryside grew
larger until Maw could see for miles. He saw the small French
towns scattered throughout the countryside, and, in addition,
could see the enemy. He thought as he watched the enemy location,
"It's strange, but just over there there are men who are trying to
kill me—men I don't even know." While he was deep in thought,
an enemy plane suddenly approached from the east, firing at the

balloon. He heard the bullets whiz by. His friend yelled, "Let's get out of here," and he leaped over the side, leaving Chaplain Maw alone in the balloon. The sounds of the bullets told him he didn't have much choice except to jump. Before he did, however, he prayed, giving God a thousand reasons why he should live and why his parachute should open. Over the side he went, and felt the rush of air against his face as the parachute was jerked from the bag and began to open. He had a frightening few seconds, but when he looked up and saw the bright white parachute above him, he sighed and said two words, "Thanks, Lord."

Herbert B. Maw:
Combat Conditions During World War I

During World War I, much of the fighting was done in trenches. According to Chaplain Maw, trench warfare was a miserable experience.

Chaplain Maw felt that the worst living environment that the doughboy of World War I encountered was that of living in the trenches filled with mud—mud up to his ankles. The soldier never felt dry or comfortable, and trying to sleep in the slimy, wet and murky substance was almost impossible. If he slept at all, it would be in a small foxhole that he would dig around the trench. The foxhole would be just deep enough so that no part of the body extended above the ground. In this manner he was able to sleep except during the rainy season. During the rainy season, he would wake only to find his little bed full of water.

He not only had to put up with the mud, but found unwanted guests in the trenches. The "cooties," better known as body lice, covered his clothing. The trenches were full of them, and a soldier couldn't spend more than a day in the trenches without being covered with lice which chewed upon him all the time.

Because of the miserable conditions, the soldier was sent to rest areas every few weeks where he stayed for a period of two weeks or less. There he would be deloused. His clothing would be taken from him and cleaned to get rid of all the bugs. The army called it a rest area, but the soldier didn't get much rest as the area was generally located within the range of enemy artillery which continued its bombardment.

In addition to having to live and fight under deplorable living conditions, the doughboy also faced the prospect of dying or being wounded by poison gas. The soldier, however, did not fear the poison gas as much as he feared the "mustard gas." He had a mask which protected him from the poison gas, but he had no protection against mustard gas. The Germans would spread the mustard gas over open fields, and the advancing allied army had no way of detecting its presence until one became contaminated. As the soldier marched across the field, his feet and body would get sweaty, and the mustard gas would get into his pores and burn, especially between the legs. It was a most terrifying experience to hear a soldier scream with pain. Those contaminated had to be sent to the hospital where it took, in some cases, months for them to recover from the effects of the dreaded gas.

The soldier of World War I fought under miserable conditions. Like troops who served in other wars before and after with their hardships, disease, pain and death, they concluded that *War is Hell.*

Herbert B. Maw:
A World War I Chaplain's Duty

In peace or war, a chaplain exists to serve—to serve the needs of his men. The following account describes some of the typical duties of a combat chaplain of World War I.

Chaplain Herbert B. Maw found the duty of a chaplain overseas to be quite different from what he had expected. He found that a chaplain had little opportunity to provide religious services. Religion became an individual matter overseas as the men were not allowed to assemble in large groups. The army recommended that no more than two or three men could meet together in the war zone. That caused Chaplain Maw to work with the soldiers on an individual basis rather than on a group basis, and as a chaplain, he served where his men needed him the most. In combat, they needed him at the front in the trenches. He spent almost four consecutive months under constant fire, performing a variety of jobs including administering first aid to the wounded, and in some cases, applying tourniquets to shut off the flow of blood to save the individual's life. In addition, he saw to it that the more seriously wounded were removed from the front and returned to advance medical stations for more professional attention. Some of the badly wounded men made confessions to him. A soldier after confessing his sins would often say, "Chaplain, have I done everything I should do to be saved?"

Chaplain Maw made them feel better by answering, "Yes, soldier, you have done everything that you can do to be saved." That reply appeared to make the dying man feel much better.

Other duties performed by the chaplain included keeping track of those who died, and burying the dead at the front. When a soldier was killed in the front lines, the chaplain buried him in a shallow grave near the spot where he died. He marked the grave in order that the army later could identify the body when it dug it up and removed it to a permanent military cemetery.

One of the primary duties of all chaplains lies in the area of counseling. Chaplain Maw counselled many men who were lonely and homesick, and talked to many others who were brokenhearted because they had received "Dear John" letters from their sweethearts. But, the greatest problem the men brought to the World War I chaplain seemed to be fear. Yes, some of them were so tense with fear that they lost their equilibrium. Chaplain Maw recalled one soldier who went insane. He went crazy, and started to run toward the enemy line, screaming. He had to be tackled, hit on the head and dragged back to his own lines. Many soldiers came to him because of fear. He recalled several saying, "Chaplain, you aren't scared like we are, are you?"

Chaplain Maw knew fear, but he had received a blessing which comforted him, and he replied, "I ask the Lord to protect me, and I know he will."

That reply seemed to assure the men that through prayer they would be comforted, and for a while, anyway, they seemed to lose their tenseness and fear, because they had gone to the Lord seeking help.

The World War I chaplain provided a variety of services for his men. It was a tiring job always being on the move visiting with the men, but Chaplain Maw felt good about his duty, because he had made people feel better. That's the way it is with chaplains. They make people feel better.

Herbert B. Maw:
The Armistice, November 11, 1918

World War I finally ended. The world referred to that day as Armistice Day and it became a celebrated holiday. To this day, many veterans pause at 11:00 a.m. for a moment of silence. Chaplain Maw described the last barrage.

Those who fought in the First World War will recall that in November of 1918 the word had been received that the Armistice would occur on November 7th. The fighting men rejoiced as they looked forward to peace. But November 7th came and went and no cease fire. What had happened? What had gone wrong? The men were bitter in their disappointment, and when informed that the cease fire would officially take place at 11:00 a.m. on November 11th, nobody believed it. The men had been fooled once and had gotten their spirits high, only to be bitterly disappointed. This time they would not be fooled. Nevertheless, the official word came that the cease fire would indeed occur on November 11th, but the men refused to rejoice as they didn't want to face disappointment again.

At approximately 10:30 a.m. on November 11, 1918, both sides opened up with a terrific barrage of fire power. Every cannon and gun from both sides fired for half an hour, but promptly at 11:00 a.m. the firing stopped, and World War I came to a close. Then something strange happened. Chaplain Maw recalled how everyone became excited and happy that the war was over. The Germans and the American soldiers crawled out of their trenches, and ran to greet one another. It was hard to believe that they had been mortal enemies, and that they had been trying to kill one another. Then they were there on the battlefield joking, laughing and exchanging gifts. All the hatred that had been built up on both sides suddenly disappeared. It was indeed a strange experience.

But what about those who died during the last barrage, the last unnecessary firing. What did it prove?

Herbert B. Maw:
A Tribute to the American Soldier of World War I

Chaplain Maw described the American soldiers who fought during World War I as great men. They not only displayed bravery under enemy fire, but also showed great individual character. Their character was never better demonstrated than during the occupation of Germany.

In December 1918, Chaplain Maw's unit was assigned to occupy a small town in the Rhineland near Trier, Germany. The Allied Command required the citizens of the town to share their homes with the occupying forces, and Chaplain Maw was assigned to the home of the mayor.

The German people were frightened of the Americans. They had been fed a barrage of propaganda by the German government about the brutality of the American soldiers. When the doughboys arrived, the people were living in mortal terror, because they expected the Americans to slaughter everyone of them. To the surprise of the local people, nothing of the sort happened. They noticed that the visitors took no advantage of anyone and this was a revelation to them. Had they been wrong about the Americans? Apparently they decided they had been, and after a few days, their attitude changed toward the American servicemen, and the people from two great nations, the Germans and the Americans, struck up a great friendship.

Maw became good friends with his host, the mayor, and in the course of one of their conversations, the mayor said, "Chaplain, I don't know whether or not you are aware of this, but this whole town was absolutely terrified of your people. We were terrified when we learned of your coming. Our government had told us that you were a cruel and brutal people, and we should expect the worst. You are nothing like that. In fact, your soldiers treat us better than did our own soldiers."

The chaplain recognized that statement to be quite a compliment to the doughboys of World War I.

II
LDS Naval Chaplains

Of the approximately 3,000 chaplains that served in the United States Navy[1] during World War II, The Church of Jesus Christ of Latter-day Saints provided only eight. Four of the eight served overseas, while the remainder served at various locations within the United States.

LATTER-DAY SAINT NAVAL CHAPLAINS
THAT SERVED DURING WORLD WAR II

Name	Date of Appointment as Chaplains in the United States Naval Reserve
John W. Boud	July 31, 1941
Milton J. Hess	March 10, 1942
Glen Y. Richards	September 10, 1942
A. Gifford Jackson	October 23, 1942
Rex L. Christensen	June 9, 1943
Elbert R. Simmons	November 20, 1944
Jack B. Watkins	January 14, 1945
Briant G. Badger	March 20, 1945

World War II saw the first member of the Mormon faith appointed as a Navy Chaplain. John W. Boud of Salt Lake City received his appointment July 31, 1941, and was on active duty at San Diego Naval Station on December 7, 1941, when the Japanese attacked Pearl Harbor.

Milton J. Hess:
A Mormon Chaplain Preserves the Glenn Cunningham Story

Glenn Cunningham had the distinction of being the world's fastest miler during the 1930's. He set the world's record of 4:06.7.

---

1. During World War II, Navy Chaplains also served men of the United States Marine Corps.

*That feat, in itself, was remarkable, but the story behind the man
that became a world's champion is even more memorable. Cunningham had been told by his doctors when he was eight years old that
he would be a hopeless cripple for the rest of his life. Mormon
Chaplain Milton J. Hess of Farmington, Utah was so impressed
with the famous miler that he asked him to speak to a group of
LDS servicemen at the base. The story of Glenn Cunningham's
courage and determination to overcome a tremendous handicap
was an inspiration to the Mormon chaplain.*[1]

Chaplain Milton J. Hess became acquainted with the famous
miler at the 11th Naval District Headquarters in San Diego, California. One afternoon he dropped into his office and had a talk
with him about the clean life and the Word of Wisdom.

At that time, it is quite likely every American had heard of
Glenn Cunningham. He came from a small Kansas town, and,
when eight years old, met with a tragic accident that caused the
death of his brother, and left him crippled.

It happened in 1916. He and his brother arrived at the small
schoolhouse early one morning to light the kerosene stove to warm
the school. As they struck the match, an explosion occurred which
caused the school to burn like an inferno. Glenn's clothing caught
on fire, and overcome by the flames, he collapsed. When he awoke,
he found himself at home in his bed all bandaged and suffering
terrible pain. Both legs were burned, and one was shriveled so
badly that it was three inches shorter than the other.

The doctors gave up hope and told his parents that he couldn't
possibly live, but he did. Again the doctors predicted that he would
never walk again. They told his parents that he would be a hopeless cripple. Glenn believed differently, and made up his mind that
he would not only walk, but would run as well as anyone. Over-
coming his handicap didn't come easily. It took time, work, and
determination. Every night after his parents massaged and exercised
his little legs, Glenn would continue to exercise and massage them
until he became so tired that he would fall asleep. This continued
for years, until he was able to walk on crutches. His first attempt
to walk caused him great pain, but he bore it. Later he put away
the crutches only to walk with greater pain, but he overcame that
also. He started running, and by the time he became a junior in
high school he made the track team, and as a senior, he became its
star.

---

1. Letter, Milton J. Hess to Harold B. Lee, 13 January, 1945.

Because of his athletic ability, he won a scholarship to the University of Kansas where he became a long distance runner, the mile being his specialty, and in 1931, he won the NCAA title. Three years later at Princeton University, with 25,000 screaming fans watching, Glenn Cunningham ran his greatest race and set the world's record for the mile at 4 minutes, 6.7 seconds. That was the man with whom Chaplain Hess talked about the clean life.

"Glenn, I understand that you do not drink alcoholic beverages, indulge in any form of tobacco, and abstain from drinking tea and coffee. Is that right?"

"That's right, Chaplain. In fact, I don't even drink Coca Cola. I don't believe in putting poison in my body."

"Glenn, I'm a Mormon, and our Church has a commandment called the Word of Wisdom. It states that man should not partake of alcohol, tobacco, tea or coffee. Did you know Mormons believed that?"

"No, I didn't, but it's a good rule."

"We have lots of young Mormons here at San Diego. I was wondering if you wouldn't mind speaking to a group of these young men regarding your beliefs toward taking care of one's body."

"I'd love to."

Chaplain Hess set up the fireside and he spoke to the young servicemen. A total of 618 showed up to hear him talk on how he overcame his handicap. He also spoke on the importance of the body and how he treated his. He gave an inspirational talk, one of the finest ever heard on the subject of courage and the Word of Wisdom. His talk had a great impact upon the men, because it came from a third party, so to speak, one who was not a member of the Church.

As the chaplain drove Glenn home that evening, he told Hess of an incident that occurred to him while in a major city several years before. "One day while sitting in my hotel room in New York City after a track meet, the phone rang and a person asked me if he could come up and talk with me for a few minutes. I consented, and when the man came in he said, 'Glenn, I don't want to take up much of your time so I have this contract made out for your endorsement of our _____ tobacco. You sign here and you can name your own price.' "

"I looked the man straight in the eyes and said, '*I don't know how much money your company has, but it hasn't enough to get me to put my name on that contract.*' "

Milton J. Hess:
A Sailor Healed Through Faith[1]

And again, to some it is given to have faith to be healed;
And to others it is given to have faith to heal.
And again, to some is given the working of miracles;
                    Doctrine and Covenants 46:19-21

Priesthood holders who are asked to administer to and bless
the sick recognize that their faith and the faith of the one being
blessed are essential ingredients in the power of healing. Chaplain
Hess asked a very sick Latter-day Saint sailor, "Do you have the
faith?"

On Christmas eve 1944, Chaplain Hess received a telephone
call from the naval hospital informing him that a critically ill
young man named Leroy Osler from Nephi, Utah wanted to see
him. He asked for the chaplain by name, but Hess didn't know
him. Nevertheless, he went to see him at the hospital and learned
that he had scarlet fever. The doctors had placed him in the isola-
tion ward, and in order to see him, Hess had to put on a hospital
gown and a face mask. A nurse then escorted him to his bedside.
Osler had an extremely high fever and looked very sick. The chaplain spoke to him for a moment before he interrupted saying,
"Chaplain Hess, would you administer to me?"
"Do you have the faith to be healed?" he asked.
"Yes, I do."
"Then I will do it."
He had his oil with him, but had never performed both the
anointing and sealing by himself. He called upon Heavenly Father
to give him the strength, faith and power to help this young man
and as he sealed the anointing with a blessing, he received the con-
firmation from the spirit, and felt that this boy would be all right.
After the blessing, they chatted for a few moments, but because of Osler's weakened condition, Chaplain Hess knew he wasn't
in any mood for small talk so he left and went home.
Two days later, he happened to be in the hospital for another
reason, but while there, decided to check on Leroy Osler. He went
to his ward, and before the chaplain could ask how he was, a nurse

_____

    1. Interview of Milton J. Hess by Richard Maher, October 17, 1974,
Charles Redd Center for Western Studies, Oral History Project: WW II LDS
Chaplains.

who had been on duty the night he visited Leroy rushed up to him all excited and said, "Chaplain, a very unusual thing happened to Osler. When you came in to talk to that boy, his fever was 105, and just a few minutes after you left, his temperature went down to 99 degrees. It was like a miracle, a real miracle."

Yes, nurse, it was a miracle, and he knew the reason why. She didn't. She didn't know anything about the Mormon Church. She didn't know about the power of the priesthood. She didn't know that his amazing recovery was due to the will of the Lord. She didn't know of Seaman Osler's belief that "he who has faith to be healed will be healed."

J. Duffy Palmer:
Prayers Are Answered at Iwo Jima

While in a Hawaiian hospital recuperating from wounds received at Iwo Jima, Marine Sergeant J. Duffy Palmer wrote to LDS Chaplain John Boud telling him of his experience at Iwo.[1] The following four accounts are based upon J. Duffy Palmer's experiences on Iwo Jima.

I want to tell you how great the power of prayer really is, and what great comfort there was in knowing our Heavenly Father was with my brother and me at all times on Iwo Jima.

Every night and morning and usually many times between, my brother Belton and I would lay in our foxhole, clasp each others hands and pray to our Heavenly Father for wisdom, strength, courage and protection from all adversaries, whether seen or unseen. I want to tell you he always answered our prayers, and many times we received that strength, courage, or that special protection.

On one occasion we dug in and got settled for the night when word reached us that the enemy had started to counter-attack in full force. We prayed hard and as humbly as we knew, because we were frightened, so much that we seldom stopped shaking and trembling. We asked the Lord to provide our unit with the strength to stop the enemy forces. After a few hours of battle, we stopped the attack, and we knew that the Lord answered our prayers directly. With our hearts full, we thanked our Heavenly Father for all his goodness.

The Lord answered our prayers on another occasion when I received a very dangerous assignment from my commanding officer.

---

1. *Church News*, July 7, 1945.

Our unit had dug in near some Japanese markers. The Japanese placed markers in all areas on the hill to enable them to know the range and zero in on us with their artillery and other fire power. When our forces came in contact with or close to those markers, the enemy opened up with everything they had, and by using those markers as a guide, made their fire power extremely accurate and a menace to the marines.

My commanding officer came forward to speak to me. "Sergeant, do you see those markers out there on your left flank?"

I saw three very plainly visible markers, and also knew the enemy could see them from any location on the hill above, and they could rain down their fire power on anyone trying to destroy them. I answered, "Yes, Sir. I see them."

"I want you to take some men and go out there and cut them down."

Reluctantly I answered, "Yes sir."

After he left, I gathered my men together and explained the assignment. They said nothing. They were all so young. One only sixteen—I was the oldest man in the unit at twenty-three. As I looked in those young faces I saw fear—fear such as I had never seen before. I didn't have the heart to ask any of them to go out to what appeared to be certain death.

I went to my foxhole with Belton, and asked "Will you go with me to cut down those markers?"

"Duffy, you know I will. I will go where and when you give the word."

We worked out a plan. We decided that I would cut the markers down and Belton would give me cover. We knew that we couldn't stop the mortar shells or the artillery, but we felt he could cover me from any rifle fire. Before leaving, we said our prayers. We prayed for strength and courage to accomplish the task, and for protection from the enemy.

As we left the foxhole, something strange happened. All the Japanese firing stopped. It became quiet. We went forward and got into our positions according to our plan. I crept forward until I reached the markers, and cut them down as Belton covered me. However, there was no need, because no one fired at me. But, no sooner had we returned to the safety of our foxhole, the enemy opened fire once again. We rejoiced and thanked our Heavenly Father for so miraculously answering our prayers and protecting our lives.

How great are the blessings poured out upon those who diligently seek his help.

Belton Palmer:
He Served to Save His Brother

The Songster wrote, "...The load doesn't weigh me down at all; He ain't heavy, he's my brother. Yes, he's my brother." Without regard for his own life, Belton Palmer went through heavy enemy fire three times to save the life of his brother, Duffy. This account was sent to Chaplain Boud by Duffy Palmer as he recuperated from his wounds in Hawaii.

My brother Belton and I hit the beach at Iwo Jima under intense enemy fire. I tried to get my men off the beach as fast as I could to keep them from getting hit. As we worked our way up a hill with enemy shells and artillery fire falling all around us, one of the corporals who had been quite close to me coming up the hill said, "Duffy, I'm getting out of here. It looks as though the entire Japanese Army is trying to kill you."

"O.K., go ahead."

Three days later that same corporal returned and said, "Duffy, can my squad dig in by you?"

"I thought you wanted to get as far away from me as you could."

"I did, but if ever I saw a man with a charmed life, it's you. Can I dig in next to you?"

I told him he could. Then I reflected on what he had said about my having a charmed life, and thought, "No, not charmed, but guided and blessed by one higher, oh, much higher than I."

The battle raged on and our unit found itself under continuous heavy fire. I was about 25 yards ahead of my unit and moving up when a mortar shell landed at my head so close that the blast of dirt completely covered me. A marine in a foxhole just to my left got killed, and my platoon sergeant came forward to help. He picked up the rifle of the marine who had just been killed, and looked back toward me shaking his head thinking, "they got Duffy." When he returned to the line, my brother asked him, "Is Duffy okay?"

The platoon sergeant didn't have the heart to tell him what he really thought. He said, "I think he's okay."

At about that moment, I crawled out from under the dirt, and looked over the edge of the hole and saw Belton. Yes, he was looking for a sign from me indicating that I was okay. I waved, assuring him I was alright.

The fighting on Iwo Jima was tough. Nevertheless, American Marines moved forward slowly against a very determined enemy. I received orders from the platoon leader, a Lieutenant, to move my men forward. I moved ahead about 25 yards of the main lines with my men following right behind. I told them that I was going to move forward again, and I wanted them to hold their positions until I motioned for them to move up. I left my foxhole and ran forward. I couldn't find any shell holes nearby for cover. The closest one was about 50 yards ahead and I ran full speed until I dove into one and felt safe. I knew I had to find a better way before my men could advance so I peered over the edge of my hole. As I signaled the men not to come up, I got hit! The bullets hit my neck, entered my chest, and came out my back. I tried to call for help, but I could not use my voice—no sound would come out.

I turned to my Heavenly Father for help. I knew that I was hit badly and that I didn't want to die. As I prayed for a long time, begging for my life, the Lord saw fit to restore my voice. The first words that I muttered were, "No God, not now, please not yet." Belton sensed that I was in trouble and he jumped to come to my aid. The Lieutenant grabbed him saying, "It's not possible to help your brother. I saw him raise up and he got hit in the head, there is no sense of both of you getting killed. You can't get through. No one could get through."

He didn't know my brother. No power on earth could have prevented him from coming to my aid. Belton was always there. All through the battle, he had watched over and protected me in everything I did. Time and time again he had covered me as I moved from foxhole to foxhole giving orders to my men or words of encouragement. In everything, he has been the most wonderful brother any fellow could have. After we are through this life, I hope he might say the same for me.

Unconcerned about his own safety, Belton headed out from the lines, with bullets flying all around him. He ran most of the way through the most intense enemy fire. No one believed that any mortal could get through, but Belton did—not once, but three times. Three times he went back and forth—risking his life for me, his brother. When he arrived, he knew that I was hit bad. He tore off my shirt and administered first aid. Then he annointed me with oil and blessed me before returning for a corpsman saying, "hang on Duffy, I'll get help and we'll get you out of here." He went back through heavy fire and returned with a corpsman who gave blood plazma to me. Belton made a third trip to get our

The Palmer Brothers in combat gear. Belton (left) went through intense enemy fire on Iwo Jima to bring his severely wounded brother, Marine Sergeant, Duffy (right) to safety.

troops to open fire on the hill above and, once again, made it through heavy fire. He told the marines to cover him and the corpsman as they were going to bring me out, and they did.

Three times my brother risked his life to save me. He went into an area that no one thought was possible to go through even once without being killed. Why was he able to do it? Because there is nothing impossible when God has his protecting arm around you. On that day, and at that place, he had his protecting arm around us.

Belton has remarked several times since Iwo Jima that he thought the reason he had been in the Marine Corps was just to save my life.

Mormon Chaplain Gifford Jackson arrived on Iwo Jima several months after the initial invasion, and while there, heard the story of the two Palmer brothers. He learned that they joined the marines together and made a pact that they would never leave one another. Because of marine tradition, they separated when Duffy was promoted to Sergeant, only to be reunited again when they demanded to be put back together on the beaches of Iwo Jima. Could Belton's remarks be true that he served only to save his brother?

Corporal Durkin:
It Works! It Works! Prayer Works!

Prayer had always been an important part of J. Duffy Palmer's life. However, there are countless others that do not pray at all. A fellow marine, Corporal Durkin, was just such a man. J. Duffy Palmer related the following account to Chaplain John Boud.

Just prior to landing at Iwo Jima, Belton, myself, and Tony Jarvis of Snowflake, Arizona attended a general Protestant service aboard our troop ship. The chaplain spoke on the subject of prayer. He said, "...Forget it men if you can't pray. It isn't that important. You do the fighting and I'll do the praying, and we will march through this together..." After the service, I spoke to him about his philosophy on prayer. I told him that he was wrong and that prayers are answered. He disagreed and we got into an argument. Unknown to me, a member of my company, Corporal Durkin overheard the argument. He was not a member of the LDS Church, but one evening, when the going got rough on Iwo Jima, he jumped into the foxhole Belton and I shared and said, "Sarge, I heard what you said to that chaplain on board ship. Is it true? Can God really save us through prayers?"

"You bet He can. I've seen His hand at work many times."

"Sarge, I need help. I'm frightened. Will you teach me to pray?"

That night, the three of us offered our prayers together. He felt better, and left saying, "Thanks, guys."

The next morning, a mortar shell landed directly in Corporal Durkin's foxhole, but failed to explode. In the middle of the battle-field with bullets flying everywhere and mortar and artillery shells exploding all about, the corporal jumped up yelling, "It works! It works! Prayer works! It really works!" He was so excited he didn't realize the danger he was in. Everyone thought he went crazy. Finally a marine nearby grabbed him and pulled him down and got him back into his foxhole.

Later, when the battle activity quieted down, the guys kidded him about his behavior. They told him that it wasn't his prayer that saved his life, but it was due to poor Japanese workmanship that caused the shell not to explode. They laughed at him, but no one could tell Corporal Durkin differently. He had a testimony that the Lord does indeed answer prayers.

J. Duffy Palmer:
I Don't Want Any Rum!

Even when facing possible death. Marine Sergeant J. Duffy Palmer refused to break the Word of Wisdom. He related the following incident to Mormon Chaplain John Boud.

After being wounded on Iwo Jima, my brother Belton and a navy corpsman took me back of the front lines where I was transferred to a hospital ship. Once aboard, I was placed in a ward with others. From the time I was wounded they kept plasma running in my arms. The doctor brought over a goblet of liquid and asked, "Would you please take some of this?"

"What is it?" I asked.

"Rum."

"No. I don't want any."

"Sergeant, you had better have some. You are going into shock, and if that happens, you don't have a chance."

The doctor kept insisting and I kept refusing and then stated, "The Lord has seen me through this far. He will see me the rest of the way."

The Lord did, and over the years I often wondered why he spared me.

The Lord works his will in many ways. It is the author's opinion that perhaps the Lord saw in J. Duffy Palmer a great spiritual leader, and that some time in the future He would call him to devote his time, talent, and leadership to him. He did. J. Duffy Palmer is presently the President of the Syracuse Utah Stake.

Bob Lee and Clarence Gale:
By Example and Precept

In 1943, Chaplain Milton J. Hess served with the Seabees in the Aleutian Islands. He tells the following story about two young

Mormons he met while assigned there, and the indelible impression that their behavior had upon him.[1]

Two very young servicemen, Bob Lee and Clarence Gale, who were perhaps 17 or 18 years of age, arrived in the Aleutians in 1943 as part of a replacement group. The army assigned them to share a tent with four other men. They belonged to a variety of religious denominations, and of the six in the group, two belonged to the Mormon Church, two to the Protestant Religion, one to the Catholic Church, and one was unaffiliated. During their first night together, one of the Mormon boys felt a desire to pray, but didn't know whether he should or not. He didn't know the others very well and wasn't sure how they would react and feared they might ridicule him. As he contemplated his dilemma, he heard one of the men say, "Quiet, Tex is saying his prayers." There on his knees with his head bowed, was Tex, the other Latter-day Saint, saying his prayers as though he were in the privacy of his own bedroom. Upon viewing Tex's behavior, the Latter-day Saint who lacked the courage to pray made a vow that he would never again be afraid or ashamed to pray in public. The next night both he and Tex knelt to pray while the other four watched in silence. On the third night as the two Mormons knelt to pray, one by one the other four boys joined with them in prayer. From that time on all six of the boys said their evening prayers on their knees together. In addition, each night they read and discussed the Bible. Thrilled from what he had witnessed, Chaplain Hess wrote, "I have often thought that God may have suffered this war to be in order that our youth might be scattered throughout the entire world in the work of disseminating this Gospel by example and precept. After seeing so many similar instances of the missionary work of our men in the service, I believe that the Church will make great strides as a result of this war."

Jack Dempsey:
I'm a Mormon Too

Jack Dempsey, the former heavyweight champion of the world, was visiting the fighting men in the Pacific during the second World War when LDS Chaplain A. Gifford Jackson had the oppor-

---

1. Letter, Chaplain Milton J. Hess to Thomas E. McKay, September 30, 1943.

tunity to meet him. The following is an account of that brief meeting.[1]

Chaplain Gifford Jackson spent many months on the island of Guam. During his stay on the island, he was introduced to Jack Dempsey, the former heavyweight champion of the world, by another chaplain. "Chaplain Jackson, I'd like you to meet Jack Dempsey."

They shook hands and Jack said, "Nice to meet you, Chaplain."

The Chaplain continued saying, "Chaplain Jackson is a Mormon Chaplain."

Jack Dempsey thrust out his hand and replied, "Well put'er there again chaplain, I'm a Mormon too."

A. Gifford Jackson:
The Attitude of a LDS Soldier Amputee

Often the difference between success and failure, happiness and sorrow, is one's attitude. Chaplain Gifford Jackson had an experience at Guam Island in 1945 where he met a man with a special attitude.[2]

One day while working in my office, I received a telephone call from one of the doctors at the hospital. He said, "Chaplain Jackson, we have a Mormon boy over here who is in bad shape. He was wounded on Okinawa and has lost both legs, one above the knee. He also lost four fingers on one hand. He would like to see a Mormon chaplain, can you come over?"

"Yes, I'll be right there." I left my office and drove to the hospital thinking, "What am I going to say to this young man?" I knew that he would be depressed. What could I say to a man who had suffered the way he had? I could think of nothing to say. When I arrived at the hospital I felt uncomfortable and quite helpless. As I approached his bed, he must have known that I was the Mormon chaplain because when I was within 15 feet of his bed, he smiled and said "Chaplain, it could have been worse."

With those few words I felt completely relieved and thought, "Both legs gone and part of his hand blown off, and he puts me at ease! He must be quite a guy." And he was. His special attitude

---

1. Personal Interview with President A. Gifford Jackson, October 27, 1975.
2. Ibid.

inspired others in the hospital. For example, one young man had to have his foot amputated. The doctors did everything they could to save it, but to no avail. It had to come off. The young man went into a state of depression until the LDS boy went to visit him. His special attitude and outlook convinced the young man that losing a foot wasn't any reason to give up.

That young Mormon serviceman returned home and went to accounting school. He was able to provide for his wife and daughter, and became active in disabled veterans activities.

Yes, attitude makes the difference.

Harrill S. Dyer:
How Blessed is that Word of Wisdom?

Chaplain John Boud convinced the commanding chaplain at San Diego of the truthfulness of the Word of Wisdom. Chaplain Dyer once said, "Jack, how blessed is that word of wisdom!" The Mormon chaplain relates the following experience.[1]

The commanding chaplain of the 14th Naval District, at San Diego, was Harrill S. Dyer. No finer gentlemen ever lived. Although he represented the Methodist faith, we became good friends. I taught him much about the beliefs of the Mormon Church. He became especially impressed with the Word of Wisdom. I suspected his great interest was due to his being a heavy smoker. At that time, he smoked between two and three packages of cigarettes a day. After learning about the Word of Wisdom, he quit smoking, and, like a reformer, tried to get everyone he knew to stop also. He would tell everyone how bad it was for their health. He was, however, unable to give up smoking permanently and after a couple of months, the tobacco habit was too much for him to overcome— and he started again.

Just prior to my receiving orders assigning me to Hawaii, Chaplain Dyer had a heart attack and was rushed to the hospital. When I visited him, he said to me, and I shall never forget those words, "Well, Jack, I guess you win. The doctor told me I can never touch cigarettes again." And I don't believe he ever did.

---

1. Interview of John W. Boud by Richard Maher, October 18, 1975, Charles Redd Center for Western Studies. Oral History Project: WW II LDS Chaplains.

Bill Andra:
Good Character Pays Dividends

One must learn in life to accept personal responsibility and the consequences of the decisions one makes. One LDS marine on Guam did just that, and, by doing so, showed his character. Chaplain A. Gifford Jackson had the following experience.[1]

During 1944 on Guam, Chaplain Gifford Jackson met Bill Andra, a very devoted Latter-day Saint. During Bill's spare time, he would go to headquarters and look through the service records of the men of the 3rd Marine Division. He would list the names and units of all those who came from Utah, Idaho, and Arizona. He would then seek them out to find out if they were members of the Church, his purpose being to get all Mormons to the 3rd Marine Division LDS services.

One evening, Bill received the assignment to police the mess line. During each meal, enlisted personnel policed the "chow line" to insure that there was no fighting or breaking into line. Usually, there were no problems, but on that particular evening a fight broke out in the line causing a great commotion. Because of the disturbance, Bill's commanding officer got involved and wanted to see the man who had been assigned to police the line. He learned that Bill Andra had not reported for duty that evening. He proceeded to investigate the matter by calling Bill to his office to get the facts.

"Bill, why weren't you on duty policing the "chow line" last night?"

"I'm sorry sir, I was at headquarters looking through some records and became so involved I didn't realize the time."

"I'm going to have to punish you, Bill, for not reporting to duty. You are going to have to spend some time in the Brig."

Bill went to the brig, but while there got a call to report to the commanding general. In the division Bill was a barber and he always cut the general's hair. He reported to the general and as he cut his hair, the general said, "Bill, why didn't you tell me you were in trouble. I would have helped you."

"Well, General, I made a mistake, and a person has to pay for his mistakes. I wasn't where I ought to have been and for that I was punished. I got exactly what I deserved."

---

1. Gifford Jackson interview.

Bill's honesty impressed the general so much that he made Bill Andra his orderly, the best assignment in the division.

Merrill Bickmore:
Life After Death

The first great land battle in the Pacific was at Guadalcanal. The victorious marines won possession of the island after many weeks of hard fighting. Merrill Bickmore, a member of the LDS Church, fought there. He later became wounded in the battle for Guam Island and returned to the San Diego Naval Hospital. At San Diego, Merrill met Chaplain Milton Hess, and related the following story dealing with life after death.[1]

Merrill Bickmore fought with the U.S. Marines at Guadalcanal and shortly thereafter, Bickmore's unit invaded Guam. He had a "buddy" named Victor. Shortly after the invasion of Guam, Merrill had a dream. He dreamed that Victor had been killed. The dream seemed so real that he woke his buddy in the middle of the night to tell him. "Victor, I had the most horrible dream. I dreamed that you were killed."

Victor replied, "Merrill, it's only a dream. Death and the thought of being killed is on everyone's mind now. Everyone has dreams like that. I'm not going to die. Go to sleep and don't worry about it."

Merrill thought perhaps he was right, that death was on everyone's mind at that time and he fell back to sleep. The next day, to Merrill's horror, Victor was killed just as he had seen it in the dream. He was shot by a sniper and died instantly.

Merrill found it hard adjusting to the loss of his buddy. He found it difficult to sleep. For a time he thought he would go crazy. He became depressed and no longer cared whether he lived or died. This continued for days and finally, one night Merrill Bickmore fell into a deep sleep. While asleep he had a dream. In the dream he saw Victor standing before him calling, "Merrill, it's me, Victor."

In his dream Merrill couldn't help but answer, "Victor, what do you want?"

"I don't want you to worry about me any longer. I'm okay. You go ahead and carry on."

---

1. Milton J. Hess interview.

The dream was so vivid Merrill awoke. He had always believed in the resurrection and life after death, but now he had a testimony of it. Victor came back to help him find the way out of his state of depression.

A few days later Merrill Bickmore received a chest wound from a sniper bullet and was returned to the United States Naval Hospital at San Diego, California. There he met a very pretty nurse and fell in love. She became converted to the Church and Chaplain Hess performed the marriage ceremony. Merrill Bickmore presently lives in the Los Angeles area. He recently served as president of the Torrance, California Stake.

Erling Jacobsen:
A Mormon Chaplain Aids a Fellow Member

When servicemen need help, they usually see the chaplain. Sometimes a chaplain can give them valuable assistance. Erling Jacobsen was lucky. He got help. The following experience happened to Chaplain A. Gifford Jackson.[1]

One day Chaplain A. G. Jackson was sitting in his office at the Receiving Ship on Treasure Island. This was where Navy personnel being transferred from one duty assignment to another would await their orders. Chaplain Jackson's office was always busy with men having all types of problems. This particular day a young blond fellow came into the office who had such an accent it was difficult to understand him. Chaplain Jackson thought to himself, this is one of the Swedes I have heard about from Minnesota.

The request this young man had was rather unusual. He wanted a three-day pass to take an ocean-going navigator's examination in San Francisco. After much questioning the following story unfolded. The young man was Erling Jacobsen from Norway. He had been on a whaling ship in the South Atlantic when the Germans invaded Norway. They received orders to put into an allied port and landed in Halifax, Nova Scotia. Erling Jacobsen was a member of the Church and because of this was able to obtain what amounted to a birth certificate and which opened the way for him to gain entrance into the United States. He was granted citizenship right away and then found himself in the Navy.

---

1. A. Gifford Jackson interview.

Chaplain Jackson made the necessary arrangements in order that Brother Jacobsen could take the examination. He passed the exam and this qualified him for an appointment as a commissioned officer. Erling went to various training schools and eventually ended up with a ship that saw duty in the Pacific.

He was an outstanding young man, almost idolized by the others aboard ship. He found an LDS girl whom he married and later was able to bring his immediate relatives from Norway to Seattle where he now makes his home and operates a successful fishing business.

Chaplain Jackson believes that Brother Jacobsen was guided to him where he received the necessary interest and help that might not have been forthcoming if he had talked to other chaplains on the base.

III
Stateside Experiences

War had raged in Europe, Asia, and Africa for two years prior to the United States formally entering into the conflict on December 8, 1941. Because of the uncertainty of world conditions, many Americans recognized the possibility that the United States might become a participant and the American Government prepared for war. In September 1940, the U.S. Congress passed the Selective

Uniforms worn by army chaplains prior to World War II included spurs. *Left to right:* Methodist Chaplain, Colonel Hall, Chaplain of Fort Douglas, Utah; LDS Chaplain, Theodore E. Curtis, Jr.; LDS Chaplain, Wayne Bennion; and LDS Chaplain, Rueben E. Curtis.

Service Act which provided for a peacetime draft, and many young Americans were drafted into military service. In addition, many serving in National Guard units were activated for a period of one year.

The rapid build-up of the services caused enormous problems for the military, including the procurement of personnel. This difficulty plagued all branches and departments including the Chaplain Corps. Many new chaplains had to be provided to meet the needs of the tens of thousands of new recruits and National Guardsmen who were called to serve. Among those called prior to the outbreak of hostilities were eleven Mormon chaplains.

The eleven chaplains representing the LDS Church served at various locations in the western United States. Major C. Clarence Neslen, a former mayor of Salt Lake City, served on active duty at San Luis Obispo, California with the 145th Field Artillery. Utah Governor George H. Dern had appointed him a chaplain of the 145th in 1926. Major Theodore E. Curtis and First Lieutenant George R. Woolley of the 115th Engineers were also assigned to San Luis Obispo, California. Called to active duty, Captain Reuben Curtis, who had served as a civilian Conservation Corps Chaplain for several years, was assigned to Camp Ord, California. Another civilian Conservation Corps member, First Lieutenant Reed G. Probst, was called to active duty and assigned to Fort Lewis, Washington where the army stationed many young Mormon soldiers. Captain Robert G. Gibbons served at the recreational center at Fort Douglas, Utah. First Lieutenant Orlando S. McBride, a chaplain in the Arizona National Guard, was stationed at Fort Sill, Oklahoma. The War Department attached First Lieutenant Howard Clark Evans to the Air Corps at Salt Lake City, Utah. First Lieutenant Milton G. Widdison served on active duty at Fort Warren, Wyoming, and John W. Boud, the first Mormon naval chaplain, was assigned to San Diego, California.

As the war progressed, thirty-four other Latter-day Saint men were to serve as military chaplains. The accounts recorded in this chapter tell some of their experiences while serving in the United States.

Theodore E. Curtis, Jr.:
Chastity

"Only one thing can stop the spread of venereal disease, and that is chastity." (Mark E. Petersen)

The leaders of the Mormon Church constantly teach its members, young and old, male and female to be morally clean. Does it pay off? Chaplain Theodore E. Curtis had an experience which indicates it does.

Mormon Chaplain Theodore E. Curtis, Jr., was stationed at San Luis Obispo in the autumn of 1941 when Major General Storey, the commanding general of the 40th Division, called his staff together to express his concern for the sudden increase of venereal disease throughout his division.

At that meeting, he asked the division chaplain who was not a member of the Mormon Church, "Chaplain, why is it that we have had this sudden increase of V.D. in our division?"

"I don't know sir."

"Well, can you tell me this, how is it that we have three regiments that have hardly any problem with V.D. compared to the others which are plagued with it?"

"Which regiments are those sir?"

"The 115th Engineers, and the 145th and 222nd Artillery."

"Well sir, those are Utah National Guard regiments made up largely of Mormons. The Mormon Church has a high standard of purity, and it teaches its young men and women to keep themselves clean. I believe that the lives of the men in those three regiments exemplify the teachings of the Mormon Church."

General Storey replied, "I wish to God that those teachings were the accepted teaching of the United States as a whole."[1]

Theodore E. Curtis, Jr.:
An Effective Communication System

While stationed at San Luis Obispo, California, Chaplain Theodore Curtis, Jr., because of his position as chaplain at the nearby military installation, attended meetings with members of the San Luis Obispo Ministerial Association. The following interesting experience occurred at one of those meetings.[2]

At one of the weekly meetings of the San Luis Obispo Ministerial Association, a subject of great importance was discussed which caused association members to take a firm stand on a

1. *Some Experiences—World War II Period of Service*, Chaplain Theodore E. Curtis, Jr. (Unpublished), p. 3.

2. *Ibid.*, p.6.

particular issue. The clergymen felt it so important that they wanted all their members to be aware of the topic and to take a stand with them. However, they recognized a problem existed trying to inform all their people because many did not attend church on Sunday. Therefore, a discussion began on how to inform everyone in the congregation. The ministers presented several ideas, but none seemed appropriate or workable. Finally one asked, "Chaplain Curtis, how would your church handle the situation?"

Chaplain Curtis arose and walked to the chalkboard and said, "the Mormon Church has a definite system to disseminate information. For example, if the leaders of the church had a message that they considered of such universal importance that they wanted each member to receive it, the following would happen." Chaplain Curtis proceeded to draw an organizational chart on the blackboard showing the complete line of priesthood authority from the First Presidency to the individual member. "The First Presidency would contact approximately 200 Stake Presidents who in turn would inform the bishops in the stake. The bishops would call the three priesthood leaders in the ward, and the priesthood leaders would get in touch with the approximately 40 ward teachers under their area of responsibility. Finally, the ward teacher would contact the individual family for which he was responsible and relay the message."

"In addition to the use of the priesthood line, the organization at the ward level could also work through its Relief Society. The Relief Society is a women's organization, and, like the priesthood ward teacher program, has a program similar to the men's. It is called the visiting teaching program. The visiting teachers in the ward have the responsibility to contact all the women of the ward at least once a month."

"Gentlemen, using the procedure as outlined, every member of the Mormon Church would be provided with the information that Church leaders wished them to have within two or three days."

"Amazing!" exclaimed one clergyman.

The religious leaders of San Luis Obispo had listened attentively and courteously to the Mormon chaplain. When he finished, they expressed their appreciation for the information, but Chaplain Curtis could sense an unasked question lingered uppermost in their minds: *but how do you get all those people to do it?*

Reuben E. Curtis:
Prayer Stopped Their Profanity

Early in 1942, Chaplain Reuben E. Curtis' unit, the 13th Engineering Batallion of the 7th Infantry Division, was assigned to

*Gilroy, California with instructions to patrol a certain portion of
the California coast to insure that no Japanese infiltrators reached
the shores of the United States. Chaplain Curtis relates the following incident that occurred at Gilroy.*[1]

Serving with the combat engineers was quite an experience.
They were a rough group of men. One of their most noticeable
traits was their swearing. The problem however, wasn't limited to
the enlisted men as the 50 officers assigned to the battalion also
swore constantly. The language used by the officers embarrassed
the commanding officer, Lieutenant Colonel Hall, because he felt
that officers not only served as leaders, but were gentlemen, and
their swearing detracted from that image. One day he called me
to his tent and said, "Chaplain, what do you think about the
language that the officers use?"

"It's terrible."

"I agree, and I would like you to do something about it."

"Me, what can I do about it? You are the commanding
officer. Why don't you order them to stop?"

"Chaplain, you are right. I am the commanding officer and
I'm telling you to do something about it."

"Yes sir." I left recognizing the tough assignment he had
given me. I began to think—how do I stop these men from swearing?
I felt that I should visit with some of the officers and discuss the
problem. Much to my surprise, the men didn't realize that they
swore. They were not aware of their habit. One replied to my
questions, "I didn't notice that we swore that much." Another
said, "Really, do we swear that much?" A third responded, "Oh,
come on chaplain, you're kidding."

I seemed to be getting nowhere in finding a solution so I
went to the Lord for help. I learned early in life to take my
problems to Him and ask for His help. I prayed asking for inspiration to find the right answer and in a very short time the Lord
placed a thought in my mind that gave me the solution to the
problem.

I went to the commanding officer and said, "Colonel, next
time you come to eat in the officers mess, ask me to say Grace."
It was customary for the officers, including the commanding officer,
to eat at the officer's mess. It was also customary for all men to
stand at attention when the commanding officer arrived at his
place at the table.

---

1. Interview of Reuben E. Curtis, Jr. by Richard Maher, March 1, 1974,
Charles Redd Center for Western Studies. Oral History Project: LDS Chaplains
of World War II.

"What do you want me to do that for?"

"Sir, you gave me an assignment to stop the men from swearing. I believe I have found the solution to the problem but I need your cooperation."

"Okay, chaplain, I'll do what you ask this evening."

That evening Colonel Hall came into the officer's mess. Many of the men were already seated and eating. As he approached his place at the table, they all stood at attention. He turned to me and said in a tone loud enough that everyone in the mess could hear, "Chaplain, would you mind saying Grace?"

They all looked surprised, but as I moved forward to pray, they all bowed their heads in reverence while I gave a very simple prayer to the Lord.

After the prayer, the room became very quiet. No one spoke. It was one of the quietest meals I ever sat through. The commanding officer noticed the change of atmosphere. "Chaplain Curtis, what did you do to change the mood? Why is it so quiet?"

"Sir, men don't want to swear or profane after being brought into the Lord's presence with prayer."

Prayer began to affect the lives of the officers. We started to bless the food at each meal, and because of prayer, the conversation changed to more uplifting topics.

Rueben E. Curtis:
The Lord Answered His Prayer

In 1942, Chaplain (Major) Reuben E. Curtis served as the assistant division chaplain of the 7th Infantry. When the division chaplain received a transfer, it looked as though Chaplain Curtis would become the new division chaplain but his commanding officer refused to appoint him to the position. The following story tells of that incident. [1]

Shortly after World War II began, the 7th Infantry Division spent several months in the California desert training for what most assumed would be the invasion of North Africa. At that time, Chaplain Reuben E. Curtis served in the position of assistant Division chaplain, and held the rank of major. When the division chaplain received an assignment to another area, Reuben felt certain that he would be his replacement because he had the rank and the qualifications for the position. Shortly after the senior

---

1. *Ibid.*

chaplain's departure, Chaplain Curtis received word that the commanding general, Albert E. Brown, wanted to see him. As he entered the general's office he assumed that he would walk out as the new head chaplain of the 7th division.

Chaplain, (Colonel) Reuben E. Curtis, the highest ranking Mormon Chaplain of World War II, served with the 7th Infantry Division experiencing combat at Attu, Kwajalein, Okinawa and the Philippines.

"Chaplain Curtis," the general began, "you are the ranking chaplain in the division. I want you to know that your work is superior and I have no complaints. You ought to be the new division chaplain but I'm not going to offer you that position."

"Why not?"

"Because you are a Mormon."

"What do you mean you are not going to appoint me the division chaplain because I'm a Mormon. Who do you think you are?" He stood there yelling at a two star general because he was roaring mad.

"Now wait a minute chaplain. Calm down. Don't get excited and hear me out. I'm just afraid that your being a Mormon might cause some unnecessary waves throughout the entire division. I hope you understand. I'm sorry, but I am going to write to General William R. Arnold, the Chief of Army Chaplains, requesting a replacement."

Chaplain Curtis was so angry that he told General Brown what he could do with the chaplaincy before he left his office. He returned to his quarters feeling both miserable and furious. In time he calmed down and in the privacy of his tent knelt before the Lord and said, "Now, Lord, what is the trouble here? I am qualified, and he told me that he would like me to be the division chaplain, but, just because I am a Mormon, he isn't going to appoint me to the position. Why don't you do something about it?"

It felt good praying, and losing that bitterness he had within himself. Nevertheless, Chaplain Curtis still hoped that his prayers might be answered. About a week later, the commanding general called him to his office and handed him a letter. "Chaplain Curtis, read this!"

The letter came from the Chief of Chaplains in Washington, D.C., and read: "I have noted your request for a division chaplain. I have been informed that you have a Chaplain Reuben Curtis in your division. Our records indicate that he meets all the qualifications and we would like you to appoint him as the division chaplain of the 7th Infantry."

The Lord answered his prayer.

Lyman C. Berrett:
Then the Shoes Fit

The first assignment of many World War II army chaplains took them to Harvard University, Cambridge, Mass. to attend chaplain's school. Much of the training dealt with physical activities such as marching and drilling, the purpose being that chaplains served with their men, and they had to be in excellent physical condition in order to go where their men went. The chaplains spent as many as three to four hours a day marching all over the Boston area. An essential ingredient to insure proper marching is

in the fit of the shoes that the soldier wears. The following story
told by Chaplain Lyman Berrett tells of an incident that occurred
at Harvard.[1]

While training at Harvard University most of the chaplains
held the rank of First Lieutenant. Our drill instructor had the rank
of a buck sergeant, but he made it appear that he had the authority
of a five star general. He was an Irishman named O'Shaughnessy,
and I will never forget my first experience with him. Several hundred of us lined up outside Perkins Hall waiting for drill training to
begin. A buck sergeant confronted us and called us to attention
saying, "My name is Sergeant O'Shaughnessy, and I don't care
what kind of rank you guys have got. During drill, you are under
my command. I'm the commanding officer, and you'll do everything I say. Is that clear?"

No one replied. He apparently expected an answer because
he shouted, "Gentlemen, I don't hear you."

We got the message and returned a loud, "Yes, sir."

He continued, "If I order you to march into some strange
places, you follow orders. Is that understood?"

We shouted in unison, "Yes, sir."

He explained a variety of moves one makes when marching,
and after an hour or so, he decided to take us on our first drill.
He marched us to the Charles River which was located next to the
campus. It took us ten minutes to get to our destination, and as we
came upon the Charles River he halted us on the grass next to the
river. His next command was "left face." As I turned left, I saw the
Charles River about 40 feet away. He then called "forward march,"
and we headed toward the river. I waited for an order telling us to
halt, turn right, or left, or to the rear march but none came. All
I heard was "hup two, hup four," as we walked toward the river.
I didn't know whether to stop or not, and I'm sure the other chaplains became confused also, but I remembered what he had said an
hour before, "If I order you to march into some strange places,
you follow orders. Is that understood?" That's exactly what Sergeant O'Shaughnessy had in mind, and there in Boston, Mass., an
army buck sergeant marched three hundred army officers into the
Charles River. It was a shocking experience, but we obeyed him.
Finally, as the water reached my knees, he yelled out, "halt." As

1. Interview of Lyman C. Berrett by Richard Maher, October 10, 1975,
Charles Redd for Western Studies, Oral History Project, LDS Chaplains of
World War II.

I stood there knee deep in water, I thought to myself, "This man must be crazy." We stood there for a few moments when he shouted, "about face" and marched us out onto the grass. He looked at us with an amused expression on his face, and said, "now gentlemen, we will walk until those shoes are dry, and if any of you get corns or blisters, you can sue me."

No one got any corns or blisters, and when the shoes dried out, they were the best fitting shoes I ever had. I hated to see them wear out. Sergeant O'Shaughnessy wasn't crazy after all.

Phillip Karl Eidmann:
A Soldier's Faith

Often when medicine fails, faith succeeds. Chaplain Eugene Campbell tells the following account of a soldier's faith in the Mormon elders.[1]

"This young man is a Mormon priest, and the only reason I can give to account for the fact that he is alive today is his great faith in the power of the Mormon elders who came and administered to him when I had given up hope."

The speaker was an army captain, the commandant of the camp hospital; his audience was a group of army doctors who had gathered to hold a clinic before sending the patient to another hospital, and the soldier he was talking about was Pfc. Phillip Karl Eidmann of St. Paul, Minnesota. His story is one of faith and courage, and of God's goodness.

His connection with our Church has rather an unusual beginning. Although his father was Catholic and his mother Protestant, when asked to state his religion during registration for junior high school, he put down Mormon, although he had never been inside of a Latter-day Saint Church at the time. He was a great student, and made a thorough study of most of the religions of the world, and became firmly convinced that Mormonism is true.

His assignment in the army took him to Lincoln, Nebraska, and after attending one or two meetings, he amazed the branch president by applying for baptism. When asked what he knew about the Church, he was able to give its whole history and discuss its doctrines. Then he was baptized and began an active career in the Church. When his division was training at Camp Rucker, Alabama, Phil was branch president of the Latter-day Saint group there.

---

1. *The Improvement Era*, September, 1945, p. 496.

One afternoon while on maneuvers, Phil felt sick and reported at the dispensary for treatment. He was told that he had a temperature of 105 degrees, and immediately was rushed to the hospital. Before long it was determined that he was a victim of the dread disease, infantile paralysis, and inside of twenty-four hours he was completely paralyzed. His parents were notified, but were told that it would be useless for them to attempt to see him because he could live only a few moments at the longest. Phil had asked that two of his buddies, who were elders, be notified, and the division chaplain complied. Phil said that although he felt himself slipping, he knew he had to hang on until the elders came. One of the elders was scheduled to leave on a train, and the commanding general ordered that the train be delayed so that the elder could go and administer to Phil. Finally they arrived and performed the administration. By morning the doctor could notice some improvement. He ordered that Phil be placed in an iron lung, and he remained there for eleven days and was finally able to breathe without it.

When I met him and heard his story, he was in the hospital at Ft. Benning, Georgia, awaiting shipment to Hot Springs, Arkansas, for further treatment. His body was still paralyzed, but he was regaining the use of one hand. The amazing thing to me was his cheerful outlook on life. He was full of plans to attend B.Y.U., in a wheel chair, if necessary, and then go on a mission. He had absolute faith in the power of the priesthood and a sure knowledge of the goodness of God. My life is better for having known him.

Lyman C. Berrett:
She Had Fourteen Husbands

No other subject sets Mormons apart from other groups of people more than polygamy. During the 19th century the practice of polygamy as part of the Mormon religion caused the LDS Church to be at odds with the U.S. Government and its people for over half a century. Chaplain Lyman Berrett got involved with a polygamist while stationed at Camp Grueber, Oklahoma during the winter of 1944-45.[1]

Camp Grueber, Oklahoma served as a training camp for soldiers scheduled to go overseas. In most cases it was the last stateside assignment for the serviceman. I served with the ordinance battalion and one day one of the clerks placed a letter on my desk. I

---

1. Lyman Berrett interview.

noticed it immediately because it wasn't addressed to me, but addressed "Chaplain, Camp Grueber, Oklahoma." The letter came from a soldier who had previously been stationed at Camp Grueber before going overseas. The letter, in part, read:

"Chaplain:

I have reason to believe that the girl to whom I am married is also married to my buddy. We got to comparing pictures of our wives, and, we had the same picture of the same girl. We compared notes and found we met her at the same place, and got married under the very same circumstances. Would you please look into it?"

I knew I didn't have the ability to handle such a problem. I decided that it would be best handled by the military police. I took the letter over to the Provost Marshall's office, and after a short wait, was escorted into his office. I handed him the letter saying, "Sir, I have a letter that I think you ought to read."

He read it and said, "Chaplain, don't be too shocked. This isn't an unusual happening around here. But, this problem is not within my jurisdiction. It is a matter for the FBI, not the military. By the way, Chaplain, how would you like to go with the FBI agent and see how these situations are handled? I think you will find it very interesting."

"Yes, Sir, I think I'd like that very much."

He made a phone call and set up an appointment with an FBI agent. We met and went to her apartment. Her address was contained in the letter and, also the names of the two husbands. When we arrived at the apartment, the FBI agent knocked upon the door and soon a very attractive young woman opened the door. She was the same girl in the picture. The FBI agent said to her. "Mrs. _____ ." He used the name of one of her husbands.

She answered, "Yes, what can I do to help you?"

"I'm with the FBI and your husband is being investigated for a top secret clearance. May we come in and ask you a few questions?"

"Of course." She escorted us in and as we sat down, the FBI agent asked, "How long have you been married?"

"About six months."

"Do you know where he is stationed now?"

"I only know the APO number, because he isn't allowed to tell me anything else."

The agent had very smoothly put her at ease by asking her very simple questions and then addressed her using the other husband's name. "Now Mrs. _____, what is your husband's middle name?"

She hadn't noticed that he used the other soldier's name and she replied giving him the information.

He had trapped her very neatly, and said, "Now wait a minute. Are you Mrs. _____ or Mrs. _____? How many men are you married to?"

She was caught. I could see it in her face. The expression changed to sheer fright. She went to pieces and sobbed for several minutes. After she calmed down she admitted that she was a polygamist. "I have a total of fourteen husbands. Getting married to soldiers is a very easy way to make a living. All I had to do was find a soldier who was going overseas and marry him. He would be gone a long time, and perhaps, might even get killed. I've been able to collect the allotment checks, and if he died, I'd get an insurance check. I found it easy getting men to marry me. I looked for the marrying kind. I would seek them out, and because they were uncertain about the future they would fall in love and we would get married. That's all there is to it."

"What were your plans after the war when they would be coming home?" the agent asked.

"I'd just get lost. The United States is a big country."

The agent took her into custody and as we left he said to me, "Chaplain, this is not uncommon. We are working on these kind of cases all the time."

I felt sorry for all the husbands that were married to women like that and never knew the truth. But, I had to look at the humorous side of the incident also. Mormons were known for polygamy, and there at Camp Grueber, Oklahoma, a Mormon chaplain helped uncover a polygamist.

Wendell O. Rich:
Let's Look Like American Soldiers

Pvt. Wendell O. Rich spent six months at Camp Sibert, Alabama during the spring and summer of 1944 for basic training. Camp Sibert, in addition to being a training camp, also housed a number of German prisoners of war. They had their own compound and appeared to be an elite group of soldiers as they demonstrated their marching ability daily. Their commanding officer drilled them for the purpose of keeping them in good physical condition, but also to remind the American recruits that German soldiers made a formidable enemy. Pvt. Rich tells of an experience he had which demonstrated the personal pride of the American soldier.[1]

My company, which consisted of approximately 200 recruits, had spent several days on field manuevers, and, as we returned to our barracks, we looked forward to getting some much needed rest. In order to get to our quarters, we had to pass an area where several hundred German prisoners of war were held.

We were marching completely out of step, and looked more like a bunch of refugees rather than soldiers. Nevertheless, as we approached the German compound a new life seemed to emerge in everyone. I knew as did the others, that our unit couldn't let the enemy soldiers see us in such a deplorable condition. As we came into view of the area, our drill sergeant shouted, "Dress it up, look sharp, get in step, hold those heads and rifles high and let's look like American soldiers."

Fatigue left me, and we started to sing as we marched. I felt excited because I knew we looked superb. When the singing stopped, I could hear the heels of 200 men's boots making a thud in unison as they pounded the pavement. As we passed the German compound, I noticed them watching us, and I felt like turning to them and saying, "Look, this is what the American soldiers are like."

It took only a few moments to pass their compound and get out of sight. Once out of sight, weariness seemed to get the best of everyone, and we trugged along the rest of the way to our barracks.

I don't believe that as a group we ever marched that well together as we did for those few moments when we passed the German soldiers because of our pride in being American soldiers.

Wendell O. Rich:
Shootout at Fort Devens

While attending Chaplain's school at Fort Devens, Mass., Chaplain Wendell O. Rich challenged the gunnery officer to a rifle match. Chaplain Rich tells of the outcome of that match.[2]

---

1. Personal interview with Wendell O. Rich, December, 1974, July and August, 1975 at Salt Lake City, Utah.

2. *Ibid.*

It was a beautiful New England summer day, and I was in the officer's mess chatting with a group of men who happened to be discussing the subject of marksmanship. The men argued whether or not it was easy to become a marksman. Both sides of the issue were discussed, and several felt that learning to shoot a rifle wasn't as difficult as the range officer claimed. The gunnery officer believed that it was difficult to shoot a weapon with proficiency. He felt it took a great amount of training before a person became a marksman. Because the range officer seemed so serious, I thought I would have a little fun with him and I interjected, "Oh come on, Captain, shooting can't be that difficult."

"Chaplain, weapons aren't your business. They are mine, and I know better."

I thought that I would make the forum a little more interesting and issued him a challenge, "I'll bet you dinner tonight that I can outshoot you with no more than a few minutes practice."

"Chaplain, I don't want to take your money."

"What's the matter, Captain, are you afraid I might win?"

"Okay, Chaplain. You asked for it."

The others in the group wanted to go out to the range and witness the match. The wager brought an aura of excitement to the topic. We all went out to the firing range. The captain provided me with a rifle and I looked at it and asked, "Would you mind showing me how it works?"

"Certainly." He explained the various parts and how to hold it and sight in a target. He fired a round at the target and came close to hitting a bullseye. He handed me the rifle saying, "Good luck, Chaplain."

The group watched my every move. I took my time and aimed very carefully. I squeezed the trigger and hit the bullseye dead center. Everyone looked astonished, including the gunnery officer. I think he squirmed a little and everyone applauded my good fortune. I turned to him and said, "See, I told you it wasn't very hard." He didn't know what to say and I aimed again and fired several more shots at the target, hitting the bullseye every time. I turned laughing, "Imagine that! I guess I'm just lucky."

"Chaplain, I think you're putting me on."

I laughed, "You are right, Captain. I'm an expert rifleman. I've been shooting a rifle since I was a ten year old boy in Idaho. By the way, you don't have to buy my dinner."

He smiled, "Chaplain, I'd love to buy your dinner."

Wendell O. Rich:
The Soldiers Come Home

How does one feel when he arrives in his homeland after a long absence? Shortly after World War II ended in Europe, the troops began returning to the United States. The following story tells what happened aboard a troop ship transporting a group of soldiers home.[1]

It was cold upon the Atlantic on that October day in 1945, but nobody noticed. The 2,000 men aboard the *SS Rushville Victory* had fought the Germans from Normandy to final victory, and as the ship edged its way closer to New York Harbor, a quiet excitement existed on board. The chaplain of the *SS Rushville Victory* was LDS Chaplain Wendell O. Rich of Logan, Utah. He will always remember that day.

It was his first trip bringing American soldiers home from Europe. He sensed the excitement as the ship approached the coast of the United States. He looked out to the horizon and saw a speed boat making its way toward them. It was a converted PT

Soldiers aboard the *SS Rushville Victory* returning home after months of hard fighting in Europe.

---

1. *Ibid.*

boat and on board he noticed a small army band, and a group of WAC's. The loudspeaker rang, "The boat approaching to starboard is bringing out the New York Harbor Pilot who will guide the ship into port. We are approximately two hours from New York Harbor." A tingling sensation seemed to pass through everyone as they heard those words "two hours from New York Harbor."

The speed boat came next to the troop ship, and let the pilot aboard the *SS Rushville Victory*. Every man on board went to starboard to see what was happening, and the ship appeared to make a decided list in that direction. The band aboard the speed boat played The Star Spangled Banner, the WAC's sang, and the men shouted and cheered. It was an exciting time, but because of the bitter cold, the speed boat headed back to shore after the short welcome, leaving the men with their own thoughts about going home.

Ambrose lighthouse soon came into sight, and behind it on the horizon was America. Being too excited to go below, every soldier remained on deck in spite of the chilling weather. The two hours to reach the narrows of New York Harbor seemed an eternity, but finally the ship entered the harbor of New York City.

Its entry into New York Harbor was spectacular. The captain ordered every stitch of signal flags to be hung from the halyards. The ship looked like it belonged in a fourth of July parade. The 2,000 soldiers were being saluted by New York City as steamboats, battleships, liners, tugs and ferries started to blow their whistles and horns continuously as the troop ship made its way toward the dock leading a triumphal procession.

It was dusk, and the floodlights on the upper works of the ship were lit. The master of ceremonies went to the microphone on deck, and addressed the men aboard. "Fellows, I'd like to be a little serious for just a moment. We are approaching that Grand Old Lady in the harbor. I'd like our small band to play The Star Spangled Banner while we all face her and stand at attention." The men caught the spirit of the moment, and in a second, their mood shifted from one of great joy to one of seriousness. They removed their hats and stood at attention quietly and proudly as the band played the national anthem. The boats surrounding the ship stopped blowing their whistles and horns noticing the behavior of the men aboard the troop ship. Then unasked, a soldier who had a most beautiful voice went to the microphone and sang,

"God bless America, land that I love
Stand beside her and guide her

Through the night with a light from above.
From the mountain to the prairie
To the ocean white with foam.
God bless America, my home sweet home."

When he finished, everyone stood motionless. Then someone in the crowd yelled, "We want our chaplain."

Chaplain Rich pushed his way through the crowd to the microphone and stood there looking upon the faces of 2,000 great American soldiers. The master of ceremonies said, "Chaplain, maybe you can say the things for us we would like to say."

In the quietness and stillness of the moment he called upon Heavenly Father in private and silent prayer to guide him with the words that he would say. He prayed and when he finished there wasn't a dry eye in the group. The harbor was so still you could hear splashing as the ship's bow cut through the water. Chaplain Rich prayed for 2,000 bareheaded men with tears in their eyes while New York Harbor waited in silence. It seemed an eternity, but approximately two minutes passed when the master of ceremonies came forward and said, "Thank you, Chaplain, that's the way we all feel about it."

Wendell O. Rich:
Prayer Brings Inspiration

Chaplain Wendell O. Rich worked with the wounded and sick while assigned to the Fort Hamilton Army Hospital in New York City during 1946. He witnessed much horror caused by the war. He met the wounded, not just in body, but in spirit as well. He saw men without limbs, and others who lost their minds.

With the aid of inspiration, Chaplain Rich helped one wounded soldier recover. He tells the following story:[1]

I remember one particular soldier who had lost his arm to the shoulder. He has been depressed ever since his mishap and appeared to make no progress toward getting well. He ate little and spoke to no one. I visited with him many times but he just laid there staring at the ceiling. He never acknowledged my presence. For some reason, I became interested in him. I did some research and learned that he came from the midwest and had a very special talent. He had been a gifted pianist and had hoped one day of becoming a

---

1. *Ibid.*

great concert pianist. But, with the loss of his arm, he would never be able to fulfill that dream, and therefore, he lost his will to live.

I wanted to help him but everything I did produced no results. He responded to nothing. Each night in prayer I asked God to help me help him. Finally one evening I received the inspiration that I had been seeking. I went to his ward and made my way over to his bed. It was a large ward with perhaps twenty other patients, and, as I worked my way to his bed, I chatted with the other soldiers in the ward. They were always happy to see the chaplain. I reached his bed and leaned over in such a way that he couldn't but notice me. I said, "Hello, soldier." I waited a moment for a response but none came. He continued to stare like he always had. For just a moment I thought that maybe what I was going to say might not work, but I continued, "Soldier, there are many other things you can do with a piano besides be a concert pianist. Did you ever think of composing music?"

Did you ever think of composing music? Just a few words, but the right words. Those inspired words changed that soldier's life. Immediately a light flickered in his eyes. He turned as though he had just received a revelation and said, "That's right. I can compose music, can't I?"

He began to play the piano again. He used only one hand but played beautifully. Soon all the wards in the hospital wanted him to come and play to them. He became an inspiration to all and travelled throughout the hospital raising the morale of others.

I received my release from the army prior to his leaving the hospital and I don't know whether he ever became a great composer or not, but I would have predicted that with his attitude he would be successful in life.

Wendell O. Rich:
The Wounded Marched

After World War II ended, New York City honored the return of the victorious American servicemen and women with one of New York City's famous "ticker tape" parades. Tens of thousands of soldiers, sailors, and marines marched as tons of paper dropped on them from the skyscrapers along the parade route. Viewing the parade were 200 men who were convalescing at the Fort Hamilton Army Hospital in New York City. LDS Chaplain Wendell O. Rich accompanied them to the parade and tells the following story:

New York City officials reserved an excellent location along the parade route for a number of wounded soldiers from the local military hospital. Several of the soldiers wore their uniforms. One group of six men seated together wore on their uniforms the patch indicating that they had belonged to the famed 101st Airborne Division. Three of them used crutches and had placed them next to their chairs. They appeared quite excited because their unit, the 101st, was taking part in the parade and they anticipated seeing many of their buddies.

We arrived early and had to wait a couple of hours for the parade to begin. At parade time there wasn't an inch of space as far as I could see. Both sides of the street were filled to capacity. Finally the parade began. The bands marched, with them tens of thousands of soldiers, sailors, and marines. They marched shoulder to shoulder filling the street as hundreds of thousands cheered. Trucks and tanks rolled down the pavement. The tanks were so heavy that they crushed the manhole covers as they passed over them.

As the 101st Airborne Division came into view, the six men who had once belonged to that unit stood as though they intended to salute their group as it passed. Somehow I sensed that they planned on marching with them. I went over to the six and said, "You can't march."

One replied, "Chaplain, that's our outfit. Our buddies are out there. We've got to march."

"I can't let you march. How would you get back to the hospital?"

"Chaplain, please let us go. Our friends will see that we get back."

I didn't know what to say or do. Their eyes pleaded with me and I felt inspired to let them go. "Okay, go ahead."

Soon the 101st approached. I hoped I had made the right decision as I watched them go out to meet their unit. With hundreds of men marching in precision coming towards them, they seemed to know exactly where to go. The paratroopers made room for them. I noticed one soldier grab and hug one of the wounded as he got in line next to him. One of the men on crutches fell, and before he could get up, two men of the outfit picked him up and carried him on their shoulders along the route.

What a sight. I saw grown men cry to see their friends and buddies once again. I witnessed their joy, their tears, and their expression of love that they had for one another and the 101st

Airborne Division. I shall never forget what it meant to a few men just to belong to that great military unit.[1]

Wendell O. Rich:
Faith, A "First Principle" of the Restoration

Chaplain Wendell O. Rich visited the Hill Cumorah near the end of World War II. He tells the following story about faith in the restoration of the Gospel.[2]

> *Faith implies such confidence and conviction as will impel to action....*Belief is in a sense passive, an agreement or acceptance only; faith is active and positive, embracing such reliance and confidence as will lead to works. Faith in Christ comprises belief in Him, combined with trust in Him. One cannot have faith without belief; yet he may believe and still lack faith. Faith is vivified, vitalized, living belief....This principle becomes therefore the impelling force by which men struggle for excellence, ofttimes enduring vicissitudes and suffering that they may achieve their purposes. Faith is the secret of ambition, the soul of heroism, the motive power of effort.
>
> —Dr. James E. Talmage
> *The Articles of Faith*
> pp. 96, 97, 103

It was near the end of World War II. A fortunate break in my duties as an LDS Army Chaplain aboard the army transport *SS Rushville Victory* had brought the realization of a life-long dream. With me was the mother of an LDS serviceman I had just met at the Smith farmhouse. We were standing, as had so many before us, at the foot of the lane leading up the gentle hillside to the Sacred Grove. We paused at the foot of the lane, each filled with his own thoughts of the grove that lay above on the rising flank of the hill.

A century and a quarter ago a young boy in his fifteenth year had walked this dusty lane before us. He was in our thoughts as we climbed slowly upward and turned near the top into the cool depths of the grove, enjoying every moment.

On just such a day as this young Joseph Smith had sought the solitude of this grove of trees. From this young man's act of

---

1. *Ibid.*
2. From the book *Our Living Gospel* by Wendell O. Rich, published by Bookcraft. Copyright Bookcraft, Inc., 1964. Used by permission.

LDS Chaplain Wendell O. Rich (front) standing with a friend. The ship *SS Rush-ville Victory* in background.

faith had transpired events which have made this bit of ground as sacred as that where Moses stood before the burning bush in the desert of Sinai. Joseph's visit here was an expression of faith, faith that God would honor the promise of the scriptures. He trusted that God would resolve a boy's confusion whose plea was simply to know the truth. The dilemma in his young mind echoed the confusion of countless thousands of others who have struggled in the same spiritual darkness.

We stopped at a little clearing in the grove. From a tiny circle of blue sky above us a brilliant shaft of sunlight cut through the green background of the leaves into the shadows beneath the trees. As I opened the record of the experience of that morning, long before, only the sound of the birds and the crickets broke the silence of this quiet place. Meanwhile, the grey-haired mother beside me was humming a verse from a well-remembered song:

> Oh, how lovely was the morning
> Radiant beamed the sun above.
> Bees were humming, sweet birds singing,
> Music ringing through the grove,
> When within the shady woodland
> Joseph sought the God of love;...

She smiled and then sat down at the foot of one of the trees. Turning the pages of the scriptures we read again the story of a boy's adventure in faith which was to become the opening scene of the Dispensation of the Fulness of Times. The boy Joseph's own words seemed most appropriate in the grove:

While I was laboring under the extreme difficulties caused by the contests of these (the local) parties of religionists, I was one day reading the Epistle of James, first chapter and fifth verse, which reads: *If any of you lack wisdom, let him ask of God that giveth to all men liberally, and upbraideth not; and it shall be given him.*

Here we paused for a moment to recall the next two verses from James, so significant in Joseph's actions of that day, "But let him ask in faith, nothing wavering. For he that wavereth is like a wave of the sea driven by the wind and tossed. Let not that man think that he shall receive anything from the Lord."

Never did any passage of scripture come with more power to the heart of man than this did at this time to mine. It seemed to enter with great force into every feeling of my heart. I reflected on it again and again, knowing that if any person needed wisdom from God, I did; for how to act I did not know, and unless I could get more wisdom than I then had, I would never know; for the teachers of religion of the different sects understood the same passages of scripture so differently as to destroy all confidence in settling the question by an appeal to the Bible.

Joseph's earlier words show the depth of his confusion: "In the midst of this war of words and tumult of opinions, I often said to myself: What is to be done? Who of all these parties are right; or, are they all wrong together? If one of them be right, which is it, and how shall I know it?" Confused and disillusioned by the teachings of men, there remained to the boy only the refuge of prayer.

At length I came to the conclusion that I must either remain in darkness and confusion, or else I must do as James directs, that is, ask of God. I at length came to the determination to "ask of God," concluding that if he gave wisdom to them that lacked wisdom, and would give liberally, and not upbraid, I might venture.

So, in accordance with this, my determination to ask of God, I retired to the woods to make the attempt. It was on the morning of a beautiful, clear day, early in the spring of eighteen hundred and twenty. It was the first time in my life that I had made such an attempt, for amidst all my anxieties I had never yet made the attempt to pray vocally.

"But let him ask in faith, nothing wavering," the scripture says. Here, somewhere near where we stood, the faith of a fourteen year old boy was put to an acid test that could have shaken the spiritual strength of a mature man. Many have "wavered" and fled with much less excuse than this.

>After I had retired to the place where I had previously designed to go, having looked around me, and finding myself alone, I kneeled down and began to offer up the desire of my heart to God. I had scarcely done so, when immediately I was seized upon by some power which entirely overcame me, and had such an astonishing influence over me as to bind my tongue so that I could not speak. Thick darkness gathered around me, and it seemed to me for a time as if I were doomed to sudden destruction.
>
>But, exerting all my powers to call upon God to deliver me out of the power of this enemy which had seized upon me, and at the very moment when I was ready to sink into despair, and abandon myself to destruction—not to an imaginary ruin, but to the power of some actual being from the unseen world, who had such marvelous power as I had never before felt in any being—just at this moment of great alarm, I saw a pillar of light exactly over my head, above the brightness of the sun, which descended gradually until it fell upon me.
>
>It no sooner appeared than I found myself delivered from the enemy which held me bound....

What unspeakable wonder must have been in the eyes of the boy as he turned to the light which had descended into the midst of the grove. Never had the searching faith of a mortal been more richly rewarded.

>When the light rested upon me I saw two Personages whose brightness and glory defy all description, standing above me in the air. One of them spake unto me, calling me by name and said, pointing to the other—*This is My Beloved Son. Hear Him!*

—Pearl of Great Price
Writings of Joseph Smith
2:11-17

It was not in the heart of either of us to talk further about this wonderous event. Just being in this sacred place was a spiritual experience. We stood there quietly, feeling we were in one of God's own temples. That which had occurred here did not belong to the boy Joseph alone. It belonged to us and to all mankind. Quietly we left the grove, feeling a deep assurance that our faith could be rewarded too, not in such a transcendent experience as had his, for this had been a hinge-point in mortal history, but nevertheless rewarded, quietly and effectively, in our own lives whenever we should "ask in faith, nothing wavering."

Reuben Curtis:
Bill—A Nobody?

Reuben Curtis became the chaplain of the Veteran's Hospital in Salt Lake City at the end of the Second World War. In that capacity he met thousands of veterans and was called upon to conduct many funerals. The following story is about one of those funerals.[1]

On one occasion, a young couple visited Chaplain Curtis at the Veteran's Hospital and asked him to conduct a funeral service for a veteran named Bill. He was a relative of theirs. They mentioned that Bill had had a high regard for the chaplain even though Chaplain Curtis did not remember him.

Chaplain Curtis felt that he should learn something about the deceased man before he eulogized him. He went to his neighborhood to make inquiries. At the door of one of the neighbors he said to the woman who answered, "I hate to bother you, but I'm Chaplain Curtis, and I'm going to conduct the funeral services for your neighbor, Bill. What kind of a person was he?"

"Bill was no good. He was anti-everything. I'm sorry about his death, but he was a nothing."

He continued his search for information and spoke to another lady, "What can you tell me of Bill?"

"Bill caused nothing but trouble in his life time. The neighborhood will be a better place to live without him."

He sought a third party and received a similar reply. "Bill was a no good drunk."

The chaplain found himself involved in a real dilemma. He didn't learn of one nice thing about Bill. How could he give a

---

1. Reuben Curtis interview.

sermon? He felt that Bill must have done something nice during his lifetime, but if he had, no one noticed.

Finally the day of the funeral arrived. The services were to be held at the funeral parlor. Inside the chapel, the chaplain looked at Bill as he laid in the casket and couldn't help feel a little sad for the deceased soldier. He also felt a little sad for himself, because at the moment, he hadn't decided on what he would say. As he looked in the casket, he overheard two of Bill's brothers talking nearby. One commented, "Look at old Bill. For the first time in his life he is all dressed up and has no place to go."

Now Chaplain Curtis knew what he had to say, and as the time arrived for him to speak, he arose noticing the large crowd in the chapel. That surprised him because he didn't think Bill had any friends. He saw some of the people he interviewed and he felt reasonably sure that they came only to hear what he had to say about Bill, not to pay their respects. He spoke softly saying, "Today we are going to bury Bill. I guess most of you feel that Bill was a nobody. I want you to know that he wasn't a nobody. He was a very important person, at least to his Creator. Why did everyone dislike Bill? I can't answer that because I didn't know him. What made him the way he was?" He hesitated a moment so his words could be pondered. "Did you, his family, and you, his neighbors, ever try to help or even understand him? Did you treat him as a nobody until he actually came to believe he was?" Chaplain Curtis noticed many in the chapel began to look uneasy and saw several squirm. He continued speaking about eternal life and the kingdom of God and then sat down. Bill was carried out and to the hearse and on to the cemetery. As the chaplain started to leave, one of the relatives who had asked him to speak said, "Chaplain Curtis, you really laid into that group. Why?"

"Well, I just felt Bill might have turned out differently had his family and friends treated him as they should—as a child of God."

Mrs. Alben Borgstrom:
America's Only Four Gold Star Mother

During World War II, it was customary for American families to display in their windows a small silk-like banner containing any number of blue stars. Each star indicated the number of members of that particular family serving in the military. If a gold star shown in the window, it meant that a loved one had died in the service of his country. One Mormon family displayed four gold stars, the

*Borgstrom family from the Tremonton, Utah area. They lost four
of their six boys—all within six months of each other, and all
killed in action. Only one American family gave more, the Sullivan
family who lost all five of their sons at one time when their ship
went down at sea.*

*During wartime, when men are killed in action, they are
buried in the area where they die. After the war, the military
makes a great effort to return their bodies to their loved ones, and,
in June 1948, the four Borgstrom boys came home with full military honors. World War II LDS Chaplain Leon Flint played a part
in the ceremonies.[1]*

Mr. and Mrs. Alben Borgstrom had to relive the agonizing
past once again during that June of 1948. Their four sons were
coming home, home in flag-draped caskets, home to them and the
land they loved, the land for which they made the supreme sacrifice.

It had only been four short years earlier that the family had
been stricken with grief learning of the death of their sons, Clyde,
Elmer, and the twins, Rolon and Rulon, all within a six month
period.

March 17, 1944: U.S. Marine Clyde Borgstrom was killed in
action in the Solomon Islands. Age 28.

June 22, 1944: Elmer Borgstrom, a member of the United
States Army, gave his life while serving during the battle for Italy.
Age 30.

August 8, 1944: Somewhere in the skies over Germany,
Rolon Borgstrom was killed while flying a mission for the U.S.
Army Air Corps. Age 19.

August 25, 1944: Rulon, a member of the U.S. Army, died
while fighting in France. Age 19.

Now they were coming home. Their neighbors and family
remembered the tall, husky lads well. They had a reputation for
being hard workers and one neighbor commented "They would
rather go to war than hide behind cows."

Their father, Alben, recalled, "Every cent they ever earned,
they turned over to their mother. They were willing workers, and
when they left for the service, they knew farming from A to Z."

Their mother remembered, "They were all active in the Church.
They were great on hunting and fishing. They liked the open spaces.

---

1. Leon Flint interview. *Salt Lake Tribune* and *Deseret News*, June 26,
27, 1948. *Life Magazine*, July 19, 1948.

I remember Rulon broke his leg skiing a year before he went into
the service. You know how daring boys can be, and they seemed
never to be afraid of anything. They weren't angels, but they were
good wholesome boys."

Others couldn't help but remember as the four shiny army
vehicles escorted by the Utah Highway Patrol stopped at the Shaw
Rogers Mortuary in Garland, Utah where the caskets were placed
around the walls of the viewing room, and over each hung an en-
larged picture of the dead heroes.

Shortly the parents arrived. Their mother, a graying matronly
woman, gave way to obvious grief shortly after entering the room
while other relatives sobbed. She was heard to say, "If it were not
for the priesthood, I simply could not have been here today."

An honor guard stood by as the visitors, relatives, and friends
passed by the four caskets. The next morning the bodies were
taken to the stake house for funeral services. Many prominent
individuals played a part on the program including General Mark
Clark, representing the Army, the governor of the state of Utah
and a former World War I Mormon chaplain, Herbert B. Maw, and
the president of the Mormon Church, George Albert Smith.

LDS Chaplain Leon Flint offered the invocation as more than
2,000 persons jammed the large brick stake house and others
crowded onto the green lawn outside, listening to the services over
loud speakers which the army had installed in anticipation of a
large crowd.

Governor Herbert Maw expressed the state's "deepest sym-
pathy." He said, "It seems that the good things in life always
require great sacrifices."

General Mark Clark, former commander of the U.S. 5th Army
and leader of the American forces through the tortuous Italian
campaigns during World War II eulogized them. He said, "Their
devotion to duty helped save our liberty and made the name of
Borgstrom synonymous with freedom. For us they willingly gave
life itself. They achieved what very few of us dare hope will be our
fortune, a share in the shaping of destiny. I pray that we will main-
tain the American way of life, in the future, that we shall not fail
those valiant defenders whom we honor today. To preserve them,
we, as individuals, must match the patriotism of these brothers.
That patriotism was woven in many patterns—there is in it a call
of service arising from love of country and from its principles of
citizenship as taught in our schools and in practice of our lives."

President George Albert Smith offered hope to the bereaved
little family. He reminded them of the resurrection "where all

worthy persons will be reunited." Pointing to the alter, President Smith said, "The mortal remains are here but they are not here. They may be where they can see what goes on here today. I don't know about that, but we have assurance that they are safe in paradise until the morning of resurrection. This knowledge robs death of its sting." He reminded the family, "You have so much to look forward to. So much to be thankful for. Only if this were the real end, would the event be a sorrowful one."

The service ended with the presentation of three bronze stars, one air medal, and a good conduct medal to the family. Then many of the group moved on to Bear River cemetery, near Tremonton, to bury their mortal bodies in a final resting place. The cemetery was crowded as Chaplain Flint dedicated the graves, and three volleys were fired. The flags were removed from the caskets and the buglers played taps. The flags were presented to Mr. and Mrs. Borgstrom and their two sons, Boyd who had served with the Marines and the other son, Eldon. The colors were then retired and the family returned home. Home with the knowledge "if this were the real end, the event would be a sorrowful one...."

IV
The War in the Pacific

The surprise attack at Pearl Harbor by the Japanese on December 7, 1941 crippled the United States Naval Fleet in the Pacific. Japanese military forces advanced across the southern and southwestern Pacific capturing the Philippines, Singapore, New Guinea and the Netherlands East Indies. A bleak outlook faced the American people early in 1942 as victory over Japan seemed far into the distant future. In June 1942, the first American victory and the turning point of the war occurred at the battle of Midway. The naval battle resulted in a standoff between the Japanese Navy and the U.S. Navy, but caused the Japanese Navy to retreat from the area.

Shortly thereafter, the first major land battle in the Pacific occurred at Guadalcanal. Mormon chaplains were in evidence there and elsewhere in the Pacific. Captain George Woolley, a Mormon chaplain, served at Guadalcanal with the United States Army troops as they mopped up after the 2nd Marine Division departed for a well-deserved rest. In addition to Guadalcanal, Latter-day Saint chaplains served in all major battles in the Pacific including Attu, Kwajalein, Biak, Iwo Jima, the Philippines, and Okinawa. A total of 21 Mormon chaplains served in the Pacific War.[1] Several of them spent 30 months or more in the area. Two won the Silver Star for bravery, three were awarded the Bronze Star for outstanding service, and one was wounded at Okinawa and awarded the Purple Heart.

The 21 Mormon chaplains who served in the Pacific during World War II were:

LDS CHAPLAINS WHO SERVED IN THE PACIFIC DURING WORLD WAR II

Name	Branch of Service	Area Where Served
Theodore E. Curtis	U.S. Army	New Britain, Guadalcanal & Philippines

---

1. A total of 45 Mormon chaplains served during World War II.

Name	Branch of Service	Area Where Served
George R. Woolley	U.S. Army	New Britain, Guadalcanal, Philippines
Reuben E. Curtis	U.S. Army	Attu, Kwajalein, Philippines, Okinawa
Reed G. Probst	U.S. Army	Australia, Biak, New Guinea, Philippines
Howard C. Evans	U.S. Army	New Caledonia, Okinawa
Milton G. Widdison	U.S. Army	Okinawa, Korea
John W. Boud	U.S. Navy	Midway
Milton J. Hess	U.S. Navy	Aleutian Islands
Gerald L. Ericksen	U.S. Army	Saipan, Tinian
Anthon Jackson	U.S. Navy	Marianas, Guam, Iwo Jima
Hyrum A. Hendrickson	U.S. Army	New Guinea
Marsden Durham	U.S. Army	Philippines, Okinawa
John W. Fitzgerald	U.S. Army	Saipan, Philippines, Biak
Samuel George Ellsworth	U.S. Army	Philippines
Ray L. Jones	U.S. Army	Okinawa
Lyman C. Berrett	U.S. Army	Okinawa, Cebu, Philippines, Japan
Wilford E. Smith	U.S. Army	Okinawa, Japan
Roy M. Darley	U.S. Army	Philippines, Japan
Vadal W. Peterson	U.S. Army	Philippines
Warren Richard Nelson	U.S. Army	Korea, Philippines
Albert O. Mitchell	U.S. Army	Philippines

Many of the Mormon chaplains serving in the Pacific found themselves involved directly in combat. A typical example of combat conditions could best be described by Reuben Curtis, the younger brother of Chaplain Theodore Curtis and the Division Chaplain for the 7th Infantry Division, who served at Attu when the United States Army recaptured it from the Japanese.

"The landing was a thrilling experience: sitting on a case of bangalore torpedoes in a fast landing barge, surrounded by scores of others that churned the water into a frenzy of angry froth, heading through the dense fog towards—we knew not what. Chaplains accompanied their troops into the front lines and, unmindful of their own security visited groups of men, bringing comfort and

cheer, holding services for individuals and small groups as the opportunity presented itself, providing such things as hot drinks, clothing, medical supplies, etc. In such quantities as could be obtained
from any source."[1]

He reflected upon his experiences at Attu:

"It is true that one can be at peace in the midst of conflict
and the true tranquility and calm comes from within and has
nothing to do with the noise and violence of our poor deluded
civilization. One day I sat upon a rock on a hillside reading from
the New Testament and not many yards away a fierce battle was in
progress. The artillery was belching forth red hot steel, and tracer
bullets from machine guns and small arms criss-crossed the valley
like a Fourth of July fireworks display gone crazy.

"Again, I climbed a mountain range and recovered the body
of an aviator who had crashed. Unable to get the body down the
steep slope I dug a grave on the hillside, and with uncovered head,
sang a hymn and held a simple graveside service. I could see in
every direction and all seemed so peaceful and beautiful that I
could hardly bring myself to believe the distant roar was anything
but thunder and the flashes of fire anything but lightning."[2]

Another affliction suffered by the American fighting men in
the Pacific was the jungle weather. Chaplain Theodore Curtis told
of the unbearable conditions on New Britain as follows:

"The equatorial sun is mercilessly beating down upon the tent.
The limp canvas, sagging in the oppressive heat, attracts and focuses
the stifling rays in near unbearable concentration. Dust particles
hang in the air, listless, inert. Perspiration streams from every pore
in a futile effort to reduce body temperature.

"Myriads of insects—flies, knats, mosquitoes, and other less
well-known but equally pestiferous bugs, multiply the torment.
The searing afternoon intensifies their determination to make life
as unbearable as possible. The sea also has entered into the tempo
of the day—its brassy surface adding reflection to direct heat."[3]

A third example of adversity sustained by the G.I. in combat
was characterized by Mormon Chaplain L. Marsden Durham as
follows:

"Combat has been rough. For nights on end we 'slept' in foxholes: in water up to our heads and we were grateful when it rained

---

1. Journal History of The Church of Jesus Christ of Latter-day Saints,
July 17, 1943, located in Church Historian's office. Hereafter this collection
will be referred to as Journal History.

2. *Ibid.*

3. Theodore Curtis, *Experiences During World War II*, p. 19.

only two inches a day. I've crawled over rice paddies and bogs with mud shoulder deep moving along by placing a stretcher on the surface, crawling its length, and then repeating the process. You can imagine our difficulties with the wounded. But through all the trials, I didn't hear a complaint from the men. The wounded were heroic in the acceptance of their misfortune and I am all admiration for the pluck and grit of the American soldier."[1]

Chaplain Turner:
He Wouldn't Abandon the Wounded

Latter-day Saint Chaplain L. Marsden Durham felt that chaplains had a special place in the minds and hearts of the combat soldier. While serving in combat during the battle of Leyte, he said, "In garrison life, I learned that a chaplain had a certain worth. In combat, I found, however, that worth enhanced and magnified for in combat a chaplain can be the spark-plug and nerve center of the organization. The men rely on him. His very presence on the battle scene is an asset, and a smile to that, a word of prayer with another, and a comforting arm thrown about still another combine to fortify and replenish the spiritual needs of the men."

Mormon Chaplain Reuben Curtis, serving with the 7th Infantry Division during the battle for Attu, tells the following story about one of the chaplains under his supervision—a very special chaplain.[2]

The battle for the isolated island of Attu in the Aleutians was tough. Time Magazine described it as "One of the hardest battles U.S. soldiers ever fought." After the American forces licked the enemy, the cleanup for remaining Japanese soldiers began. Army officials estimated that at least 1,000 were scattered throughout the island. They broadcasted daily, trying in vain to get the holdouts to surrender. Apparently, the Japanese chose to die fighting rather than surrender. Before attacking, however, the rival soldiers filled themselves with saki, a form of alcohol, which made them drunk. At 2300 hours on a very dark night, the American soldiers heard a frightening sound in the darkness that sent chills up and down their spines as the enemy charged, yelling and screaming in Japanese. The Banzai charge came as a surprise to the American defenders. The G.I.'s fired, killing many, but the Japanese kept

---

1. *Church News*, March 3, 1945, p. 9.
2. Reuben Curtis interview.

coming with the suicidal charge. In some areas, they broke through the American defense, causing confusion among the U.S. soldiers.

Near one of the areas that the enemy broke through, a medical tent to treat the wounded had been established. One of Chaplain Curtis' subordinates, Chaplain Turner, a member of the Protestant faith, attended thirteen patients confined to the hospital. As the rival forces advanced toward the tent, an American officer called to Chaplain Turner. "Chaplain, can I see you for a moment?"

The chaplain went outside to see him. "Chaplain, the Japanese have overrun our position, and we are falling back. You had better get out of here quickly. They are right behind me and coming fast."

The chaplain replied, "What about the men in the hospital? Can't we evacuate them?"

"I'm afraid we can't. I don't know where all my men are yet. When the enemy broke our lines, my troops scattered, and I doubt if I could get any of them back in time to save the men in the hospital, but you have time to get out. Come with me."

"Thanks anyway, but I'll stay with the men."

"Don't you understand, Chaplain? It's too late to do anything for them and you'll only throw away your own life if you stay."

"Sir, if these men ever needed me, it's now. I can't leave them."

The officer understood. He looked with admiration into the chaplain's eyes, and handed him a pistol saying, "Maybe this will help." As the officer departed, he heard the chaplain telling the thirteen men in the tent that it was time for prayer. He heard no more.

By morning, the battle was over. The Banzai attack had killed a number of Americans, but had completely destroyed the Japanese as a force on the island. A patrol found Chaplain Turner and all thirteen of the hospital patients dead. They had been killed by machine gun fire, but not without a struggle. Chaplain Turner had died fighting. He was found with a pistol in his hand, and on the ground laying near him were several dead Japanese soldiers.

For his courage and devotion to his men, Chaplain Turner was awarded the nation's third highest military award, the Silver Star.

Reuben E. Curtis:
If You Follow the Teachings of This Book...

Prior to World War II, the major religions in Japan consisted of the following: Buddhism, Shintoism, and Christianity. It was estimated that only 300,000 of the 73,000,000 Japanese belonged to the Christian Church, and one of those served with the Japanese

army on Attu. The following story about that one is told by
Reuben Curtis.[1]

Often I traveled with the men of the 7th Division on patrol.
I enjoyed going. It gave me an opportunity to visit with men in the
field, and also a chance to receive some stimulating exercise. While
on one of those patrols we were startled as a young Japanese
soldier jumped out of a hole in front of us. It was a miracle that he
didn't get shot. He was dressed like a medical officer, and the
sergeant in charge of the patrol motioned him to come over and to
drop his weapon. He didn't appear to have any as he started forward. He had his hands raised in the air, and as he came toward us,
he suddenly reached into his jacket. As he did, the sergeant fired
his rifle, killing him. He thought that the young man was either
booby trapped or that he might be reaching for a weapon. We ran
to the dead man, and very carefully examined him. We found no
hidden weapon nor any booby trap. I thought, what did he have
in his jacket pocket that was so important? Why did he do such a
crazy thing? I searched him and found a book in his jacket pocket.
To my surprise, it was a New Testament. What in the world would
a Japanese soldier be doing with a New Testament? I examined the
book, and inside found a picture of his mother and a note from his
father which read:

"Son, this New Testament belonged to your mother.
She loved this book. Whether we win or lose this war won't
make any difference, but if you follow the teachings of this
book, you will ultimately win in the end."

That surprised us, it made us feel bad that he had died needlessly. The soldier who had killed him felt especially bad and
muttered trying to vindicate himself, "I thought he was reaching
for a weapon."

We tried to console the sergeant, but to no avail. It wasn't his
fault. I knew that. What else could he have done? What else would
he have thought when the soldier reached in his pocket?

I took possession of the Bible, hoping someday to return it
to the young Christian's father. However, I returned to the United
States prior to the occupation of Japan. I had been in the Pacific
for 3 years without being home, and jumped at the opportunity to
return to the states. I had intended to return, but the war ended

---

1. Reuben Curtis interview.

and I received my release while home on leave. Nevertheless, I gave
the book to my assistant who later became the chaplain of the 7th
Infantry, Chaplain Curtley, and he did return it to the young man's
father.

I'll always remember the message contained within, "...Wheth-
er we win or lose this war won't make much difference, but if you
follow the teachings of this book, you will ultimately win in the
end."

Norman Ahern:
A Covenant at Baptism

*On Sunday, March 5, 1944 at Guadalcanal, Chaplain Theodore
E. Curtis, Jr. conducted a fast and testimony meeting for members
of the LDS Church. Latter-day Saint soldiers, marines, seabees, and
airmen came many miles from widely separated units to attend the
meeting. Chaplain Curtis described the meeting as thrilling and
inspiring. The following accounts are based on two testimonies at
that meeting.[1]*

*Baptism: "The covenant of salvation," a moment to remember
in one's life. The following account describes one convert's covenant with the Lord.*

Norman Ahern, a young marine, had already seen plenty of
action in the Pacific. His unit was on Guadalcanal resting and getting
ready for more combat. He held the office of Priest in the Aaronic
Priesthood, and acted delighted when asked to bless the Sacrament.
Something about Norman caused Chaplain Curtis to watch him as
he said the Sacrament Prayer. The chaplain noticed Norman ignore
the card with the printed prayer by placing it aside. He watched him
as he closed his eyes and tilted his head toward heaven and expressed
the prayer as reverently and impressively as one could ever hope to
hear it.

After the Sacrament was blessed and passed to the membership,
the testimony meeting began. As the men would stand and bear
their testimony, he noticed Norman absorbing every word with an
attentive look. As time passed, the young marine stood to bear his
testimony. He told the congregation that he belonged to the Hawthorne Ward, Granite Stake, in Salt Lake City, and that he had been
converted to the Church the previous April, April 1943. He became

---

1. Theodore Curtis, *World War II Experiences.*

interested in the Church through the MIA. Norman participated in the basketball program, and before long became convinced of the truthfulness of the Gospel. When he told his parents, however, they refused to allow him to be baptized. He was disappointed, but continued attending meetings until he enlisted in the Marine Corps a few months later. Because becoming a member of the Church was so important to Norman, his parents finally relented and gave him their permission and blessings to join. He was baptized the night before he left for "boot camp," and the bishop ordained him to the office of Priest.

He continued, "Brethren, this is the first Sacrament meeting I have had the opportunity to attend since I joined the Church. You don't know how wonderful it was to have been able to bless the Sacrament. Today was the first time I have ever performed any Priesthood ordinance. While I prepared myself for the prayer, I thought about the covenant I made with the Lord the night I got baptized. It was a silent covenant. After the bishop ordained me a Priest, I said "Lord, I covenant with you that I will be prepared and worthy to officiate in any priesthood ordinance expected of a priest whenever I might be called upon. I'm proud to say that I have kept that covenant."

Marine Ahern's unit shoved off a few days later for another combat assignment. Chaplain Curtis had a feeling that the Lord would be with him. He didn't see Norman again until he returned home and met him in Salt Lake City when he attended his missionary farewell. Norman received a mission call to serve the Lord in France.

J. David Carson:
A Sister's Prayer Saved His Life

Inspiration comes to he who lives close to the Lord. The following account tells of just such a case: a soldier's sister, while living close to the Lord, received a revelation that saved her brother's life.

Sergeant J. David Carson served as the LDS Group Leader of Group IV on Guadalcanal. He bore his testimony on that Sunday morning in March 1944, and told the following story:

Two of my buddies and I became separated from the rest of our unit during a furious Japanese counterattack. It was a tough battle, and we took refuge behind a mahogany tree for temporary safety. Believe me, it was very temporary! The enemy bullets pinged in the front of the tree while the fire from the machine guns shot off the small branches on the tree causing them to fall on us. We were scared. It seemed that it was the three of us against the entire Japanese army, and they were winning. The fire was so intense that we didn't dare look out from our cover. The situation seemed hopeless. We knew it only was a matter of time before the enemy would come and get us. They knew our position and had us pinned down. Aware that we had to make a decision, I turned to the others and said, "we have got to get out of here. If we stay, it's certain death. It will be only a matter of time before they come and get us. I'd think we should make a break for it."

One of the others spoke, "I agree, it's suicide to stay here and it may be suicide to go, but I'm with you Sarge."

"Gentlemen, I suggest we say a prayer before we go." We decided that we make a break in five minutes. During those five minutes, I said my prayers and prepared myself to leave. Those five minutes passed slowly but finally I gave the signal and we ran as fast as we could. Bullets seemed to hit all around us, but not one hit us. We made it—we made it back to our unit in one piece. Brethren, I know that I am here today because of divine intervention, because a month later while at a rest camp, I received a letter from my sister. The letter read in part,

> Dear David,
> ...I hope you are all right because a strange thing happened this evening. I suddenly became overwhelmed with a feeling that you were in danger, extreme danger. I felt that I must pray for you and I did. I prayed more fervently than I had ever prayed before...

Brethren, my sister received that revelation and prayed for my safety the very same day at the same moment that I was behind that mahogany tree. I am alive today because of the faith and the prayers of my beloved sister.

Reuben E. Curtis:
They Could Not Drive Christ From Their Hearts

During World War II, Chaplain (Lieutenant Colonel) Reuben E. Curtis of Salt Lake City served with the 7th Infantry Division in several major battles including Attu, Kwajalein, the Philippines, and Okinawa. An experience he received at Kwajalein was so unique that the national radio program "Church of the Air" asked him to tell of it on its Easter Sunday program 1944. The following is that broadcast:

Announcer: While the battle for the Marshall Islands was still in progress a Christian Chaplain with the 7th Army Division was conducting services on Kwajalein. He is here today, to tell a remarkable story of the undying faith of a little band of natives who joined American soldiers in the worship of almighty God. Come in, Lieutenant Colonel Reuben E. Curtis, of Salt Lake City.

Chaplain Curtis: The Easter story I am going to tell you actually happened a short time ago during the conquest of Kwajalein in the Marshall Islands. One afternoon, while the big guns boomed a short distance away, I was holding a worship service with a small group of soldiers near the seashore when a large contingent of Marshallese natives who were being evacuated from the battlefield to a place of comparative safety approached. They seemed a pitiful group as they filed up, tattered and torn, dirty and dazed and hungry, men, women and children with tired faces and dragging feet, each carrying a little ragged bundle containing all of the earthly possessions they had been able to save.

We were singing the old hymn, "Rock of Ages," and as they came near they began to join in, softly and timidly at first, singing in their native tongue. As soon as we had finished I was approached by an elderly native with a long, white mustachio. Through an interpreter he said that his name was Lemokto, that he had been educated by early missionaries and that he was acting as their pastor. He asked that their group be permitted to hold a prayer service that evening as they were thankful their lives had been spared and remarked that the Japanese had long since confiscated their chapel for a storehouse and had forbidden them to hold any worship services and that they hadn't had any services of any kind for a long time. Permission was, of course, immediately granted and he asked me to join with them.

They busied themselves with washing out their clothes, bathing, curling the little girls' hair, and soon were transformed into a pretty respectable looking group. Their wide, friendly smiles were punctuated with sparkling rows of even, white teeth. They opened their little bundles containing everything they owned in this world, and to my surprise the things they had saved as being the most precious were the Bible and a number of hymn books printed in the Marshallese language.

During the service that evening we sang a few hymns and I spoke to them briefly, through an interpreter. Then old Lemokto arose and holding the Bible in his hand began to speak in a soft, earnest voice. He told how the missionaries had come to them over eighty years before and had converted them to Christianity. Then he said about twenty years ago the Japanese had come and about nine years ago the missionaries left. His voice filled with quiet scorn as he reviewed how the Japanese had taken their church and forbidden them to worship. He said, "They told us they had driven Christ away and that he would never return." Then, placing his hand on his breast, he said, "Our faith in God is from deep in here. They could never drive Christ from our hearts and we knew that He would come back to us. Now the American soldiers have come and have driven the Japanese away and brought Christ with them. We again have our liberty and are free, again, to worship God."

I believe this little episode is a forerunner of what will soon happen all over the face of the earth as millions of weary people are freed from the yoke of the axis. All over the world people have refused to give us, in their hearts, the hope that Christ brought to the human race nearly two thousand years ago. Dictators have tried to destroy the Christian religion, but you can never drive Christ out of the true Christian heart and today on this Easter Sunday all over the world, American soldiers are meeting in little groups, worshipping together, praying together and hoping together that their task will soon be done, with a faith that will spur us on until we have rid the world of tyrants and oppression and have secured a lasting peace wherein the brotherhood of man is universally recognized and wherein justice and mercy reign supreme.

Lenice Brady Field:
"We Make Bad Men Good and Good Men Better"

LDS Chaplain George R. Woolley served with American forces in three major battles, Guadalcanal, New Britain, and the Philippines. While on New Britain, he met, converted, and baptized a young man. Chaplain Woolley tells the following story about how the gospel improved one man's life.[1]

1. Interview of George R. Woolley by Richard Maher, March 16, 1974, Charles Redd Center of Western Studies. Oral History Project, World War II LDS Chaplains.

While stationed on New Britain, a young man by the name of Lenice Brady Field came into my office. He said, "Chaplain, may I speak with you?"

"Sure, I'd be glad to talk with you."

He continued, "Well, it's like this. I've been to your church three times." I recalled seeing him there, but he always left before I had a chance to talk with him. "I was brought up to believe in the Baptist religion. My mother is a very staunch Baptist, and I attended the Baptist Church. Although I never felt satisfied, I went for my mother's sake. When I joined the army, I thought I would have a chance to attend many different religious services and find one that would satisfy me. Since I've been here on New Britain, I have attended every service I could and I still didn't feel satisfied. I found that going to all those services is like going late to the 'chow line,' because when you get to the serving table, all they have left is a dry crust of bread. That's the way I have felt since I have been searching for a church to satisfy me.

"About three weeks ago, I left a service feeling awful. It appeared as though the Lord didn't want me to believe in Him. On my way home from the meeting, I crawled under a bridge and knelt down and I asked my Heavenly Father to please help me find the right Church. I heard about your church, but heck, I wasn't interested in any Mormon religion. But, as it turned out, yours was the only one left that I hadn't gone to on New Britain. In desperation, I went to your service and I liked it. The following Sunday I went again, and yesterday, I attended for the third time. That's why I'm here. That's what I want to talk to you about. How can I become a member of the Mormon Church?"

I baptized Lenice Brady Field a few weeks later in the Pacific Ocean. Another Mormon chaplain, Theodore E. Curtis Jr., confirmed him a member of the Church.

A short time after his baptism, Lenice's commanding officer, Lieutenant Drin, sought me out, "Chaplain Woolley, I don't know what you've done to that man Fields, but you've done something. He used to be a pretty good soldier, but now he's the best damn soldier in the outfit, and it's all happened since he's been coming over here to see you."

"Lieutenant, I'm glad to hear that. In the Mormon Church, we have a saying and it goes like this: "The gospel makes bad men good and good men better. It's true isn't it?"

Chaplain George R. Woolley, Assistant Chaplain of the 40th Infantry Division, was a veteran of several campaigns in the Pacific including Guadalcanal, New Britain, and the Philippines. In 1928, he became a chaplain because the President of the Mormon Church, Heber J. Grant asked him to serve in that capacity.

Lenice loved the Church, and became an excellent soldier. A few months later while fighting in the Philippines, his unit got down and several of the men in his unit had been shot and were lying out in no-man's land. They needed help, and Fields went out to get his buddies. He managed to bring back five of them by crawling out and carrying them to the lines on his back. He went out to get a sixth man, but he didn't return. He was hit by enemy fire and killed instantly.

The army buried him at sea, and for heroism under fire, Lenice Brady Field was awarded posthumously the military's second highest honor for valor, the Distinguished Service Cross.

Theodore E. Curtis, Jr.:
"We Hitchhiked In Style"

War is hell, but somehow there seems to be time for some very funny experiences. The following humorous experience happened to Chaplain Theodore Curtis while on New Britain.[1]

Last week Lt. William Reddie (115th Engineer Batallion) and I went on another interesting hike. From the end of the road at Borgen Bay we followed jungle and beach trails for about 15 miles. This we covered the first day. One was a river, narrow, but over our heads. We made it across. Other rivers, shallower, were waded. The sand we got in our shoes had an abrasive action on our feet and walking became quite uncomfortable. So, after going through three native villages and taking numerous pictures we made camp, slinging our hammocks between coconut trees.

The next morning we were still tired. The hike back seemed most unattractive, as we were tired to start with. We walked down to the beach to reflect upon our problem.

What we saw looked like a page out of the National Geographic. A large outrigger canoe, complete with nine natives, a large square sail, and a pile of supplies was sailing by. Vigorously and authoritatively we beckoned them to shore. After giving each native a small present we asked the one chap who could understand a little English ("pidgeon English") to take us to our camp—fifteen miles down the line.

We hitchhiked in style, reclining comfortably on the platform over the canoe, with our backs against the supplies.

The old gent had his wife, three daughters, son, and three neighbor boys along. The breeze died down and the sail was furled. Two of the girls, one in each end of the canoe, poled us through the shallow water. It was a sight! My guess is that the girls were about 15 and 17 years of age. The group had been on their way for three days from Sumilani, the islet where they have their village—a series of shacks on stilts.

These were the most "native" natives I have ever seen. The mother, the two girls who were poling, and their little sister were dressed a la Garden of Eden, substituting a tuft of grass for the more classical fig-leaf. The men were clad in "G-strings." The little boy had nothing on.

---

1. Theodore Curtis, *Experiences.*

The natives carried their supplies on a platform made of small poles built over the central part of the canoe. This platform also served as a base for the mast. At one corner of the floor was a sheet of tin where the embers of a small fire were kept glowing. The embers were used to light their cigarettes. They rolled their own. These homemade smokes were about eight inches long, the tobacco sort of a black twist, the covering—old newspaper. Galima, the eldest daughter, was adapt at the job of rolling.

They all were chewing betel, with "combung," a homemade lime preparation. They were hospitable souls and offered us some. We appreciated their generosity, but declined it.

The young man who could speak a little English (of sorts) became very friendly. He wanted to know if I had a "Mary," native for "woman." I replied: "One Mary, America." He said he had two Marys and a shack for each of them. The way the conversation was going I was afraid that he was leading up to offering me a present of his sister, Galima. Though she is an expert at paddling and poling a canoe, I could hardly believe she would make a practical addition to my household. So I changed the subject. It was a friendly gesture on the part of her brother.

The little boy was staring at me intently. Pretending not to notice him, I nonchalantly removed my upper partial plate, looked at it, and replaced it. The boy nearly fell off the canoe in his astonishment. You should have seen his eyes pop.

Wildly gesticulating and jabbering noisily, he gathered the clan about me, and made motions for me to do it again. It was necessary for me to repeat the operation ten times before they were satisfied. If I would have made it to their islet they probably would have made me Number One Chief, and given me a full quota of Marys.

We returned to our base camp in much better condition than we would have been had it been necessary to walk back.

Gerald L. Ericksen:
Priorities When the Ship Goes Down

"Do not overpack the luggage you plan to take with you when you leave this world, for we simply cannot get most mortal things by celestial customs: only the eternal things are portable." (Neal A. Maxwell)

Often one hears, "I don't have time" or I don't have the money." In most cases those statements are nonsense. People

make time and have enough money to do as they please. It's a
matter of priorities. The following account told by Gerald L.
Ericksen deals with priorities in one's life.[1]

Our convoy received word that its destination was the Saipan
area. At that time, Saipan was a Japanese stronghold, and we knew
we would be involved in a major battle. But the U.S. military
forces had prepared well, and we had a tremendous amount of
ships in the convoy—so many that it startled the mind to see such
military might anchored in the lagoon waiting for other ships to
join the fleet.

After a few days of waiting, we departed for our destination.
It was a dark, raining night when the ship's engine started and the
ship moved slowly out to sea. I fell asleep, but a few hours after
leaving the lagoon, a crash woke me. It was three o'clock in the
morning, and the collision knocked me to the floor. It was dark
and raining outside, and I couldn't see anything. I didn't know
whether we had been torpedoed or rammed. It was a scarey feeling
as the voice of the executive officer, Mr. Steel, blared over the
loudspeaker, "Prepare to abandon ship—this is not a drill." This
alarm was repeated over and over, and I knew this wasn't a drill
because when we drilled the loudspeaker always called out, "Prepare to abandon ship—this is a drill." This was real, and it frightened
me that I would have to abandon the ship.

Because we had drilled coming over for just such an emer-
gency, I knew exactly where I had to report. Before leaving for my
station, I got a few items. I had just been reading Eddie Ricken-
backer's book about his ordeal at sea. "If it ever appears as though
you are going to be on a life raft in the middle of the ocean, be
sure you have covering for your body, particularly your head. In
addition, you should have lots of water." As I recalled those words,
I got my helmet and some other clothes. I wanted to make sure
my body was covered. I then made sure my canteen had water,
and to be safe, I filled up a couple of extra canteens to take with
me just in case I had to spend some time in a life raft. The other
men in the stateroom headed for their stations, but I observed one
of them frantically gathering all the cartons of cigarettes he could
find. He was a chain smoker and I wondered how long he and his
cigarettes would last on the open sea.

---

1. Interview of Gerald L. Ericksen by Richard Maher, 1974, Charles
Redd Center for Western Studies. Oral History Project: World War II LDS
Chaplains.

I went on deck and learned that we were just outside the lagoon that we had left earlier in the evening. The captain had gotten separated from the convoy in the bad weather, and rather than break radio silence, or try to find the convoy in waters infested with Japanese submarines, the captain chose to return to the lagoon. On the way in, he went aground, and that was the crash we felt.

For precaution purposes, the men abandoned ship. I managed to stay aboard and watched the entire evacuation. It went smoothly and no life was lost nor were there any injuries.

I've often reflected upon that experience, and especially about the man whose only thought was to take his cigarettes with him. He would not have survived very long in a life raft upon the high seas, but those cigarettes were most important to him. From that experience, I learned the importance of priorities in one's life. What is really important? Is it the boat? The automobile? The camper? or the skimobile? I try to remember Elder Neal A. Maxwell's prophetic words, "Do not overpack the luggage you plan to take with you when you leave this world, for we simply cannot get most mortal things by celestial customs: only the eternal things are portable."

Gerald L. Ericksen:
"You Mormons Are Way Ahead..."

LDS Chaplain Gerald L. Ericksen spent many months on the island of Saipan during World War II. He received the Bronze Star for outstanding and meritorious service while on that island. One of the highlights during his tour was the building and dedication of a Mormon chapel. He tells the story of that project here.[1]

On Saipan, all branches of the military were represented including the 4th Marine Division. Many Mormon men served with the 4th Marine Division. One day, a group of marines approached me and suggested, "Chaplain Ericksen, why don't we build a chapel here on Saipan, a Latter-day Saint chapel?"

"I never thought of that, but it sure sounds like a great idea. I'll have to talk to the commanding general about it."

The more I thought about it, the better I liked the idea. It excited me, and as I approached the general, I knew that I would be disappointed if he told me we couldn't build one. I went into

---

1. *Ibid.*

his office and said, "Sir, I'm a member of the Mormon Church, and we have quite a few men assigned here on Saipan. The men wanted to know if they can build a chapel, a Mormon chapel here on the island."

He thought a moment, and replied, "That sounds like a fine idea. We have Protestant chapels, and we have Catholic chapels. Why not have a Mormon chapel? Go ahead and build it."

That's all he said. I was elated when I returned and sought out the men. I told them that the general had approved of the request. They felt great, and we started to build immediately. It took approximately four months to build. We had many skilled construction men in our group which made the job easier. The men not only built the chapel, but built a sacrament table, a pulpit, a secretarial desk, and all the benches. They did a fine job, and when completed, we invited the general to attend and speak at our dedicatory service.

Mormon marines from the 4th Marine Division outside their newly constructed LDS chapel on Saipan. Front row, left is Chaplain Gerald L. Ericksen. The tall marine smiling (center, rear) is L. Tom Perry of the Council of the Twelve.

The Mormon chapel on Saipan attracted much attention from other military personnel, including other chaplains. We had a sign by the side of the road about 40 yards from the chapel. It read, "LDS Mormon Services—Sunday, 1000-1730; Wednesday, MIA 1800. One chaplain passing by the chapel came in to visit with me and said, "You Mormons are way ahead of me. As yet, I have no adequate place in which to hold religious services."

I recalled part of what he said, "You Mormons are way ahead..." and I thought, but didn't say it, "That's right, Chaplain, we are way ahead."

Gabriel Dell Piano:
A Convert on Saipan

The World War II period brought many new members into the Mormon faith even though the missionary program of the LDS Church was curtailed. Few full time missionaries were called to service because of the war. In their place went members of the military. Their example caused the conversion of many members of other faiths in all areas of the world to the gospel of Jesus Christ. The following account related by Gerald L. Ericksen is one such incident.[1]

One Sunday as I prepared the chapel for the evening service, a young marine approached me and said, "Is this where they are holding the Mormon preaching service?"

"Yes it is. Would you like to join us tonight?"

"I would like that very much. I've heard a lot about you people, and I thought I'd like to learn more."

"By the way, I am Chaplain Gerald Ericksen."

"I'm Gabriel Dell Piano. I'm from Boston, and I'm a member of the Catholic Church."

I showed him around our chapel. Shortly others arrived, and the sacrament service began. After the service, I spoke to him. "Did you enjoy the service?"

"Yes I did. It was very nice."

"Is there anything you didn't understand?"

"No, your service was nice and easy to follow."

"Would you like to come back again? We hold an MIA meeting Wednesday evening."

"Yes, I'd love to. I really enjoyed tonight's service."

---

1. *Ibid.*

"Tell me, why did you come tonight?"

"I happen to share a tent with two Latter-day Saint marines. I've observed something different about them. They do constructive things. They write letters home. They read good books. They work with crafts. They find opportunities to help others. I have been very impressed with what I have seen, and I felt that any religion that can train men to do constructive things is worth looking up and finding more about. That's why I'm here, Chaplain. I'd like to know more. I'd like to know more about the Mormon religion. I'd like to know how your Church develops men like those two young marines."

"Well, Gabriel, I think that's a good reason for coming, and we'll be glad to teach you of the Church."

Gabriel eagerly learned the gospel and soon was baptized and confirmed a member. He left Saipan for parts unknown, and I didn't see him for several years. Then one day while walking down the street in Provo, I saw him. He recognized me, too. He had a very beautiful young lady with him whom he introduced as his wife. I asked, "How are things going? What's happened to you since Saipan?"

He said, "Everything is fine. I went home after the war, and told my parents that I joined the Mormon Church. They weren't pleased and sort of disowned me. So I decided to come out to Utah and attend BYU."

Gabriel Dell Piano is presently a professor of psychology at the University of Utah.

Gerald L. Ericksen:
Why Did That Good Mormon Boy Die?

"I am the resurrection, and the life: He that believeth in me, though he were dead, yet shall he live: And whosoever liveth and believeth in me shall never die."

John 11:20, 26

Members of The Church of Jesus Christ of Latter-day Saints understand death. They realize it is part of a divine plan. A Mormon knows that when he dies, he lives again because of the atonement of Jesus Christ. The following account about the death of a young Mormon on Saipan is told by Gerald L. Ericksen.[1]

---

1. *Ibid.*

The Japanese Air Force bombed the airfield on Saipan often. After one bombing raid, I received a telephone call from a marine officer in charge of a detachment located near the airfield. His unit had the responsibility of defending the field. He said, "Chaplain Ericksen, I understand that you are an LDS chaplain, is that correct?"

"Yes, I'm a member of the LDS Church."

"During the raid last night, one of my men got killed, and he happened to be a member of your Church. I thought you might like to come over and take care of him."

"Thank you for being so considerate, Captain. I'll be right over."

I went over to the airfield, and found the captain. I made the necessary arrangements for the burial, and we struck up a conversation. "Chaplain Ericksen, I've been thinking about something since that boy was killed last night. In all my years in the Marine Corps, that was the finest young man I ever met. He was always dependable, he was bright, alert and honest. He could handle responsibility. He was everything one could expect or want in a young man. And yet, he was the only one that got killed last night during that raid. Now, would you explain that to me?"

What a question! How could I hope to give him an answer? I wondered about all the other young Mormon boys, the pride of Zion, who went to their death prematurely during the war just as this young marine had. Nevertheless, I felt I had an opportunity to explain to him the Mormon concept of death, and I replied, "I don't know why he died. It could have been he was in the wrong place when the shell hit, or he might not have been able to get to his foxhole in time. Captain, I don't know the reason he was killed, but I'm not alarmed over his death. In the Mormon Church we believe in eternal life and that death isn't final. We believe that when one dies, he lives again, because of the atonement of Jesus Christ. We believe that it is the way one lives that counts, not how and when one dies. If he lived a good life, he hasn't anything to worry about in the next world. I want to assure you, Captain, that that marine lives. He is not dead. He is just living in another place."

"That's a beautiful way to look at death. I'll bet the people in your Church don't have the traumatic experiences that I have known others to go through, because they don't understand death."

"Captain, I think you are right."

Reed G. Probst:
The Silver Star

The Silver Star is the nation's third highest award for valor. It is awarded to any person who, while serving with the armed forces, is cited for gallantry in action not warranting the Medal of Honor, the Navy Cross or the Distinguished Service Cross.

Two Mormon chaplains won the Silver Star for gallantry during World War II. Chaplain Theodore E. Curtis, Jr. was awarded his for gallantry during the battle for the Philippines. Chaplain Reed G. Probst won the Silver Star for gallantry under fire on June 8, 1944 while serving with the 41st Infantry Division during the battle for Biak Island. His citation reads in part as follows:[1]

> "...with severe artillery fire bursting all around him, Chaplain Probst stood in the open without protection, and calmly conducted in a normal manner, funeral services for those killed in action. While the area around the beachhead was smothered with fire, Chaplain Probst moved about without regard for his safety giving aid and assistance to the wounded...."

The above behavior was typical of Chaplain Probst. When LDS Chaplain Roy M. Darley arrived in the Philippines in 1945 to replace Chaplain Probst, he learned the following from one of the officers in the unit: "Chaplain Probst was fearless. It amazed us to watch him in action. He seemed to have had a guardian angel with him at all times, because he would go out to aid the men with shells exploding all around him, and bullets whizzing by, but he never was hit. He would just go out under intense fire and drag men back to the lines. Everyone in the outfit knew that if he were hit and lying out on the battlefield, the chaplain would go to him and bring him back. He was a great man."[2]

Theodore E. Curtis, Jr.:
The Silver Star

LDS Chaplain (Major) Theodore E. Curtis, Jr., for gallantry in action against a strong enemy position overlooking the Dulig-

---

1. *Church News*, 3 March 1945.

2. Interview of Roy M. Darley by Richard Maher, December 2, 1974, Charles Redd Center for Western Studies. Oral History Project: World War II LDS Chaplains.

Labrador Road, Luzon, Philippines Island on January 10, 1945,
was awarded the Silver Star. The citation reads in part as follows:[1]

LDS Chaplain (Major) Theodore E. Curtis, Jr. being presented the Silver Star
by Major General Rapp Brush, Commanding General of the 40th Infantry
Division. The young lieutenant standing at Curtis' left was killed by a sniper
not long after the picture was taken.

"Chaplain Curtis attached himself to one of the platoons
of the assault force, which almost immediately came under
heavy enemy small arms and mortar fire. During the engagement, one of the men was mortally wounded by shrapnel,
and the area in which the man was lying was constantly under
enemy fire. Chaplain Curtis, disregarding the fire, made his
way to the wounded man, said a prayer for him, and remained
with him until someone came to help remove the man to
safety. Chaplain Curtis personally helped to carry the wounded
man from the area. He was always in the thickest part of the
fight, which lasted over an hour, and his conduct and bravery

1. Theodore Curtis, *World War II Experiences*, p. 24A.

while under fire served as an inspiration to the officers and
enlisted men engaged in the attack...."

Jerome Hartley Horowitz:
An Inspiring Letter to a Jewish Mother

*The following letter was obtained from the personal file of
Theodore E. Curtis, Jr.*[1] *While he was in Manila, Chaplain Curtis
attended a Sunday service of the large LDS Servicemen's Group
a short time after a conference had been held. After the meeting
he attended, he got a copy of the letter a Jewish convert had
written to his mother (a very orthodox Jewish lady) on Mother's
Day, 13 May, 1945:*

Dearest Mom,

I guess this is a fitting time for me to express my gratitude for all you've done for me in the last 23 years. But it's a
hard thing to put into words. I guess a fellow amounts only
to what his mother trains him to be. You're not perfect and
you've made mistakes; yet you're largely responsible for making me what I am. And I wouldn't trade that for anything in
the world. I can't possibly do enough for you to make up for
all you've done for me. But I do think there's a continuity in
people's lives from generation to generation, and that the
way for me to make up for your love and sacrifices is to try
to do the same for my children.

Today I went to a General Conference of all the Mormons in the Philippines who could get to Manila. 271 of us
paced into a small church—soldiers, sailors, marines, seebees,
WAC's, nurses, Red Cross workers—privates to colonels. On
the program were prayers, songs by a choir and soloists,
general singing, poetry readings, and 12 speakers. A wonderfully inspiring and exhilarating spirit filled the atmosphere. The
meeting itself was scheduled to last two hours and it ended
on time!

Then we all piled into trucks and drove out to some
colonel's home, where there was supper (including ice cream,
layer cake, and fresh apples) and socializing for everybody.
Transportation home was arranged for all. Everything went
off smoothly, easily, on schedule. There was enough punch
and ice cream for everybody.

---

1. Theodore Curtis, *World War II Experiences*, pp. 26, 27.

But what moved me most deeply was the people. I can only say that Mormons seem to live on a higher plane than the rest of the world. There were no misfits, no undesirables, no maladjusted individuals. Something about each person made me proud to be among them. The faces were clear, open, friendly, generous, intelligent, alert. There was no hubbub or loud laughter, but there was lots of smiling and cheerful talk, and people shook hands with a firm grip as though they really meant they were glad to know you. Neither was there any drinking, smoking, cursing; and, although as a group the girls were exceptionally good looking with clear eyes and healthy complexions, no one was on the make. Each person seemed to have a feeling of self-respect and of his own worthwhileness, that made him ready to respect the next fellow.

Many outsiders say they can't understand why the Mormons, who seem to be so exceptionally well adjusted and intelligent, and who live such worthwhile lives, can accept the silly doctrines of their church. But the Mormons claim, and I agree with them, that it's those very doctrines that make them what they are.

Loads of love,
Jerry.

Jerome Hartley Horowitz, who wrote the preceding letter, was born 21 November 1921 in New York City. While stationed in the service in the Philippines he had the good fortune to share the tent (or quarters) with several LDS servicemen who were living their religion. He was baptized 3 June 1945 at Alalang, P.I. by Stayner W. Call (Elder), confirmed by Chaplain W. Richard Nelson (Seventy), and ordained a Deacon by Lt. J. Morris Richards, 3 June 1945.

Denmark Jensen:
Observing Christmas with Mercy

Chaplain Reuben Curtis was among the first American soldiers to land during the invasion of the Philippines at Leyte. He was awarded the Bronze Star for meritorious service during the campaign. A very close friend, Captain Denmark Jensen from Idaho, also assigned to the 7th Infantry Division, had an unusual experience in the Philippines which Chaplain Curtis relates. [1]

---

1. *Church News,* February 24, 1945.

On the day before Christmas, 1944, Captain Denmark Jensen called a group of his men together. The group had been assigned patrol duty. Captain Jensen said, "While you are out on patrol today, I don't want you to kill any Japanese soldiers unless it's absolutely necessary. If you locate any, notify me. I'll take it from there. Is that clear?"

It seemed rather an odd order, but the men knew and respected their commanding officer. He had proved himself. He had fought with them at Attu where he was charged with the responsibility of operating a battery of seventy-five howitzers. Their position had been discovered by the enemy, and soon the Japanese tried to destroy his unit by shelling it with seventy-five millimeter bursts.

The first casualty on the Holtz Bay side of the Attu operation occurred in Mark's battery as the result of that action. One of his men was hit, and his arm torn from his shoulder. Mark ordered his men to stay in their foxholes, because of the artillery fire, and, fully exposed to the view of the enemy, dashed to the side of the wounded man. The man was hysterical. Mark quieted him, dressed his wound out there in the open, and stayed with him for about fifteen minutes until he died. This was the first battle casualty the men had seen, and they all wanted to withdraw. But, Mark had other ideas. He located the enemy position and ordering his men to "dig in good" set up a counter barrage. With utter disregard for his own safety, he moved from position to position, inspiring his men as they returned the fire destroying the enemy guns. His only concern was for the lives of the seventy men for whom he was responsible.

During the Kawajalein campaign Mark displayed the same remarkable degree of courage and leadership, and further endeared himself to the men he commanded. They would follow him anywhere, and even though the order seemed strange, they would obey it.

Toward evening of that day, the men on patrol located a Japanese soldier hiding in a small hut, and instead of tossing in the usual grenade, they sent for Captain Jensen.

Mark arrived at the sight and saw the hut directly in front of him. Without regard for his safety and all alone, and in full view of the hut, Mark approached it, shouting, "Soldier, I want you to surrender. No one will hurt you. We don't want to kill you."

The Japanese soldier came out of the hut, carrying a grenade and his rifle. Mark took the grenade from him, disarmed him, and led him back to camp.

The next day, Christmas Day—Mark issued the same order to another group going out on patrol. "Remember, do not kill any enemy soldiers."

During the course of the day, the patrol found a Japanese soldier bathing his feet in a small mountain stream. The group sent word back to Captain Jensen. He hurried to the area, and saw the enemy soldier bathing his feet with his rifle by his side. The captain, unobserved, crept upon him, and after a short struggle, took his rifle from him, and led him captive down to his waiting men.

That night in the camp, one of the group asked, "Captain, why did you needlessly expose yourself to such great danger when we could have killed both of those Japanese soldiers with so little risk?"

"Men, we've been killing them for over two months now. It didn't seem right to me to kill even a Japanese soldier on Christmas Eve or Christmas Day—the time we have set aside to commemorate the birth of our Lord and Savior."

Theodore E. Curtis, Jr.:
A Simple Prayer for a Catholic Boy

During World War II, the U.S. military classified chaplains into three denominations: Roman Catholic, Jewish, and all others including Mormons as Protestant. Chaplains frequently helped men of other faiths. Chaplain Theodore Curtis, while serving in the Philippines, aided a Catholic boy during his last moments of life.[1]

Toward the close of the campaign on the island of Negros Occidental, in the Philippines, we had our most bitter and longest period of heavy fighting. The platoon I was traveling with was ambushed. The enemy killed several men and wounded several others. One of the wounded had his chest opened up with shrapnel. He wore a little medal on a chain around his neck indicating that he belonged to the Catholic Church. He didn't lose consciousness and I knelt down next to him, trying to comfort him. I knew that he soon would be dead and there was no Catholic chaplain in the area to administer last rites to him. I felt he needed something, and I had memorized a prayer, "The Act of Contrition" for just such an occasion. I knew that the prayer meant a great deal to the Catholics, and as I leaned close to him, I said, "Soldier, repeat after me, "The Act of Contrition.""

---

1. Theodore Curtis, *World War II Experiences*, p. 24.

I said the words slowly, giving him time to repeat each word after me.

> "Oh my God, I am heartily sorry for having offended Thee, and I detest all my sins, because I dread the loss of heaven and the pains of hell. But most of all, because they offend Thee, my God, who art all good and deserving of my love. I firmly resolve, with the help of Thy grace to confess my sins, to do penance, and to amend my life. Amen."

The prayer comforted him as I hoped it would. He died, but I couldn't help but notice that the boy died with a smile on his face.

I continued with that platoon for the rest of that particular foray. Most of the men in that unit came from New York and were Catholics. They knew that I wasn't a Catholic chaplain, but had watched me pray and comfort that Catholic boy during his last moments of life. For the rest of the time I spent with that platoon, I had to all but fight with those Catholics to carry my own pack, or to dig my own foxhole. They were grateful for what I had done, and that was their way to express their appreciation.

I wrote to the widowed boy's mother telling her what had happened, and informing her that her son had repeated "The Act of Contrition" before he died. I also mentioned that I had arranged for a Catholic Priest to do whatever he felt necessary at the grave. I received an answer, a letter of appreciation. The letter was written in broken English, and contained what appeared to be dried tears on the paper.

Albert O. Mitchell:
"The Best Darn Church in the World"

LDS Chaplain Albert O. Mitchell served in an unusual role as an army chaplain. He served aboard a transport ship, the S.S. Kinkaid, and, in that capacity, spent more time aboard a ship than did the eight Mormon Navy chaplains combined. The following experience happened aboard his ship somewhere in the Pacific.[1]

----

1. Interview of Albert O. Mitchell by Richard Maher, July 23, 1975, Charles Redd Center for Western Studies, Oral History Project: LDS Chaplains of World War II.

Chaplain Mitchell and several other officers aboard the *S.S. Kinkaid* were in the officer's mess eating when some very loud voices interrupted their lunch. Several of the crew were coming through a porthole using some very foul language. The *S.S. Kinkaid* was a merchant ship consigned to the U.S. Navy for the duration of the war. Its officers and crew were not U.S. Navy personnel, but civilians. One of the civilian merchant marine officers in the room looked at Mitchell, the ship's chaplain, and very caustically said, "Hey, Chaplain, doesn't look like religion has done much for those boys. In fact, they are probably worse than they would be if they had never heard of religion."

Before Chaplain Mitchell could make a defense for religion, one of the other men at the table, a steward by the name of Brown and a non-member, said, "They are not swearing and profaning because of religion. They are doing it in spite of religion. Religion doesn't teach them to do that. Religion doesn't teach men to fight or to gamble. Religion teaches a person to be good, and to do good."

Religious services held aboard the troop ship *SS Kinkaid* in the Pacific. LDS Chaplain Albert O. Mitchell front row — first left.

"I hate to disagree with you, because I have yet to find a good religion. All religions are greedy. They are always passing the hat and looking for contributions. What has religion ever done for anybody?"

"Let me tell you what religion does for people, said the steward. "Years ago I was in Idaho, and I knew a man who had a very serious accident. He became incapacitated, and couldn't work for the entire summer. He had a large farm. It was too large for his wife and their small children to handle. He might have had a problem had it not been for his Church. The men in his Church came to his aid. They worked his farm the entire summer. He didn't have to do anything. That's true religion!"

"What religion was that?"

"The best darn religion in the world. The Mormon religion."

David Weeks:
"Move Over, Corporal"

The last great land battle in the Pacific occurred at Okinawa. Several Latter-day Saint chaplains served with the combat forces there including Reuben E. Curtis, Howard C. Evans, Milton G. Widdison, L. Marsden Durham, Lyman C. Berrett, Ray L. Jones, and Wilford E. Smith. During the battle for Okinawa, a group of LDS servicemen met on the first Sunday of the month and held a testimony meeting. One particualr soldier, Elder David Weeks from Smithfield, Utah, bore his testimony that morning. Chaplain Reuben Curtis tells the following story based on Elder Weeks' testimony.[1]

Corporal David Weeks had been in combat on Okinawa for several weeks. His unit came under an extremely heavy mortar barrage which lasted for days. It was a frightening experience. In the foxhole located next to him was his sergeant, an old army man who had trained himself to display no fear before his men and, thus, win their confidence. As the shelling increased, Elder Weeks began to pray, and the heavier the bombardment, the louder he prayed. The sound of his voice caught the attention of the sergeant who yelled to him, "Corporal, what are you yapping about?"

In order to be heard above the noise from the shelling, Elder Weeks had to yell, and a conversation began between the corporal and the sergeant in the midst of exploding bombs. "I'm scared, Sarge," shouted the corporal.

"Who are you talking to over there?"

"I'm praying."

"What for?"

---

1. Reuben Curtis Interview.

"For protection."

"Do you really believe that God will hear your prayer, and give you protection from those shells?"

"I know he will."

A moment of silence ensued before David Weeks saw his sergeant jump out of his foxhole and head for him. He jumped in with him and said, "Move over, Corporal, if you are so sure God will take care of you, I'll be safe as long as I stay close to you."

Elder Weeks couldn't get rid of him. The sergeant stayed for two days until after the bombardment ended, and the sergeant left saying, "Thanks, Corporal, we'll have to do it again sometime."

Wilford E. Smith:
"If I Join Your Church, I'll Be Out of a Job"

Chaplain Wilford E. Smith had many interesting discussions with a Methodist chaplain on Okinawa. In the course of their discussion, the Methodist surprised Chaplain Smith with what he had to say.

While assigned to a replacement depot in Okinawa, I shared a plywood shack with a Methodist chaplain who smoked cigars all the time. He smoked them one after another. As we got to know one another, we became very good friends. We very often had intimate conversations and spoke freely on any subject. In the course of one of our discussions, I said, "Chaplain, you are a hypocrite."[1]

Startled, he answered, "What do you mean by that remark?"

"You smoke! And I know that you had to take an oath that you would not smoke or drink before your Church would allow you to become a minister."

At that time every Methodist minister had to take an oath that he would never drink or smoke. Several other Protestant denominations had the same policy also. He replied, "Yes, that's right, but everybody knew the oath was taken under duress. Nobody took it seriously. It was just one of the rituals that you had to go through."

"Yes," I said, "but I think it's demeaning when one takes an oath if one doesn't intend to honor it."

---

1. Interview of Wilford E. Smith by Richard Maher, July 23, 1973, Charles Redd Center for Western Studies. Oral History Project: LDS Chaplains of World War II.

I got the better of him in that discussion as he didn't even bother to reply. That was the kind of discussions we had.

During the course of our relationship, I often attended his services to listen to him preach. He was a fine preacher. One time after a sermon, we started one of our discussions, and I said, "Chaplain, did you know that you preach Mormonism?"

To my surprise he answered, "I know I do. You have the only true Church." I nearly fell off my chair when I heard that remark. "How in the world did you come to that conclusion?"

"For two years, I had a returned missionary for my assistant, and we often discussed religion. He persuaded me that the LDS Church is the only true Church."

He spoke very nonchalantly about it so I asked, "Why don't you get baptized?"

"Chaplain, I am a minister by profession. I love what I'm doing, and I honestly believe I'm doing society a lot of good. You don't have a paid ministry, and if I join your church, I'll be out of a job."

I felt disappointed because of his response, but I knew that a seed had been planted. Maybe some day this good man would forsake the world and enter the waters of baptism.

Sister Tomano Kumagai:
She Waited 21 Years to Partake of the Sacrament

LDS Chaplain Lyman Berrett of Salt Lake City, Utah, had many memorable experiences while serving as a chaplain during World War II, but none more memorable than the story of Sister Kumagai. [1]

Chaplain Berrett went to Japan with the 77th Infantry Division as part of the occupation forces. The 15,000 troops of the 77th Infantry were scattered over the large area of Hokkaido, the northernmost island of Japan. One of the major cities was Sapporo which had a population of approximately 1,000,000 people including a member of the LDS Church, Sister Tomano Kumagai, the only Mormon in the area.

Before the war, Sister Kumagai had a job working for the local newspaper, *The Hokkaido Times*, as an interpreter. She had had no contact with the LDS Church for many years, because of the policies enforced by the Japanese government. It pleased

---

1. Lyman Berrett Interview, and letter from Mr. Bert M. Busath.

Mormon Chaplain Lyman C. Berrett while stationed on the island of Hokkaido, Japan.

her to know that American servicemen would soon be coming to Sapporo for she knew that some would be Mormons.

She prayed to the Lord that he would guide her to some members of the Church. The Lord answered her prayers by aiding that faithful member of His Church to meet an American soldier, Bert M. Busath, in a very unusual manner.

Bert M. Busath, an LDS soldier stationed in Sapporo, Japan, with the air section of the 902nd Field Artillery Battalion of the 77th Division, had the opportunity to attend a dinner, because two pilots decided at the last minute not to go, and asked Busath and another mechanic to go in their place. During the dinner, tea, saki, and cigarettes were offered, and each time, Busath refused.

The airport manager noticed that he declined and became curious. He asked, "Why don't you want these things?"

Busath answered, "Because of my religion."

"What religion is that?"

"The Mormon religion."

To Mr. Busath's surprise the airport manager replied, "I know a lady of that religion."

"A Japanese lady?"

"Yes."

"Do you know where she lives?"

The manager gave him her address, but the street addressing system in Japan was very difficult for a foreigner, so Busath asked the manager. "Would you call her for me, and ask her to meet me at a place that I know?"

The airport manager set up an engagement for the next day, and, in order to get to the appointed place, Sister Kumagai had to walk two miles through several feet of snow to meet him. She was delighted to encounter a member of the Church, and asked, "How can I obtain the Sacrament?"

Bert Busath replied, "Our group holds Sacrament services each Sunday on the base, and I'm sure I can get permission for you to attend with us."

He did, and on the following Sunday, Sister Kumagai met with the LDS group. To her surprise, the LDS group leader and she had worked together in staging entertainment for the troops, but neither knew that the other was a member of the Church. She told the men that she had not received the Sacrament for 21 years, and as she partook, all the men in the group found it difficult to hold back the tears in their eyes as they watched that sister take the Sacrament.

Sister Kumagai described the event, "When I took a piece of bread, and a cup of water at Sacrament meeting after 21 years, tears flowed from my eyes until I thought they would never stop."[1]

Elder Busath felt that the beauty of her story is that Sister Kumagai lived her life in such a manner that her friends knew of her religion even after 21 years without the priesthood in her life.

Bert M. Busath presently lives in Salt Lake City and is employed as a printer for the Newspaper Agency Corporation. He is married and has three sons and one daughter. Two of his sons are returned missionaries and the other is planning to serve when old enough. Mr. Busath has held many positions in the Church, and presently is a Temple Worker in the Salt Lake Temple.

Lyman C. Berrett:
Sin Is Sin In Any Language

Elder Orson F. Whitney said, "Sin is the transgression of divine law...He sins when he does the opposite of what he knows to be right."

When one commits sin, the light of Christ bears witness to that transgression no matter what language one speaks. Chaplain Berrett had the following experience dealing with remorse.

During the occupation of Japan, Chaplain Lyman Berrett obtained the services of a Japanese woman to clean his quarters. Although her name translated into English was "A child of the snow." Chaplain Berrett called her Mary.

At that time many citizens of Japan were literally starving to death, including Mary. Because of her situation Chaplain Berrett obtained and gave her a generous quantity of rice and gesha crab-

---

1. *Ensign*, August 1975, p. 41.

meat. She did not, however, use the food as she had wanted. She violated military regulations and sold it on the black market. Her remorse for doing wrong caused her to write the following letter.

チヤラプリン 様

私はなんいか耻しいことを致しましたでもう
私は泣いてお詫び申上げます。私は今まで責か
と思ったことは有りません。
私は全然そんな気持は有りませんでしたけれど
お友達がみらして 私のおちさ人が大きな学校で
いくらでもお金をもすかり漬ってくれないかと
言ひますので、今是非入用などといふわけ
では有りませんが。つい その日は、そ人をこ負
になりました。でも、それは大分前のことで
今には正男も学校に行き様すし、やがて運動
会にでもと。今は全然 そんな気持もないに
ろへ、この度 言葉には耻して もう チヤプリニ
様のところで働かせて戴したへ心底しい気か
いたします。一時的にもせよ、人の言葉に動か
され、悪る心を起したことを。悔いて悔いて
も、悔いなりません。
どうぞ 悠を悔許れさいませ.

The above letter in Japanese translated reads as follows:

Chaplain,

What a shamed woman I am. I beg your pardon in tears. I have never thought to sell. I never thought, but my friend come and says, "My uncle is wealthy and he will pay enough so won't you sell?" I don't need money just now, but my friend says, "Anasas (her son) will go to school soon and it will help you on athletic meeting." And I was moved by this word. I am shamed and couldn't work any more at your house. I am a foolish woman moved by such a word. I am crying for my sin, please pardon me.

Reverend Jiro Tsneta:
"Man Shall Not Live by Bread Alone"

During the occupation of Japan, Chaplain Lyman Berrett's unit, the 77th Infantry Division, was assigned to the island of Hokkaido. He shared a house with six other American servicemen including Elder Paul H. Dunn. They had a Japanese woman clean their house, and had plenty to eat. Chaplain Berrett tells of a man who used his food for a nobler purpose.[1]

We ate in a mess hall a few blocks from our quarters. We brought food home from the mess hall to eat at our leisure. One evening, one of the bakers called me aside and said, "Chaplain, how would you like a couple of loaves of baked bread to take home with you?"

"Oh, that would just be great."

"Here they are." He handed me two loaves of freshly baked bread. I could feel it's warmth and the aroma made me hungry. I looked forward to eating them later that evening.

While walking to my quarters, I saw a friend of mine approaching, Reverend Jiro Tsneta. He was a congregationalist minister. He had received his training for the ministry at the University of Southern California and spoke perfect English. We met earlier, and, because of our having similar professions, we struck up a cordial relationship.

At that time Japan was in bad shape economically. United States bombers had destroyed much of the country and many of the Japanese people suffered for lack of food and shelter. I thought it a good idea to share one of my loaves with him and his family. As he approached I said, "Good evening Reverend."

"Good evening, chaplain."

After some small talk, I said, "Reverend, I have two loaves of freshly baked bread here, and I'd like to share one with you and your family."

He hesitated for a moment and said, "Chaplain, I can't thank you enough. It's wonderful of you to share your food with me."

His sincere reply to my offer made me feel good. I felt as though I had done something good for someone, I thought what it would be like in his home that evening when he brought home that bread. Wouldn't his family be excited! Yes, I felt good, and

1. *Ibid.*

that evening as I finished my loaf, I couldn't help but think of the Tsneta family enjoying their bread.

A few days later I ran into the Reverend again, and asked, "How did your family enjoy the bread the other night?"

I expected him to reply that they enjoyed it, but to my surprise he said, "They didn't get much of it, but they enjoyed what they got."

Puzzled, I asked, "How come?"

"Well Chaplain Berrett, I haven't had the opportunity to have bread at our communion service for seven years. I hope you don't mind, but I used that loaf of bread for the communion."

Maxine (Tate) Grimm:
The Hand of the Lord

When we do all we can and it isn't enough, the hand of the Lord will reach out and get the job done. Chaplain Roy M. Darley had that experience in Japan in April 1946.[1] Brother Darley relates the following story:

Three Mormon chaplains, Vadal Peterson, Warren Richard Nelson, and myself, stationed in Japan, met and organized a three day LDS conference in Tokyo to coincide with the general conference being held in Salt Lake City in April 1946. We spent several months planning and organizing the event. We prepared it in such a way that the word would reach every Latter-day Saint serviceman in Japan down to the last platoon in order that all Mormons could plan to attend the conference.

Everything was ready when a problem arose. The commanding general for the Honshu area didn't issue orders releasing the men. The only ones that could attend the meeting were those stationed in the Tokyo and Yokohama areas because they were located nearby. Nevertheless, the conference was to proceed as planned. and the night before conference, I boarded the train in Okayama in a depressed mood, and headed for Tokyo. The train was approximately fifteen cars long, and in the particular car that I entered I happened to see a very good friend of mine, a Red Cross worker named Maxine Tate.[2] I sat down next to her and said, "Maxine, what are you doing on this train?"

"I'm going to Kyoto. What are you doing on this train?"

---

1. Roy M. Darley Interview.
2. Maxine is now Maxine Tate Grimm and resides in Tooele, Utah.

"I'm going to the conference in Tokyo."

"Oh, how is it going, Roy?"

"Terrible, Maxine, just terrible."

"Why? What happened? I heard everything was going great."

"We haven't been able to get orders to release the men to attend conference. No orders have come out of corps headquarters giving the men permission to go."

"That's too bad. I don't know whether you know it or not, but I know the commanding general quite well. When I get to Kyoto, I'll go and see him and see what I can do."

"Thanks, Maxine. That might help, but the conference begins tomorrow."

We chatted as the train rolled toward Tokyo. She got off at Kyoto, and went immediately to see the commanding general. She found him, and told him of our plight. "General, do you know that the Mormons are holding a conference in Tokyo and you haven't issued any orders releasing these men to attend. Don't you think you ought to?"

Within an hour, a communique went out releasing all Mormons from duty in Japan, Okinawa, Korea, and China to attend the conference. In one area, the military dispatched a special train which the Church members called "The Mormon Special" to take the men to Tokyo. It traveled from the southern tip of Honshu, picking up Mormons all the way to Tokyo. In addition, the army ordered the train to remain in Tokyo during the conference so that the LDS servicemen would have a place to sleep. Maxine thought of everything.

The conference was a great success thanks to Maxine Tate and the hand of the Lord. Was it just by chance that out of all the trains that travel to Tokyo I got on the one that Maxine Tate was on? Was it by chance that she just happened to know the commanding general well enough to visit with him and ask him to release all the Mormons in the Far East in order that they could attend the conference? I don't think so. I think it was the hand of the Lord. The hand of the Lord reaches out when you do your best, and just sort of gets the job done.

L. Marsden Durham:
The Death of a Mormon Chaplain[1]

Only one Latter-day Saint chaplain lost his life during World War II, L. Marsden Durham. Another Mormon chaplain was with

---

1. John Boud interview.

him when he fell to his death. Chaplain John Boud relates the tragedy.

LDS Chaplain John Boud, and L. Marsden Durham became friends during Chaplain Durham's stay on Hawaii. Chaplain Durham had been wounded during the battle for Okinawa, and returned to Hawaii to recuperate. He had previously been awarded the Bronze Star for meritorious service during the battle for the Philippines, and later was awarded the Purple Heart for wounds received at Okinawa.

When he had sufficiently recovered from his wounds, the two chaplains decided to do some sightseeing. One of the places selected to visit was the Akaka Falls. When they arrived at the falls, Chaplain Boud suggested that they visit the lower falls before going to the top. The view was beautiful as they looked over the falls and down on the dense jungle below. The lower falls stream was only two or three feet wide, and Chaplain Boud stepped across the stream to find a suitable spot to take a picture. As he turned he saw Chaplain Durham step. He didn't quite make it across as he apparently stepped on some slippery rocks, causing him to lose his balance. As he fell, he made a desperate grab at some clusters of grass, but the clumps of grass couldn't prevent him from falling over the cliff.

Chaplain Boud ran to the edge, but couldn't see him below. The falls jotted out, and the foilage below was too dense. People came running to see what happened. Chaplain Boud didn't have time to explain—he had to get to Marsden. He searched for a way down, but couldn't find one. He had to go the long way around. He prayed with all his heart that his friend would be alive as he fought his way down a steep canyon wall and through the dense jungle. He finally arrived at the spot below the falls approximately two hours later. He didn't see Marsden anywhere. He saw a pool, and thought maybe he landed in the water. Chaplain Boud jumped in looking for the body. He didn't even think to remove his camera. He searched the entire pool, but could find nothing. He decided to search the shore again, and he found a rock covered with blood, but no Marsden. He had hoped that Marsden had not been seriously hurt and was able to walk away. He noticed an area where the grass had been worn as though someone recently walked through. Again his hopes rose hoping that he was following a trail made by Chaplain Durham. He followed the trail, and, much to his surprise, it led him back to the top of the falls where Chaplain Durham had fallen. He saw Marsden's body still and lifeless laying there. Some soldiers had found a trail to the bottom, and had brought his body up. Marsden's face was all black around the eyes, and the soldiers told Chaplain Boud that his friend was dead. Nevertheless, John Boud knelt next to his body and placed his hands on his head and blessed him that he would be made alive again, but to no avail. It wasn't to be.

Chaplain L. Marsden Durham died September 25, 1945, at the age of 26. Castle H. Murphy, an assistant coordinator for the LDS Servicemen's Committee during World War II assigned to Hawaii, wired Church leaders saying, "Marsden, choice among God's noblemen. Much loved here. Hawaii mourns."

L. Marsden Durham:
The Burial of a Mormon Chaplain

The author is extremely grateful to Castle H. Murphy for allowing the following story to be used in this publication. Castle H. Murphy, during World War II, served as one of twelve assistant coordinators in the Church's servicemen's program. He was assigned to coordinate the affairs of LDS servicemen in the Hawaiian Islands. He also served as a mission president to the Hawaiian Islands, and is presently living in Orem, Utah. The following story was written by Castle H. Murphy and used by permission.[1]

"Desire Plus Prayer Equals Proper Burial. Army Captain Marsden Durham, a chaplain from Salt Lake City called me from a hospital where he was confined with a bullet wound in his leg. When I went to visit him, he asked me, as Church co-ordinator, to intercede for him that he might be permitted to remain in Hawaii instead of being transferred to the mainland to convalesce. I wrote the necessary letters, and he was finally advised that he might remain in Hawaii. We were very happy because he was a real help to us in the mission. He directed the servicemen's choir, and all were thrilled with their music. He also assisted by teaching classes in the auxiliary organizations.

When Captain Durham had sufficiently recovered from his wound, he and Chaplain Boud took a leave of absence and went to the island of Hawaii for a trip. On September 25, 1945, I received a phone call from Chaplain Boud. He advised me that

---

1. Castle H. Murphy, *Castle in Zion—Hawaii; Autobiography and Episodes from Life of Castle H. Murphy* (Salt Lake City: Deseret Book Company, 1963, pp. 119-120.

Captain Durham had fallen over the Akaka Falls to his death and that, unless I used all my influence he would be buried on Hawaii near the scene of his death. I contacted Army General Burgin who stated, "When a man dies during war in the service of his country, his remains are interred where he passes." But after I had told the General of Captain Durham's activities in the Church, he finally said he would send his private plane to return the body to Oahu Island. This was very unusual we knew.

When the matter of temple robes was mentioned to the head chaplain of the Army, he informed me that soldiers were always laid away in the uniform of their particular service. I said to him, "Chaplain, sir, the robes of the priesthood are most sacred, and you will agree with me that there is a power higher than that of the military."

He thought a moment and then said, and I shall never forget it, "I think I understand. I shall do my utmost to convince General Burgin of that fact." Later he phoned to say that we had permission to lay Elder Durham away in the temple robes.

I then obtained permission for Elder Durham's brother, Wilby M. Durham to come to Hawaii via clipper. The manager of a Honolulu newspaper agreed to make a tape recording of the funeral service which was held in the Waikiki Ward chapel, a new building connected with the tabernacle. The recording was perfect. It was sent to the family of Brother Durham. When the funeral cortege arrived at the Army cemetery at Schofield Barracks, the rain came in torrents. We were all wet when the final ceremony was completed. I noticed the Army General standing bareheaded through it all. Many things were said to be impossible to obtain from the Army officials, but through the goodness of the Lord it was all arranged, and this result was the answer to the prayers of many."

Roy M. Darley:
A Japanese Tribute to an Occupying Army

Chaplain Roy M. Darley landed in Japan with the occupation forces approximately fifteen miles north of Hiroshima. He tells the following experience when he and the occupation forces departed Japan.[1]

I encountered a strange experience upon our arrival in Japan. There were no Japanese to greet us. The town was deserted except

---

1. Roy M. Darley interview.

for a few Japanese officials. And, as we marched to our barracks several miles from the port, we passed many Japanese homes, and there behind the curtains we could see the faces of the Japanese people looking out at us. That made us feel quite uncomfortable, but we were not aware that the Japanese government had warned their citizens that when the Americans came they would rape and plunder their women and children. We weren't aware that they were frightened of us. Out of fear, the Japanese women wore long pants, because they expected the American servicemen to rape them.

Fortunately, it only took a few days for the Japanese people to learn that the Americans were their friends.

I don't know of a people that accepted an occupying army with open arms quite like the Japanese did. In fact, when our unit left, the Japanese people turned out by the thousands to say "goodbye," and I saw an occupied nation standing in the streets and literally openly weeping because we were leaving. As I witnessed that expression of love and respect, I said to myself, "What a great tribute to the American Army that the people of an occupied country would openly weep when the occupiers left.

V
Mediterranean Theater of Operations

War raged in the Meditarranean for more than two years before British and American forces launched Operation Torch in November 1942. Operation Torch was the code name used for the invasion of North Africa. The British victory at El Alamein, followed by the invasion of American and British troops in North Africa at Oran, Algiers, and Casablanca, caused the final defeat of the German army in North Africa and its surrender at Tunis in May 1943. The allies proceeded to invade Sicily, then Italy, and finally southern France in August 1944. The Mediterranean Theater of Operations became a secondary front once the Allied Forces landed in Normandy and invasion forces moved across Europe towards Germany. The battle to defeat the enemy in Italy lasted approximately 18 months due to the stubborn resistance of the German soldiers and the leadership of Field Marshal Albert Kesselring.

Four Mormon chaplains in Italy. *Left to right:* Robert C. Gibbons, Vernon A. Cooley, Timothy H. Irons, and Eldin Ricks.

Mormon chaplains arrived in the Mediterranean Theater of Operations over a period of approximately two years. The first, Eldin Ricks, arrived in Oran, North Africa, early in September 1943. Two weeks later, he joined the invasion forces at Salerno, Italy.[1] Royden C. Braithwaite, the last Mormon chaplain in the area, arrived after hostilities ceased.

LDS ARMY CHAPLAINS WHO SERVED IN THE MEDITERRANEAN THEATER OF OPERATIONS

Name	Area Where Served
Eldin Ricks	North Africa and Italy
Vernon A. Cooley	North Africa and Italy
Timothy H. Bowers-Irons[2]	North Africa and Italy
Robert C. Gibbons	Italy
Royden C. Braithwaite	Italy

One of the great battle sites of World War II was in Italy at Monte Cassino. The Germans held the strategic Abbey of St. Benedict on Monastery Hill overlooking the allied position below. From that vantage point, the Germans were able to frustrate the allied advance toward Rome. Because of the Abbey's historical and religious significance, the allies were reluctant to fire upon it, but eventually deemed it necessary, and called upon its air forces to destroy the Monastery. Chaplain Vernon Cooley and several members of the LDS Church visited the site after the battle ended. Chaplain Cooley describes the area as follows:[3]

"Bombs literally destroyed Monte Cassino. It was a pitiful sight. The place was nothing but rubble. As we climbed, we couldn't put our feet on any part of that mountain without stepping on some shrapnel, spent bullets or pieces of hand grenades. In addition, at that time, they hadn't cleaned the debris from the area, and there was still a great amount of evidence of people who had been

---

1. Interview of Eldin Ricks by Richard Maher, August 2, 1973, Charles Redd Center for Western Studies, Oral History Project: LDS Chaplains of World War II.

2. Timothy Hoyt Bowers-Irons was the only Mormon chaplain during World War II to serve in more than one major theater of operations. He also served in the European Theater of Operations.

3. Interview of Vernon A. Cooley, October 20, 1974, Charles Redd Center for Western Studies. Oral History Project: LDS Chaplains of World War II.

killed. I saw one of the most devastating examples of total destruction by bombing that anyone could have witnessed. I'll never forget that hike up the mountain. It was one of the most sobering things that happened to me while I was over there."

Eldin Ricks:
Meeting Mormons in Italy

One of the most common traits of the Mormon serviceman during the Second World War was his desire to associate with other members of his Church. Always on the lookout for fellow believers, the LDS serviceman used an assortment of techniques to find them. The following narrative by Chaplain Ricks illustrates one such technique.[1]

I landed in Salerno, D-day plus twelve, which is to say twelve days after the invasion began. I was serving as the chaplain of the 536th Quartermaster Battalion, an all-black outfit. Being a chaplain I couldn't very well go out and advertise my denomination, but I wanted to meet with others of my faith.

With that thought in mind, I decided that whenever an opportunity arose, I would somehow let my audience know that I was LDS. An opportunity came sooner than I expected. Shortly after arriving, my unit bivouacked within a few hundred yards of a military police escort guard unit. That outfit conducted German prisoners of war to North Africa and the United States. It had no chaplain, and when the commanding officer of the unit learned that the 536th had a chaplain, he asked if I would hold services for his men the following Sunday. I told him that I would be delighted to do so and suggested that I hold a combined service for both outfits, which was agreeable with him.

On Sunday, I held a service, in fact, for three groups, the white men of the military police unit, the blacks of my own unit, and the prisoners of war who were behind a barbed wire barricade. As I ended the service, I was prompted to say, "I am from Salt Lake City, Utah. Have any of you ever been to Salt Lake City?"

One of the prisoners said, "I've heard of Salt Lake City," but that was the only response. I had assumed the device of identifying myself with Salt Lake City, where I had lived for two years as a child, would flush out any Mormons in the crowd.

---

1. Interview of Eldin Ricks.

Mormons enjoying each other at LDS Conference held at Foggia, Italy in 1945. One hundred seventy-five Mormon servicemen and women attended.

Following the service, I noticed two young military police-men lingering nearby, and after everyone had left, they came forward and one said "Pardon me, sir, we were wondering if by any chance you could be a Mormon?"

"I certainly am."

"So are we. I'm Wilson K. Anderson, and this is Leslie D. Fisher." We struck up an immediate friendship. I felt as though I had met two long lost brothers. In the course of the visit that followed, they told me how the two of them had regularly held church services of their own each Sunday morning. Their self-appointed course of study was James E. Talmage's *Articles of Faith.* In addition, with bread from the mess tent and water from a canteen, they had been having the sacrament also.

After the encounter with Anderson and Fisher, I made it a practice of mentioning "Salt Lake City" to strangers whenever the opportunity presented itself.

Oh, by the way, I would never have guessed when I met Wilson Anderson near Salerno, Italy that Sunday morning over thirty years ago, that we would later be teaching religion together at the Brigham Young University. That's the way it is though. In fact, our BYU offices are only a few feet apart.

Vernon A. Cooley:
"Sir, It's Deseret, not Desert"

LDS Chaplain Vernon A. Cooley, like Chaplain Ricks, wished to meet members of the LDS faith in Italy. He used a unique technique to locate them.[1]

"Chaplain Cooley, you spelled desert wrong. You've got an extra "e" in it."

He looked at his commanding officer and said, "No sir, the word is Deseret, not desert."

"What's a Deseret? I've never heard of it."

"It's a special Mormon word. It means honey-bee."

"Well, why are you putting it on your jeep?"

"I'm hoping that it will lead me to lots of Mormons. Any member of my Church that sees that word should know that I'm a Mormon, and hopefully, will contact me.

After his commanding officer departed, Chaplain Cooley and his Latter-day Saint assistant, Claude Burtenshaw, finished painting and took a few moments to admire their work. The painted word, "Deseret" was very visible there on the front of the jeep, but both felt that something else was needed to make certain that no Latter-day Saint in Italy would miss the jeep. The two men decided that something else should be painted on the doors to attract additional attention. They proceeded to paint a picture of the Angel Moroni on one of the doors. When they finished, the men felt satisfied that a technique had been developed that would locate a great number of Mormons. Did it work? Did it get the attention of Latter-day Saint servicemen?

Everywhere they travelled in their jeep "Deseret," LDS soldiers hailed them to a stop and approached, asking, "Hey, are you guys Mormons?" Yes, the technique worked. Chaplain Cooley and Claude Burtenshaw located hundreds of Mormon servicemen in Italy with the aid of their jeep "Deseret."

---

1. Vernon A. Cooley interview.

Three Mormon chaplains in Italy. *Left to right:* Vernon A. Cooley, Timothy H. Irons, and Eldin Ricks. Vernon Cooley's jeep, "Deseret," used to locate Church members in the area, shown in background.

Timothy H. Irons:
A Mormon Private Promoted to Chaplain

In the military, a great gap exists between officers and enlisted personnel. Private Timothy Hoyt Bowers-Irons of Nephi, Utah, had the rare distinction of being the first enlisted man in the Mediterranean Theater of Operations to receive a direct commission to the rank of first lieutenant and chaplain in the U.S. Army.[1]

Chaplain Irons had applied for the chaplaincy in 1943, but due to a paperwork delay in Washington, D.C., and an obsolete

---

1. Interview of Timothy Hoyt Bowers-Irons, July 27, 1973. Charles Redd Center for Western Studies, Oral History Project: LDS Chaplains of World War II.

quota system used by the army, he did not receive his appointment until he went overseas.

He arrived in Italy as an infantry private without knowing any members of his Church, but felt certain that several were in the area. With that in mind, he went to obtain permission to organize a meeting for Latter-day Saints. He went to see the chaplain of the depot to which he was assigned, but as it turned out, he saw another chaplain, Chaplain Edwards, the command chaplain. He entered his office dirty and grubby, because he had been out on manuevers, and as Chaplain Edwards looked him over, he said, "I'm Private Irons, sir, and I'm a member of the Mormon Church. I think that there must be other members of my Church stationed here, and I would like to have your permission to hold Latter-day Saint services in this depot."

The chaplain was very cooperative. "Sure, you can hold services in one of the supply buildings. I'll send down my personal organist to play for you. Is there any specific time you would like to hold your meeting?"

"I'll let you know as soon as I find some Mormons."

"O.K., private, you do that."

"Thanks, sir."

As he started to leave, Chaplain Edwards said, "Soldier, what did you say your name was?"

"Irons, sir."

"Are you Timothy Irons by any chance?"

Irons wondered how he knew his first name. He hadn't mentioned it. "Yes, sir, I am."

"Where have you been?"

"I've been right here in this supply depot."

"I've been looking all over this command for you."

"Why?"

"I have a telegram here for you. It's your appointment to the chaplaincy."

He handed Irons the telegram. Tim noticed the address, "Private Timothy H. Irons, Chaplain." He chuckled at the thought, "Private Irons, Chaplain." He was excited that his appointment to the chaplaincy had come through. His prayers had finally been answered and as he walked back to his quarters, he could hardly keep his feet on the ground thinking that within a few days he would be a chaplain. He decided not to tell anyone. He wanted it to be a surprise, and, in case his commission didn't materialize, he didn't want any of his "buddies" ribbing him, and calling him, "the almost chaplain."

He went back to his unit and trained as though nothing had happened while he waited for Chaplain Edwards to make the necessary arrangements with the commanding general. The next morning, he and Chaplain Edwards went to Naples in a staff car to obtain some suitable clothes for the future chaplain's swearing in ceremony. The following morning at 9:00 a.m. Private Timothy H. Irons left his quarters wearing his new shiny suntans. He returned an hour later, a first lieutenant, and a chaplain in the army. He outranked his former commanding officer who held the rank of a second Lieutenant.

He felt good being a chaplain, but his first thoughts were unkind. The First Sergeant of his unit had treated him and others in a rough manner. He often marched them out to areas where nobody could hear and cussed them out. The men didn't like him, and several of them had considered giving him a beating, but were afraid that they might end up in the stockade.

He entered the orderly room wearing his new silver bar looking for the First Sergeant. He was there, and was he surprised to see Private Timothy Irons as First Lieutenant Irons. He snapped to attention. Chaplain Irons made him stand at attention while he looked him up and down like the First Sergeant had done so often to him. But soon he realized he wasn't behaving the way a chaplain should. He said "as you were." Much to Chaplain Irons' surprise, the sergeant smiled and congratulated him with such sincerity that it made him feel bad for what he had been thinking and doing. The new chaplain learned a lesson that morning that he wouldn't soon forget. Revenge is never sweet.

Eldin Ricks:
God's Presence In A Foxhole

The soldier can't help but feel helpless during a bombing raid. He cannot do anything but wait. What does he think while waiting in his foxhole? The thoughts of one serviceman are contained in the following account as Eldin Ricks narrates his experience during his first air raid.[1]

I arrived at D company in Naples on the evening of that October day in 1943. The area had gone through a particularly vicious pounding from bombs dropped by enemy planes two nights

---

1. Eldin Ricks Journal, dated October 1943.

before. Twenty-two men of a nearby outfit had been killed within a distance of less than two city blocks. Many of the men were concerned that it might be their turn next time. I kidded some of the men, saying "I hear you guys want to see a chaplain." They laughed and admitted that they did. My sermon that evening was to be on the subject of prayer, and just after the service began we heard the droning of Stuka bombers overhead. Someone said, "It seems to me I've heard that song before," and everyone made a dive for his foxhole. This was my first experience with an air raid, but I knew enough to follow their example. Since I was just visiting the outfit, I didn't have a foxhole and was obliged to jump in with somebody else. I reached a foxhole already occupied, piled in on top of its occupant, and uttered a brief apology, "I hate to do this, you understand, but "C'est la guerre."[1] He understood.

A flare dropped not far from us. It lit the area brilliantly and gave us the uncomfortable awareness that we could be seen from above. I remarked to the soldier under me, a Corporal Whitaker, that he should be safe enough. I believed that because I felt that God still had a thing or two for me to do, and also because something would have to go through me to get to him. I kept talking and asking him questions but soon heard no more answers. I began to wonder whether it was possible that falling shrapnel—and there was a good deal of it dropping around us—could have hit him in the head, the part of his anatomy that I was not covering. But then I realized that since my knees were in his ribs, the gentle rising and falling sensation that I could feel meant he was still breathing.

At that moment I recalled a statement made by my brother, Marc,[2] the last time I saw him, "Eldin, I think that if we have enough faith we can feel safe no matter what happens—even in the midst of exploding shells."

I thought about that and analyzed my feelings. Was I scared? At that moment, a Stuka suddenly seemed to poise itself directly overhead for a dive. I was still in the midst of asking myself whether I was or was not afraid, when it came roaring down with everything it had. Then as the c-a-r-rump of falling bombs came to us from some distance away and only shook the ground, I decided that I wasn't afraid. Again another plane came over ready to dive and

---

1. French for, "It is the war."
2. Marc, Eldin's brother, is an MD practicing medicine in LaFayette, California.

again, I asked, "Am I scared?" But presently the explosion from its bombs was heard from a greater distance away, and I concluded that if that was the best the boys up there could do, I could stop holding my breath.

I raised my head for a moment and shouted to the men, "Don't be scared," but was instantly struck with the futility of the admonition. A moment later I called out again, "If you think you are bad off pity poor Corporal Whitaker, I'm on top of him." The first sergeant in the next foxhole laughed an obliging two chuckles and was silent. An air raid does strange things to people's sense of humor, I concluded.

After a while, the Jerries[1] got through having their little fun, and we crawled out and shook the dust out of our mouth and ears. It hadn't been half bad for me, but it was mighty tough on poor Whitaker underneath. After the raid we continued with our church service. Sermon topic? "Prayer." We got both practice and theory in one lesson that night.

I believe now that Marc was right, more so than I did at the time he said it. You can feel God's presence with you, even in a foxhole.

Eldin Ricks:
A Chaplain Aids His Men

A military chaplain is a very unique man. His whole purpose of being is to serve—to serve his fellow man. Chaplain Ricks, while serving with the 536th Ordinance Quartermaster Battalion, an all black unit, had occasion to give special aid to one of his men. He tells of that incident.[2]

I was in one of the outlying companies when two black soldiers rushed to report to their commanding officer who was white. They were visibly shaken and one of them exclaimed, "Some white sergeant from Texas said he was going to kill me."

The lieutenant and I jumped into a truck with the two soldiers, and we went out looking for that sergeant. We saw a sergeant walking along the side of the road, and the young black soldier yelled, "That's him."

---

1. "Jerries" meaning German military men.
2. Eldin Ricks Interview.

We stopped the truck and approached him. He carried a 45 automatic pistol. I approached him and said, "Sergeant, did you threaten to shoot this man?"

He responded with the insolent comment, "Since when does a chaplain go around trying to discipline men for some private little differences that they have?"

"Now listen Sergeant," I replied sharply. I've been chaplain of a white outfit, and I've been chaplain of a black outfit, and when I was with the white outfit, I stood up for the men and their rights. The color of skin is not the question here. The issue is whether or not you threatened to shoot this man. Did you or didn't you?"

"Oh, I was just talking a little big," he said with some semblance of humility. "I don't even have any bullets. Look!" He held up his 45 automatic and showed that there was no clip in it. "I was only trying to scare him."

We were convinced that it was only a scare tactic, a bluff, and decided to let the matter drop. Incidentally, in the wake of the incident, I discovered that my stock in that outfit went up considerably. The word seemed to have gotten around that the chaplain was the sort who would stand up for his men.

Eldin Ricks:
He Went With Me Because of My Blessing

Eldin Ricks spent several months serving as chaplain of the 103rd Station Hospital in Naples, Italy. The following narrative recounts an encounter with a wounded Latter-day Saint soldier who was a patient there.[1]

One day I was walking through a corridor of the hospital when I noticed a young soldier reading a copy of *Principles of the Gospel*. I recognized it as a Mormon publication and concluded that he must be a member of the Church. In a slightly mischievious mood, I approached him and said, "Hi, I'm Chaplain Ricks. I'm the Hospital chaplain. What is that you are reading?"

"It's called *Principles of the Gospel*, chaplain. It's a book put out by my Church."

"Oh," I said, "What church is that?"

"It's The Church of Jesus Christ of Latter-day Saints, Sir, commonly known as the Mormon Church."

---

1. *Ibid.*

"I've heard of that church. Don't you have a Word of Wisdom or something like that?"

"Yes, sir, we do."

"Do you live the Word of Wisdom?"

"Yes, sir, I do."

"I also seem to recall that your church has something called priesthood?"

"Yes, sir."

"What priesthood do you hold?"

"I'm an Elder, sir."

I felt that I played the game long enough and, sticking out my hand, said, "I'm a Seventy."

He looked at me as though I were putting him on and several moments later gave vent to his lingering doubts by asking, "Are you really a Mormon, sir?"

"Yes, I really am."

"I didn't know that we had any Mormon chaplains in the whole army."

"Well, you're looking at a real live one."

In the visit that followed he proceeded to tell me of an experience he had with a Catholic friend in his outfit. They shared a tent together, and, as well as I can remember, this is the way he told the story.

One evening I was reading my Patriarchal Blessing when my tentmate asked, "What is that you read so often?"

"It is my Patriarchal Blessing."

"What's a Patriarchal Blessing?"

"It's a special blessing that all worthy members of my Church are entitled to receive. It is a guide to our lives and makes certain promises to each person based upon the way he lives."

"Can I read it?"

"I guess it's o.k."

He read it, and in the days that followed kidded me about my blessing even in front of the other guys. Then one day a group of thirteen of us were trapped by the Germans. We had gone out on patrol, and when we were returning, we found Germans had moved into a position that cut us off from our outfit. We located a cave and hid there for the day and discussed what we should do. Everyone took his turn telling what he thought should be done. Some felt it would be better to be taken prisoner rather than try to slip through the enemy's position. When it came to my Catholic friend's turn to voice his opinion, he said pointing to me, "Whatever he decides, I'll do." I decided to make the break. All told, four of us made the break together, and we all got through safely. It's funny about my friend. He had kidded me a lot about my Patriarchal Blessing, but when the chips were down and his life depended upon his decision, he chose to go with me because of my blessing.

We never did learn what happened to the other nine.

Eldin Ricks:
All Roads Lead to Rome

In our tolerant age many religious people claim that it doesn't matter what you believe so long as you are sincere in your belief. "After all," they say, "all roads lead to Rome."[1]

Chaplain Robert Gibbons of Logan, Utah, and I were once travelling in a jeep from Milan southward on one of the many roads leading to Rome. Travelling in Italy at that time was hazardous. At one point we took a short-cut and soon came to a sign that said, THIS ROAD IS MINED. We quickly turned around and got back on the main highway. After travelling southward a few miles further, we again decided to take a short-cut. Presently we came to a large river, but it was so dark that we couldn't see the bridge. I suggested to Chaplain Gibbons, who was driving, that he stop and let me get out and explore with my flashlight. He did so. It was pitch dark, no moon was in the sky, and neither the headlights from the jeep nor the beam from my flashlight seemed to find either the bridge or the road. I walked very carefully a few yards forward and my suspicions were confirmed. The bridge had been blown out. I returned to the jeep and said, "Bob, we'll have to find another way. I guess all roads don't lead to Rome after all."

Eldin Ricks:
Pope Pius XII Receives a Book of Mormon

In August 1945, Chaplain Eldin Ricks, Mark Bowers, and two other LDS men travelled to Rome. Chaplain Ricks never dreamed that within twenty-four hours of leaving Leghorn they would have the privilege of bearing their testimony to the Pope, and, in addition, presenting him with a copy of The Book of Mormon.[2]

---

1. *Ibid.*
2. *Ibid.*

I travelled from Leghorn to Rome with Mark Bowers and two other members of the Church. We planned to visit the U.S. Mission to the Holy See as I heard that an LDS girl by the name of Beth Davis worked on the embassy staff there. When we got there, I excused myself from the group and entered the embassy grounds at about the same moment that Beth left the embassy building. We recognized each other immediately, having both been students at the Brigham Young University at the same time before the war. After chatting for a little while I mentioned that we were on our way to an audience with the Pope. The Pope was holding daily public audiences for the various foreign military personnel in Italy, and we were planning to attend such an audience. Her response was, "Oh, would you like to see the Pope?" I explained that we were planning to attend one of his daily public audiences but quickly added, "If you can arrange a private audience for us I'd love you for life."

"I can't arrange it for you, but I know someone who can."

She took me to see her immediate supervisor, a smart looking middle-aged woman, and said, "This is Chaplain Ricks. He is a member of my Church. We knew each other at Brigham Young University before the war. He would like to see the Pope and I told him that you might be able to arrange it for him."

"What can I say would be the purpose of your visit?" she asked. I thought back to the many daydreams that I had had about the prospect of one day actually meeting with the Pope and presenting him a copy of the Book of Mormon. I quickly replied, "To present the Pope with a copy of Mormon scripture."

She didn't say anything for a moment and then replied, "Well, that sounds like a good reason." She added, "Now you understand, of course, that such visits are ordinarily arranged from two to six months ahead of time. When would you like to have your visit if by any rare chance it can be arranged?"

"Well, it doesn't matter to us just as long as it's before 2:00 o'clock tomorrow afternoon."

She laughed, "I don't believe by any means it is possible, but if you will call me at 5:00 o'clock this afternoon, I'll let you know whether or not it has been arranged."

When I telephoned at 5 p.m., I was greeted with the news that an audience had been set up for our group at 12:30 the next day. It was agreed that Beth would accompany us.

We met Beth the next day, and as we drove to the Vatican, I asked her what the usual courtesies were that the Pope expected of visitors. "It is, uh, customary to kneel when you go into his presence and it is, uh, customary to kiss his ring when he extends his hand..."

"Beth," I said, "Those are two things we cannot do. Is there anything else?"

"No, that's all."

At the Vatican City it seems to me that we showed our credentials to five different sets of guards before we finally parked our jeep alongside some highly polished limousines that we assumed belonged to ambassadors or representatives from other countries. We passed through the public audience chamber and on into another chamber and then were invited by an attendant to seat ourselves immediately outside the Pope's private audience chamber.

Soon the door opened and out came Justice Jackson of the U.S. Supreme Court, who was then on his way to Germany to preside at the war crimes trials in Nuremburg. Accompanying him was the Executive Secretary of the Embassy. He saw Beth Davis as he passed and nodded to her and our party. We were obliged to wait a few minutes longer and then were conducted in to meet Pope Pius XII. There were five chairs in front of his desk, presumably arranged for the five of us, and as we entered, the gentlemen who had escorted us into the room fell upon his knees. Of course, to be polite, we ignored him, and stepped forward to greet the Pope. The Pope extended his hand in an upright position, which indicated to us that he expected us to shake hands rather than kiss his ring. At least we interpreted his gesture that way and we all shook hands with him. Whereupon he invited us to sit down. We visited for eight or nine minutes, I would judge, talking about the prospects for world peace and about his visit to the United States in 1936. Then he told us that he had some souvenirs of our visit to give to us. He told us we could have as many as we liked. We all accepted a souvenir then I said: "We too would like to leave a souvenir of our visit with you. We have visited Saint Peter's Cathedral, and there we have seen treasures brought by the rulers and representatives of many nations. Our gift by comparison is of very little value in dollars and cents, but the message it contains is of infinite value."

I then handed him a copy of the Book of Mormon and as I did so I added, "It is the Book of Mormon. It is a record of God's dealing with a branch of the house of Israel that inhabited America anciently, and the most important thing that it contains is an account of the personal visit of the Savior to them."

He hadn't said anything up to that point in my brief presentation, but now, exclaimed softly, "Do you mean that Christ was in America?"

"Yes, sir. Do you remember that Jesus said to his apostles on one occasion, "And other sheep I have, which are not of this fold; them also I must bring, and they shall hear my voice; and there shall be one fold, and one shepherd." (John 10:16)

"Yes, I do remember. I remember very well."

"The Book of Mormon tells how, in fulfillment of that promise, he visited an Israelitish remnant in America called Nephites and Lamanites." At this juncture I stepped to his desk and reached for the Book of Mormon. He handed it back to me, and I turned the corner of the page to Third Nephi, chapter eight, which deals with the calamities immediately preceding Christ's coming. I then returned the book to him and explained that Third Nephi, chapter eight tells of the calamities which occurred prior to the Savior's coming to America. I also explained that the Book of Mormon tells of a golden age of peace and righteousness that followed Christ's visit, then tells of the outbreak of war again and the final destruction of the Nephites by the group called Lamanites in 385 AD.

The Pope seemed very appreciative, at least very courteous, and said, "You mean I may have this?"

"Yes," I said, "We wish it to be our gift to you, and we urge you to read it. It is a message for all people everywhere, and we are certain of its truth."

"Thank you," was his reply. "Thank you very much."

As I have recalled that visit many times since, the feeling has always come back to me that nearly everyone in the world is interested in the Book of Mormon when it is presented for what it is—not an archaeological handbook, not a collection of Indian stories, but a volume of new evidence for the divinity of Christ that even includes a brief record of his personal ministry in ancient America.

Eldin Ricks:
Death Comes to Both the Just and Unjust

Death is not the worst thing that can happen to a man. Sin is the worst. One must remember that it isn't how one dies that's important but it is how one lives that counts. Chaplain Ricks narrates the following story:[1]

---

1. *Ibid.*

I learned that quite a few Mormons were located in the Third Division and obtained permission to travel into that division area to meet some of them. Through arrangements made by correspondence with I.O.S. Captain Hansen and Pfc. John Fretwell, the group leader, I attended one of their meetings. It was a testimony meeting, and as I heard those wonderful men bear their testimony, I distinctly remember thinking, "Surely none of these boys will ever die in battle." I imagined that the Lord would protect them. I was wrong. Several months later I dedicated the graves of four of them, four wonderful sons of God. I learned then, and I learned later, that the rain falls on the just and on the unjust.

Luther Espley:
The Voice of the Spirit Speaks, "You Must Not! You Must Not!"

Eldin Ricks, while stationed with the 103rd Station Hospital in Naples, Italy, had a visit from a British soldier named Luther Espley, who told of a remarkable experience in North Africa. This is his story.[1]

I had received a transfer to the 232nd Ordinance Base Group and was in the process of cleaning out my office when a British soldier who was rather short of stature, came into my office and asked, "Are you Chaplain Ricks?"

"Yes."

He forthwith began to weep, and because I don't ordinarily affect people that way, I thought maybe there was something wrong with him. We had been getting a lot of shell shock or exhaustion cases from the front lines, and I jumped to the conclusion that he must be one of them.

After a moment he regained his composure and said, "You're a Latter-day Saint chaplain, aren't you?"

"Yes, I am."

"You are the first Mormon I've seen in three years. That is up until an hour ago when I met Lloyd Sleight while watching a film at the Red Cross Center. He told me that there were lots of Mormons in Italy and that there was even a Mormon chaplain here in Naples. He told me where you were located, and I came up immediately. I'm sorry for being so emotional. It's just that I'm so grateful to see you."

---

1. *Ibid.*

At this juncture I almost shed a few tears myself. In the ensuing conversation he told me of a singular experience that he had had while in North Africa. He said that he had been part of a platoon that had had a number of casualties. It consisted of 83 enlisted men and one surviving officer. The platoon had nineteen trucks. In the desert they had moved into a certain position and thought they were relatively safe. Then during the night they heard a noise that made them shudder. It was Germans, lots of them, who without knowing it had surrounded the British position. The Lieutenant told his men that it was apparent that the German's were on all sides and that if they stayed it would be only a matter of time before the Germans found them. He announced his decision to try to break through the German position exactly at midnight. I will now continue the story in the words of Brother Espley, as accurately as I can recall them. "Just before midnight, I decided to get off the truck I was on and get on another that a buddy of mine was on. I got halfway between the two trucks when I heard a voice, as plainly as I ever heard anything in my life. It said, "You must not! You must not!" I whirled around to see who was talking to me, and saw that there wasn't anybody looking my way or anyone near me. And besides, the voice that I had heard was right in my ear. I didn't wait to be told again. I realized that it was the Lord or some heavenly being speaking to me, and I hurriedly put my gear back on the truck that I had just gotten off. I had no sooner done so when the drivers all started up their motors and we roared off into the night.

"I'll never forget that night. The moon was almost full, and it wasn't long before "Jerry" could see everything we were doing. To make matters worse, we drove into a German mine field, and trucks were blown up on every side. The Germans fired at us with 30 caliber machine guns and 50 caliber machine guns. They even lowered their anti-aircraft guns and fired straight across the terrain at us. In addition, they came after us in fast tanks, tanks that were almost as fast as our trucks."

I remember breaking into Brother Espley's narrative to ask him whether in view of his divine warning, he was still frightened. He replied that he was, but also believed that he would get through. I suppose he didn't know how he would get through without being wounded but clung fast to the faith that the voice meant that he would survive. I return to his story.

"It wasn't till about 5 a.m. that we stopped to wait for other trucks to join us, but none did. We then drove slowly to Alexandria,

Egypt. There we waited for a week, and still none of the others came. Ours was the only truck that got through."

I have often related this story about the British soldier. A few summers ago, after a lecture that I gave on a BYU Education Week circuit in southern California, a man came up to me and said, "Brother Ricks, do you remember me?"

He had gained a lot of weight and was older, but I said, "Do I ever? I don't remember your name, but you are that British soldier that I met in Naples, Italy in 1944."

"That's right, I am. I heard that you were speaking today, so I brought along my diary that tells of our meeting in Italy that day." He showed me his diary.

I asked Brother Espley to listen to my recollection of his experience in North Africa in order to determine whether I was still telling it correctly. I related it to him, and he assured me that my memory of the episode was correct in every detail.

John Fretwell:
Teach Me to Pray

Chaplain Ricks describes John Fretwell as "a stalwart in the faith." One of John Fretwell's assignments in the Third Division was that of a runner or messenger. A runner had to be a very reliable person as he carried messages from his unit to supporting units in front line areas. The following experience of John Fretwell's was told to Eldin Ricks. [1]

"I was in a shell hole during an artillery barrage when I heard my First Sergeant call, 'Fret, oh Fret, come here.'

"I thought that the sergeant had been hit and needed help. I bellied out of the shell hole and half ran, half crawled to another shell that he was occupying. I dived in, but when I got there I saw that he wasn't bleeding, and so I assumed that he hadn't been hit. I noticed a fig tree nearby. A shell had blasted most of the figs off the tree. I said, 'What did you call me over here for, Sarge, to pick you a fig or something?'

" 'No Fret, no Fret, it's not that at all.' He was still speaking in the same desperate voice. 'I want you to teach me how to pray.'

"I was so surprised I nearly fainted. This sergeant was the same sergeant who used to razz anybody in the outfit who wanted to go to church, not just Mormons—anybody. When we were

---

1. *Ibid.*

training at Fort Lewis, he used to say, 'What do you want to go to church for? Church is just for little kids and old ladies.' And now here he was asking me to teach him how to pray.

"I said, 'Sergeant, just talk to God like you would your own father.' 'No, Fret, I couldn't think of God like my own father. My father was no good.'

"I helped him then, sentence by sentence, to talk to God. Because he had seen some of the guys in the outfit carrying little prayer books he had had the idea that in order to pray to God you have to follow some special formula or set words. He didn't realize that all you have to do is just talk to him from the heart."

Eldin Ricks:
Mormon Japanese-Americans

The most highly decorated American military unit during World War II was the Japanese-American 442nd Battalion of the 100th Infantry Regiment. Serving among that heroic group were several members of the Mormon Church. Eldin Ricks once participated in a testimony meeting with the men of the 442nd. He relates the following story:[1]

In Italy, we had a group of Japanese-American servicemen that formed the 442nd Battalion. That unit became a much decorated unit during the war. They were involved with the landings at Normandy and then were returned to Italy when the fighting bogged down there. They were used to spearhead the drive toward Milan.

One evening, my assistant, Mark Bower, and I met with a half dozen Latter-day Saints of the 442nd. We shared our testimony with one another and also some of our experiences. I remember particularly being impressed with the fact that the gospel enabled them to feel a sense of brotherhood for members of the Church even though they may be on opposite sides in the war. One of them, for example, told how he had recently flushed out some German soldiers from the basement of a farm house. The Germans came out with their hands high in the air.

When they had rounded them all up at rifle point, this LDS soldier called out to them, "Are any of you Mormons"?

None of the prisoners responded, but bless his heart, this young Japanese-American Latter-day Saint soldier just wanted to meet a brother in the faith.

---

1. *Ibid.*

Vernon A. Cooley:
Father Cooley

*The name Cooley, in many circles, is considered to be a good
"Irish Catholic" name. Because of his surname, Chaplain Vernon A.
Cooley of Salt Lake City, Utah found himself assigned as a Catholic
chaplain twice during the Second World War.* [1]

I received an assignment to Medford, Oregon to prepare for
shipment overseas. I arrived at the camp eager to begin my work. I
reported to my commanding officer who greeted me with, "Good
morning, Father."

Puzzled, I asked, "What do you mean, Father? I'm not a
Priest."

"You're not! Aren't you a chaplain?"

"Yes, but I'm not a Catholic chaplain. I'm a Mormon, and
I'm assigned here to serve the Protestant men."

"Chaplain, we already have a Protestant chaplain. We need a
Catholic chaplain. There must have been some mixup in the assignment. You'll have to help me out, chaplain."

"But, I'm not a Priest, sir. How can I fill the job that only a
Catholic chaplain can do?"

"You can't, but you can help with some of their problems
while we wait for another replacement. They haven't had a chaplain since this outfit was organized."

He wired for a replacement, but none was available. I spent
my time helping them where I could, but felt very inadequate.
After a few weeks of training, we headed east to Camp Huksted,
New Jersey for overseas processing. I was still serving as the Catholic chaplain, and I began to get nervous. I didn't want to go overseas as a Catholic chaplain. Just prior to sailing, a Catholic chaplain
replaced me, and I was assigned to a surplus pool of chaplains. That
is, chaplains that had no assignments. I waited at Camp Kilmer for
almost two weeks, before deciding to call Washington for a new
assignment which I did. A few days later, I received an assignment,
but you guessed it, as a Catholic chaplain again. I knew that somebody in Washington D.C. had made a mistake on my records, and I
got a pass and went to Washington to straighten out my service
record. While there, I was asked if I would like to serve with the
Army Air Corps. I accepted the assignment with great delight. Incidentally, I was the first Mormon to serve with the Army Air Corps.

---

1. Vernon Cooley interview.

Eventually I landed in Italy with the Air Corps. After the war, I went to Rome often. One of the places I visited was the Vatican to see the Pope and I got rosary beads for the Catholics in my unit. They appreciated that. While at the Vatican one afternoon, I was greeted by two other army chaplains. They introduced themselves as Father _____ and Father _____.

I replied, "I'm Chaplain Cooley."

"Good afternoon, Father," was the reply.

I laughed, saying, "I'm not a Priest. I'm a Mormon."

They couldn't believe what they heard, and asked very seriously, "How could a good "Irish Catholic" name like Cooley ever get mixed up with the Mormons?"

"I don't know, but I'm sure glad they did," was my reply.

VI
The War in Europe

For several years prior to the allied invasion, the war in Europe remained primarily an air war. The Allied Forces bombed German territory day and night. Germany retalliated with their "buzz bombs." The Allied Forces used England as its major area of operations to launch the invasion upon the European continent. On June 6, 1944, the Allied Forces landed at Normandy, and after the initial breakout, moved rapidly across France, Belgium, and into Germany to bring about the formal surrender of Germany on May 8, 1945.

Seven Mormon chaplains served in the European Theater of War:

Name	*Area Served*
Leo Freeman	Ireland, England, France & Germany
Jay B. Christensen	England, France, Belgium & Luxembourg
Timothy H. Irons	France & Germany
Howard C. Badger	France & Germany
Grant E. Mann	France, Germany & Austria
Eugene E. Campbell	France, Belgium, Germany & Austria
Leon H. Flint	England, Holland & Germany

Chaplain Eugene E. Campbell gives the following vivid description of the battle front during the allies quest for victory in Europe.[1]

"On the way back, I passed our artillery outfit which was setting up for a night attack. I saw German soldiers lying dead with their heads blown off. It was horrible.

"As we had approached the Rhine, we had to go through a narrow valley. We came upon what was left of a German horse-drawn artillery outfit that had been trapped and attacked from the air. The outfit was blown to bits and there were many horses

---

1. Eugene Campbell interview.

running wild in that area and many others were lying around dead. A bulldozer had pushed the debris to the side of the road. There were still horses just standing around, stunned from the bombing, but alive.

"The German people came out from the local town, and were ransacking the supplies from this destroyed German unit. Most of the dead men had been gathered up, but some were still around. I realized for the first time the devastating forces of a bombing attack."

Delbert Barney:
Pvt. Barney—'Captain for a Day'

The following story appeared in the Church News, May 20, 1944. It was written by Samuel W. Taylor, who today, is a well-known author. He wrote this story about Delbert Barney before he became a chaplain. Mr. Taylor tells why he wrote it: "Here's a feature on a local boy, and some other Utah men are treated in it. It is not an official newspaper release. I wrote it simply because I told Barney I would, because his is a good story, and because he is admirable."

An Army Base somewhere in England—As he stepped out of the Second Platoon barracks into the hazy English sunshine, Pvt. Delbert Barney of Salt Lake City and Mesa, Arizona, was something to see. The entire platoon had helped him get ready. His brass buttons and ordnance insignia gleamed like diamonds. His broad-toed GI service shoes were like patent leather. Acevedo had pressed his uniform with the electric iron toted all the way from America in a heavy barracks bag. An apple could have been peeled on the knife-crease of his trousers, if an apple could have been found in England. Bergiel had loaned him a new necktie and had seen it was knotted right. Naegelin, a professional barber from Sacramento, had cut his hair. He was shaved down to the second layer of hide, and he'd scrubbed his teeth until his big broad grin gleamed like his buttons.

"You'll do," the Second Platoon men admitted. "You look okay." Barney, a buck private, was all fixed. For one day, he was to assume the duties and responsibilities of a captain.

This could only happen at the one place in the entire army where rank means nothing. The private, the sergeant, and the general come before God on equal terms. While on leave, Capt.

Clinton C. Chappell, post chaplain, had requested Barney to conduct Sunday religious service.

The men of the Second Platoon weren't so sure about the
whole thing. They knew Barney as a big, good-natured guy, always
smiling even when given the private's jobs of KP and latrine orderly.
He was a funny duck, too, in a way. So was Wallace Johnson, a
corporal who used to sell business office machines in Tacoma.
All Mormons were. They didn't smoke, didn't pick up the barracks
cuss words, and they didn't even drink tea or coffee. Too, they
didn't get sore when ribbed about being pure. As a matter of fact,
during a whole year in the army Barney never once had been known
to indulge in the soldier's favorite pastime, "grousing." After ten
minutes of healthy and unrestrained cursing of a dank English
morning—getting a load off his chest by bitterly denouncing the
army in general and in a long list of particulars—after a regular
ten-minute period of this many soldiers have found close-order
drill and barrack life much easier to bear.

But Barney never got sore. Back in basic training the boys
had been inclined to take advantage of his good nature, until one
day he said, grinning—and looking straight at the company bully—
"If any of you boys want to put on the boxing gloves, I'll be glad
to accommodate."

Barney was funny in another way. He had no ambition. He
didn't care if he got stripes on his sleeves. "Your corporal and
sergeant ratings don't interest me," he said frankly one day while
mopping the latrine. "I want just one thing in this army."

What he wanted was a chaplain's commission. That or nothing.
He carried on correspondence regarding it. It got to be a joke. He
thought he'd get his commission at Ft. Lewis. Then for sure while
at the Port of Embarkation before going across seas. It looked like
the thing had fallen through, or surely he would have heard. Other
months went by. And then on a gray afternoon at mail call he got
an official envelope.

His application had been passed by the commission board in
Washington. The scoffers were the first to congratulate him.

Since then he marked time, waiting for an opening. In the
army, a man learns to wait. Meanwhile, he continued active in
religious affairs, assisting the post chaplain, organizing with Johnson
a Tuesday evening Gospel Doctrine class for the LDS boys and
anybody interested. On another evening each week he and Johnson
went to a cottage meeting held in a nearby village at the home of
Sister Beatrice Rogers. Pvt. Ray J. Hermansen, a carpenter from
Salt Lake City, had organized the meetings, contacting Saints by

communication through British Mission Headquarters. Those attending included Pvts. John Errington and C. J. Christiansen of Salt Lake City, Harold B. Watkins of Ogden, and Sgt. Harold Sargent, a former ward clerk from Cedar City, Pvt. Edward J. Lewis, a research chemist from Dundalk, Maryland, and the local members included Nellie Middleton, Marie Fulton, Janet Junner, Beatrice Rogers and her daughter, Irene.

Miss Junner recently had been converted and was to be baptized by Barney.

The men of the Second Platoon knew about all this. They knew Barney was a graduate student of the School of Religion at Brigham Young University, and that he'd filled two LDS missions in Texas. As a matter of fact, Barney talked to them so much, good-naturedly trying to point out the error of some of the ways a few of them thought soldierly, that it got to be a habit to say, "Wait a minute, Barney, until I put on my boots. Your applesauce is getting ankle deep." That was a glib, easy way to answer Barney when the truth of his remarks began getting too close to home.

They knew Barney was active in church work, and with experience—but it was those bare sleeves of his OD blouse. No stripes. Not even one. Let alone brass on the shoulders. When he'd got notice of the commission board's action, Barney had said to those who were inclined to be in awe, "I'm no different than I was yesterday. A man shouldn't be judged by the position he holds." Barney was always saying things like that—platitudes, perhaps, but things of elemental truth.

The army teaches caste. Caste is necessary for discipline. Men are trained month after month to obey instantly and without question an order from a superior. In time, military caste permeates the whole strate of life and thinking. What a man says on duty is important in direct ratio to his sleeve stripes or shoulder brass, and this by natural transfer is carried into off hours and social life. An ignoramus with a third-grade education, sergeant by virtue of long military service and a loud voice, will find his opinions on science, literature and world affairs held in deep respect, while those of a Ph.D. private are discounted.

So the men of the Second Platoon were dubious as they watched Barney stride with a Bible in his hand down the company street between the barracks and the hawthorne hedges toward the chapel. Some shook their heads. One man said: "This oughtta be good. Too bad I'm not dressed up to take it in."

A few of them did go, just for the fun of it.

But on reaching the chapel, they found a different man on the pulpit. This wasn't the big easy-going guy they associated with a grin and a mop. Barney stood erect and at ease, completely in charge. As he announced his subject, "Christ's Baptism and Public Ministry," the boys noticed that even his voice was different. This was a trained speaking voice, deep and full, delivered without effort.

Presently, the men forgot it was Pvt. Barney. Speaking to them was a man in God's work, giving a message from which they could profit. This man said things to make you think. He said things that reminded you of your mother's teachings. He said things that you'd tended to forget in the rough routine of army life. He gave you a picture of life from the long range view. Existence wasn't merely counting the hours from pass to pass, picking up a girl in a pub, living for the moment. He made you realize that forever was a long, long time.

And when at the close of the services Barney stood at the door shaking hands with the uniformed congregation as it filed out, the men from the Second Platoon who'd come for a good time, gripped his hand firmly. Barney would never be quite the same to them again, no matter how many times he stood dishing out mashed potatoes in the KP line.

The men walked back silently among the Nissen huts, noticing such things as the early spring leaves and the sun in the hazy sky, and remembering one particular part of the sermon.

Jesus Christ, Himself, had owned no home, possessed no wealth, filled no office, nor held any rank.

Eugene E. Campbell:
Songfest Benediction

"For my soul delighteth in the song of the heart; yea, the song of the righteous is a prayer unto me, and it shall be answered unto me, and it shall be answered with a blessing upon their hearts." (Doctrine and Covenants 25:12)

Beautiful music lifts one's spirit, even if its sung just prior to combat. Chaplain Eugene Campbell expresses his feelings through the use of poetry after singing some hymns just before his first experience in action.[1]

We all knew that within a few days our division, the 71st Infantry, would be going into combat. We had just arrived in Europe

---

1. Eugene Campbell interview.

in January 1945, and as we prepared to go to the battle lines, we were scared because very few men in our outfit had ever been in combat before, including our commanding officers. In the tense atmosphere, tempers flared and commands were often accompanied by cursing.

Chaplain Eugene E. Campbell, a veteran of the European Theatre of Operations having served with General George Patton's Third Army shown in his dress uniform.

One evening, my assistant Corporal Tippey, a Wesleyan Methodist boy from Indiana and a few of the men met in the headquarters tent. Corporal Tippey had a nice tenor voice, and on that evening he sat up a little portable organ and began playing hymns while we sang. Each of the men in turn asked him to play their favorite hymn that they had enjoyed from their particular denomination. The men were all Christians and as the evening passed, I discovered that of the ten men that had participated, all came from different states and most came from different denominations, and all had different national heritages. That is, their heritage was from different countries of Europe. I became so impressed with the melting pot aspect of America and the unifying force of songs and religion that I wrote a poem about the experience and called it "Songfest Benediction."

Songfest Benediction

Our hearts are full tonight, Dear Lord.
For we have felt Thy Presence near
As we have sung these hymns so dear
To followers of Thee.
And as our thoughts have heaven-ward soared
On wings of song with notes so clear,
We felt the absence of all fear
In sweet humility.

Our tent has known new sounds at last,
Where curses often fill the air
Tonight we uttered sincere prayer
With reverence, unashamed.
We've sung the songs of ages past,
And burdens that we daily bear
Were cast aside with freedom rare,
And Thy sweet spirit claimed.

The problems of the world today;
How peace can come to earth again
And man can live with fellowmen
Seemed solved at one in Thee.
For we are made of common clay,
And though we differ now and then
In race and creed, we were not ten
but one in harmony.

O God, our Father; hear us now,
We need Thee and Thy guiding hands
To teach this lesson in all lands
Wherever men may be.
Eternal Father, show us how
To hearken to Thy law's demands
And cease to live as waring bands,
But as Thy family.

Eugene E. Campbell:
The People of Europe are Starving For the Word of God

*The destruction resulting from the war caused millions to
suffer—to suffer from lack of shelter, clothing, food, and from
hearing the word of God. The following account from the pen
of Chaplain Eugene Campbell demonstrates the need of God and
his words in the life of people.*[1]

"Dear Brother,

Can you believe that the day has come when an entire community of Lutherans will beg a Mormon elder to hold worship
services for them in their own church? Frankly, I never expected
it to happen, but it has happened to me, not only once, but three
times, and will probably happen several more times in the future.
Here is how it happened.

As chaplain for special troops in this division, it is my duty
to provide services for several different groups of soldiers in widely
separated areas. A few days after arriving on the front lines, I began
to go from village to village to arrange worship services for my men,
and I found that the people in these villages were also in need of
religious leadership. They are German-speaking people, and mainly
adhere to the Evangelical Lutheran faith. Most of their pastors left
with the retreating German Army, and the few who remain are
not able to serve all the people here. The people seem incapable
of helping themselves religiously, and are even letting their beautiful old churches disintegrate. As I went to the burgomeister of
each village and asked for permission to use their chapels for my
services, they found that I spoke enough German to be understood, and they asked if their townspeople might be permitted to
attend also. I agreed, but told them that I was a Mormon, not a
Lutheran. It didn't matter to them. They were starving for the
word of God, and would *welcome anyone* who could bring it to
them.

So last Sunday I held three joint soldier-civilian services. Of
course, using both languages presented a problem, but no one
seemed to mind. I spoke, prayed, sang, and read from the Bible
first in German and then in English. It was thrilling to hear them
sing their songs, and to see their eyes shining with the happiness

----
1. *Church News,* June 9, 1945.

that true worship brings. At the conclusion of each service, the burgomeister and other village notables thanked me in the name of the people, and asked me to promise to come back next week.

I couldn't help but feel that possibly a new era is dawning for our missionary work, and that after this war our missionaries all over the world will find many of the old barriers of prejudice and disinterest have been broken. I also felt to thank God for providing us with such a wise system of Church government, wherein every worthy boy and man can hold the priesthood, which gives him the authority and the responsibility to take *the lead in our Church.*

My testimony is growing stronger each day as I associate with people, both in the army and out, who have not been blessed with a knowledge and understanding of the true Gospel of Jesus Christ. How wonderfully simple it is! How clearly it points the way to happiness! How carefully our Father in Heaven has plotted the course for us!

I am also happy to report that of the more than 50 LDS men in this division, most of them are trying to live their religion, and are attending our meetings whenever possible. We are well organized and are holding meetings whenever it is possible to get together. We held some wonderful services aboard ship while coming over here, and had many non-members in attendance who showed a genuine interest in our message.

I only hope and pray that God will bless our men and women all over the world, and that he will continue to bless you in your great responsibility."

Eugene E. Campbell:
Would You Like to Have a Kiss, Chaplain?

Chaplain Eugene Campbell relates the following amusing experience he had when he misinterpreted a young woman's German. [1]

Before we arrived on the Rhine, we pushed across France, and as we first hit the front lines, we stayed in a little town called Benesdorf. It was in Alsace-Lorraine France, right in the Saar region between France and Germany. The French and Germans

---

1. Eugene Campbell interview.

have been fighting over that area since the Treaty of Verdun back in 843 AD. I was able to observe the conditions and got a bit of a feeling of how it must have been to have lived there. This family from Luxemberg said that they kept two flags in the attic, a French flag and a German flag. They didn't know which one to fly. We were friendly with this family that night and shared our K rations with them, which was a treat to them. They had some fresh eggs which they shared with us and this was a treat to us.

I had an amusing experience with a member of this family that first night. I could speak some German, having taken a couple of years of German at Snow College and I had reviewed it while working on my masters degree. I used it a little while on my mission. In Canada I commenced talking with this man and his wife, who had three grown daughters, and we tried to understand each other. We spoke in German and had a very pleasant evening. As I was putting my bedroll down on their living room floor one of the daughters came in and said, "Wollen sie ein kissen haben?" and, in my limited German, that sounded to me like "Would you like to have a kiss?" I thought, maybe those World War I stories were true about the French girls. I didn't answer her and she went out of the room and pretty soon she came back with a pillow and said, "Hier ist einen kissen." Then I discovered that the word for pillow in German is "kissen," the word for kiss is "küssen." You can see that they are pretty close, especially the way they are pronounced with the umlaut above the "u."

Grant E. Mann:
That Inner Feeling

While serving in Europe with the 42nd Infantry Division (Rainbow Division) somewhere in Germany, Chaplain Grant Mann experienced the "inner feeling" which may have saved his life.[1]

It was a beautiful spring day when Chaplain Mann arrived in a small German town. He was sitting on the doorstep of a bombed out house when a Red Cross truck arrived and passed out sandwiches, donuts, and coffee to the soldiers. While he sat there, he had a strong feeling that something was wrong. He couldn't tell exactly why, but he felt uncomfortable.

---

1. Grant Mann interview.

Chaplain Grant E. Mann, winner of the Bronze Star, conducting an outdoor service in southern Germany, April 1945.

Just then, one of the men from his unit came over to speak with him. He said, "Chaplain, I got word that my mother is dying and I want to go home. If she dies, I don't want to live."

His name was Green and he came from Illinois. The chaplain replied, "Soldier, right now it's hard to do anything because everyone is on the move. I will do everything I can do for you, but you have to remember we are at war and there are lots of 'snafus' during wartime."

"I understand, Chaplain, but you must get me home."

As they talked, a friend of Chaplain Mann's yelled, "Hey, Chappie, come here, I have something I want to show you."

He told the soldier he would be back shortly, and as he left the doorstep Green sat down exactly where he had been. Chaplain Mann felt a sense of relief come over him as he walked down the street with his friend. They traveled approximately 100 yards and entered a bombed out building. His friend showed him a record player that was intact. It was one of the old wind-up types, and there were some records there untouched by the bombing. They played a record or two and then heard the noise of a big shell coming in followed by a blast. Some yelled, "Somebody's been hurt."

They ran from the shelter and looked down the street and there where Chaplain Mann had been sitting only moments before lay the dead body of the soldier who had asked for his help.

To this day the chaplain feels certain that he was warned from beyond the veil that he was in danger, and luckily he moved. He did learn, however, from that time on that when an "inner voice speaks," he listens.

Eugene E. Campbell:
A Chaplain Captures Two Towns

While serving under combat conditions in Europe, many servicemen, including chaplains, found themselves lost behind enemy lines trying to find their military units. This was due to the front lines being very fluid and extending in all directions. Often, a military chaplain, while looking for men in his unit, would travel several miles behind enemy lines without knowing it. The following experience happened to Chaplain Eugene Campbell as he looked for his unit in Fulda, Germany. [1]

The tanks of Patton's Third Army travelled along the main highways and occupied the main cities. The infantry regiments moved forward on each side of the tank force capturing the smaller towns. In that way, Patton's army swept across Europe. On one occasion, my division was assigned to clean up the small towns on one side of the thrust and then I received orders to report to my division headquarters at Fulda, Germany.

Upon receiving the order, my driver and I headed for Fulda in my jeep. We had a carbine with us, and that was the total amount of protection we had. We were under the impression that the whole region was under American control. We were within ten miles of the city when we came to a bridge that had been blown out. We didn't know of any other way to get to Fulda, but as luck would have it, I noticed a farmer working in a nearby field, and asked him if there was another way to get to Fulda. He told me that a jeep could cross over the river on a dam by a mill a short distance away and gave us directions to get there.

We thanked him and set out for the dam. We crossed a bridge and entered a small German town, and as we headed through I noticed all the Germans hanging out their sheets. I knew that this is the way Germans air their bedding so I didn't pay much attention. After all, they do it every day. I heard some small arms fire, but it didn't seem like it was very close. We even had a flat tire in the town and stopped to fix it. We travelled on and passed through

---

1. Eugene Campbell interview.

another German town and witnessed a similar hanging out of sheets and finally arrived in Fulda, but couldn't find the 71st Infantry Division Headquarters. Instead, we found the 26th Division which was supposed to have moved on by this time. I went in to talk with the commanding officer as to why my division wasn't there and his was. He asked me, "What are you doing here?"

"I had orders to report to my unit here. What's happened to them?"

"There has been a delay and they are not here yet. By the way, Chaplain, how in the world did you get here?"

I went over to the map and pointed to it, showing him the route we took.

He smiled and said, "Congratulations, Chaplain, you just conquered two towns!"

Eugene E. Campbell:
Here Come the Mormons

One of the most notable traits about the LDS servicemen during World War II was their desire to be with one another. Chaplain Eldin Ricks attributed this to the common bonds that existed among them. They came from the same geographical area, knew many of the same people, had the same standards, and the same heritage. On many occasions, Chaplain Eugene Campbell was kidded about this trait of seeking out other Mormons. He tells the following humorous story to illustrate this: [1]

Right after the war, several chaplains from our division were dining in a little Austrian resort town of Bad Hall. While sitting at the table in one of the local inns, I saw two young LDS soldiers that I knew in our division. Because they were in another regiment, I hadn't seen them since we had gone into combat. I said to the group that I was dining with, "Pardon me. I see a couple of my Mormon friends, and I want to talk with them." I went out and visited with them for a while and when I returned, the other chaplains kidded me about this feeling that Mormons seemed to have for one another just because they are Mormons.

From that time on, wherever any strange looking group of people appeared, I was kidded. One time a group of Menonites came down the street dressed in the black coats, black boots, and broad rimmed black hats and their women all dressed in black.

---

1. *Ibid.*

Chaplain Pippen said, "Let's get Chaplain Campbell, there are some Mormons in town."

Howard C. Badger:
A Voice From No-Where

The Power of the Holy Ghost saved many LDS servicemen from certain death during World War II. The following experience was told to Chaplain Howard Badger by a young serviceman somewhere in Germany during 1945.[1]

I met a fine young LDS serviceman at one of our Church meetings. He told me that he was a courier. I knew that his was an extremely dangerous job as the couriers carried important and sometimes very urgent messages between commands. In some cases a courier had to travel through enemy territory to deliver the message.

On one occasion, he received an assignment to deliver an urgent message to another command area which required the use of a jeep. He had to travel at night which made it even more hazardous, and because he was in a war zone area, he couldn't use any lights. He could only use the cat eyes on the jeep and they were used so that oncoming traffic could spot his vehicle. It was hard driving at night along a dark road, and on that particular night, the road was extremely dark. He used the silhouette of the trees along the side of the road to guide him. He travelled as fast as he dared to, because of the urgency of getting that message through. While riding along, all of a sudden, he heard a voice say, "Stop." The voice was so demanding and clear that he couldn't refrain from obeying it. He slammed on the brakes, and his jeep skidded to a halt with one wheel hanging over a precipice. The bridge before him had been blown out, and had it not been for that voice, the voice of the Holy Spirit, he most certainly would have lost his life plunging over that ravine.

Arthur Spencer:
A Mormon Conference

Mormons love to hold meetings. While doing missionary work, one young LDS flyer received an unforgettable answer regarding Mormons and all their meetings.[2]

---

1. Howard Badger interview.
2. *Ibid.*

Chaplain Howard Badger, while serving in Marseilles, France had an interesting experience at a place called Istres which was some 30 to 40 miles from Marseilles. Several LDS servicemen served with the Air Force on the base and he travelled to Istres to provide services for them. He met a young Lieutenant, Brother Arthur Spencer, who flew as a member of a bomber crew. This young officer told Chaplain Badger that he always tried to be a missionary, and while flying one day, he said to his skipper of the plane, "Sir, I don't know whether you are acquainted with Mormons or not, but I am a Mormon, and I'd like to tell you something about our Church."

The pilot turned to him smiling and said, "Lieutenant, you don't have to tell me anything about your Church. I've met some of your men before and one thing I've learned about you Mormons is that if there are two or three of you, you hold a meeting, and if you have more than three, you hold a "conference.""

Leon Flint:
To Partake of the Sacrament

Many Latter-day Saints partake of the sacrament each Sunday as a way of life. They may even take it for granted, with the attitude that it's always there. But many who served in World War II found it wasn't always available. Chaplain Leon Flint had the following experiences regarding the sacrament. [1]

While on board the ship, Isle De France, on our way to the European Theatre of Operations, there were some 13,000 G.I.'s aboard. On Sunday after I had held the Protestant church services, I called for an LDS service aboard this ship, and approximately 40 men showed up. We held the service in the ship's chapel. It being the first Sunday, naturally we observed the fast and testimony meeting. How well I remember the many men who stood and emphasized that it was the first time in three, four or even six months that they had had the opportunity to partake of the sacrament, and how they had taken the sacrament for granted until they had no opportunity to do so. They showed great emotion for their appreciation that Sunday on the high seas of being able to observe and partake of the sacrament once again.

---

1. Interview of Leon H. Flint by Richard Maher, February 25, 1975. Charles Redd Center for Western Studies. Oral History Project: LDS Chaplains of World War II.

I have thought that this should be a great lesson to members of the Church who live where they are constantly partaking of the sacrament and are not deprived of it as was indicated in this experience aboard the ship.

Another experience occurred during the occupation of Germany. Chaplain Flint attended many meetings in Munich with both Germans and American servicemen attending. He noticed that one young American LDS nurse attended almost every Sunday. He didn't know her, but he recalled the day that she stood and bore her testimony.

She said, "It's such a joy to be here with you each week and partake of your sweet spirit. I travel 150 miles each Sunday just to come here to church and partake of the sacrament. Partaking of the sacrament is that important to me. When I take the sacrament it seems that I get through the week without any major problems and I feel the Lord's presence. When I can't get away from my unit to receive the sacrament, the week doesn't seem to be the same." How true the chaplain thought—the week just isn't the same when one doesn't partake of the sacrament on Sunday.

Howard C. Badger:
Ezra Taft Benson Goes to Europe

"If I were to choose the highlight of my chaplaincy," said Howard C. Badger, "it would be the blessing of having helped in re-establishing the organization of the Church in the war torn areas, after the war, with Elder Ezra Taft Benson."

While stationed at Marseilles, France, I received an assignment transferring me to London. I headed to London by way of Paris. I had a few days before I had to report to London, and while in Paris, I looked up Sherm Brinton, an M.D. working in a Paris hospital, and Tom Adams who was assigned to the Provost Marshal's office in Paris. They both held the rank of Captain and were in charge of the LDS Servicemen's Program in the Paris area. During a church service which I attended in Paris, it was announced that Elder Ezra Taft Benson of the Council of the Twelve was coming to Paris within a day or two with the assignment to reopen the European Missions. He had obtained permission from the proper authorities to do this. In addition, he planned to bring welfare aid to the members of the Church in Europe. My orders permitted me to stay in Paris long enough to meet him. I went out to Orley Field with a group of about a dozen servicemen to greet him. One can imagine the thrill this group of young servicemen received when they met and shook hands with an apostle of the Church, especially after having been away from home for a couple of years. Many had been away for two years or more and the only contact most of us had with the Church was reading the *Church News* and our own experiences in attending LDS services throughout Europe when circumstances permitted.

Shortly after meeting him, he told us that he was anxious to find a serviceman who could accompany him on his tour throughout Europe. He had been told by both civilian and military authorities that it would be very difficult for a civilian to arrange travel and housing accommodations in military zones throughout Europe. He had concluded it would be best to get a serviceman to accompany him. Neither Brother Adams nor Brother Brinton could make the necessary arrangements to go with him, and it appeared that no one would be able to aid him in his mission.

Then, someone suggested that I might be able to accompany him. I thought it seemed rather unrealistic that the army would cancel my orders assigning me to London in order to accompany a civilian throughout Europe.

Nevertheless, just the thought of being in Elder Benson's company seemed a wonderful privilege so I applied for the assignment. I went to the Chaplain Corps Headquarters in Paris and said to one of the senior chaplains, "I would like to have permission to accompany an apostle from my Church on his tour of Europe to reopen the missions for the Mormon Church."

"Chaplain, I have never heard of any such request being granted, but we will process your application anyway. But, it seems quite unlikely that military authorities will approve your request. Come back in a couple of days."

In a couple of days I returned, and he said, "I'm sorry, Chaplain, but there has been no word on your request."

With some concern I said, "This Church leader is most anxious to leave as soon as possible. Who can I see at headquarters who has the authority to grant me permission or turn me down."

"Well, you might inquire at the Adjutant General's office of Army Command. I'm sure someone over there can give you an answer."

I went to the Adjutant General's office and found an officer who could approve or reject my request. I was escorted into his office, and he asked, "What can I do for you, Chaplain?"

"Sir, I made out an application requesting that I accompany Elder Ezra Taft Benson of the Mormon Church on his mission throughout Europe."

"I'm sorry, Chaplain, but I haven't seen your application. What did you say was the name of that Church leader again?"

"Ezra Taft Benson."

"That name strikes a familiar note. I think I have something on that man." He pulled open his drawer and pulled out a folder. He looked through the correspondences and came to a letter. The letter came from the Chief of Staff of the Army of the United States, and it stated that Ezra Taft Benson of the Council of the Twelve of the Mormon Church would be visiting throughout Europe and stated that any assistance that might be provided by any military command would be greatly appreciated. "Well, Chaplain, it looks like Mr. Benson is some sort of V.I.P. I think that this letter is enough of an authorization to grant your request. I'll issue your orders immediately."

I received orders to accompany Elder Benson and his secretary, Brother Fred Babbel. In Paris, we purchased an army vehicle and Brother Babbel and I drove the vehicle into Holland where we met Brother Cornelius Zappy, president of the Netherlands Mission. This vehicle was to later prove invaluable in distributing welfare supplies from Salt Lake to needy brothers and sisters in Holland.

Our next assignment took us to Geneva, Switzerland where we met with Brother Max Zimmer, president of the Swiss-Austrian Mission. Part of Elder Benson's assignment in Switzerland was to get permission from the Red Cross officials for the Church to send carloads of food stuffs, blankets, clothing, and other supplies from America into Europe for the Saints. In Basel, Switzerland, Elder Benson assigned President Zimmer and myself to go to Geneva, Switzerland to meet with the Red Cross leaders. We went by train to Geneva and met with the proper officials. They immediately gave the Church permission to send its welfare supplies to Church members throughout Europe.

Following Switzerland, we headed into Germany. Germany had taken a terrible beating. Many of the cities were in rubble, and few buildings stood intact. Nevertheless, we met with the Saints in all parts of Germany including Frankfurt, Dusseldorf, Stuttgart and Berlin. We soon learned that the faith of the Saints was still strong as we went from one bombed-out city to another. Our Saints met in schoolhouses that had been bombed out and other places that one would have to go through rubble to get down to an area where a little group of Saints would be gathered in some cellar of a home or meeting place. It was touching to see their faith and their love for Elder Benson and their appreciation for his visit. Often the scenes were so touching that they brought tears to the eyes of Elder Benson when he saw the destruction and conditions of the people. Many meetings were held where there was not a dry eye as members rejoiced in hearing the message and in feeling the love emanating from the Lord's special witness at long last in their midst. We learned from many of the Saints in Europe that the aid furnished by the Church often was the difference between life and death to many members of the Church. But the most unusual thing about it was that although the Saints were grateful for the goods that were coming into Europe, their joy and appreciation were not for goods, but for the joy of having an apostle of the Church on the scene in Europe.

In addition to travelling through Germany, we travelled throughout all of Europe. Our meetings had a familiar tone of love and faith from the European members whether we visited them in Austria, Czechoslovakia, Denmark, Sweden, Norway, Holland, Belgium, Switzerland, France or England.

I had spent approximately a month-and-a-half with Elder Benson when I received army orders sending me home. Elder Benson said, "Chaplain Badger, you have been a great aid to me and my mission. I feel that you can continue to be a great help, but I know that you have been away from home for a long time, and if you'd like to go, you certainly have my blessing. But if you want to stay, you may. It's your decision."

It took only a moment to make the decision. I knew that they needed me. I replied, "I'll stay as long as I'm needed to assist you." And another month was spent with Elder Benson and Brother Babbel.

I saw the Lord's hand in that decision, because I arrived home before those with whom I would have travelled. They travelled by ship and were detained in army camps, but I flew home and arrived in Salt Lake City several days before any of them did.

I arrived in Salt Lake City on Saturday night, April 5, 1946, in time to attend the last day of General Conference on Sunday. I brought with me a letter to the First Presidency from Elder Benson. When I delivered Elder Benson's letter to the First Presidency, I was told that if time permitted, I would be asked to say a few words in conference regarding Elder Benson's work in Europe. Time did not permit, but a most unusual and thrilling experience occurred for me when Elder Spencer W. Kimball and Elder Mark E.

Peterson asked me to sit on the stand in the Tabernacle through that Sunday morning conference session—and to occupy the seat between those two great brethren, which seat Elder Benson would have occupied had he been there. This was a kindness and a wonderful welcoming home which I treasure.

While traveling with Elder Benson, I observed his masterful way of handling people. It was a thrilling experience to see the ease with which he moved among people whether one came from a high position or a lowly station in life. Their class or station meant no difference to him and he put them right at ease. For example, while in Frankfurt, Germany, we visited with the commanding general of the occupation force in southern Germany. The general had a huge office with all the pomp and pageantry to go with the position. But Elder Benson was completely at ease with him, and in command of the situation. He told the general what he needed to accomplish his task and the general gave him permission to do just as he wished.

It seemed that everything he tried to do worked, and an unseen power was helping him do what was needed to complete his mission, while others were unable to accomplish the things he could do. For instance, he wanted to go into Czechoslovakia and got permission to visit that country. But there had been members of many of the Protestant Churches whom we met who had been trying for months to get into that country. I suppose the prestige of his office, and recommendations from the Chief of Staff helped, but I feel even more that it was the fact that the Lord was with him that allowed him, a civilian, to get so much done.

We only had time to spend a day or two in any given place for the two and one-half months that I travelled with him. We met hardships, but always had the confidence and faith and feeling that the Lord was near at hand and that his work was moving forward, and it did. If anyone had witnessed as I did how inspired Elder Ezra Taft Benson was, he would know as I know that he is truly one of our Heavenly Father's chosen prophets.

VII
The Role of
A Chaplain's Wife

Doris Warren of Nephi, Utah, like many other young women from small Mormon communities expected to marry, settle down, and rear a family in and around her home town. She hadn't anticipated on that glorious day, June 15, 1940, as she and Timothy H. Irons married for time and eternity in the Manti Temple, that she was about to embark on a life of sacrifice and devotion. As the wife of an army chaplain, she received overwhelming responsibilities as she aided her husband during his career which spanned twenty years of service.

There is nothing unusual about being a chaplain's wife unless one's husband is a member of a lay church—that is, a church that does not have a professional ministry as most do. Because of this unusual situation, the Mormon chaplain has to make adjustments by virtue of becoming a professional minister. In addition, his wife also faces many challenges. She learns quickly that she must be an example to the community whether military or civilian. She must accept and play the role of a protestant minister's wife, and for a young Mormon woman from a small Mormon community, it has to be quite an adjustment. Therefore, this chapter attempts to show some of the unusual experiences encountered by Doris Bowers-Irons during her twenty years as a chaplain's wife.

Doris Irons:
"I'd Rather Be Married to a Live Captain Than a Dead Major"

Timothy Irons has the distinction of being the only Mormon chaplain to have served during three wars, World War II, Korea, and Vietnam. Over a period of 20 years' service, he and his wife experienced several separations. The following account expresses a woman's feeling while being separated from her loved one. [1]

---

1. Doris (Warren) Bowers-Irons interview.

Doris remembers her first experience with the army. Tim, like so many of their friends, had to go to war and during the summer of 1943 he received his draft notice. It terrified her just thinking about his leaving. He did, however, receive a short deferment until he planted the crops that fall. They planted approximately 500 acres, and she helped with the plowing. Plowing those acres of land gave her a guilty feeling that lasted for a long time, because each time she rode that tractor around the fields dipping the plow into the earth and turning the furrows, she knew it meant that Tim would be leaving that much sooner. She didn't want him to go, and hated the military for taking him away from her. He was gone for three years. The war, to one who waited, seemed to last forever, and knowing he served in combat areas in Italy, France, and Germany made her wonder if she would ever see her husband again. Some of the girls she knew lost their husbands in the war, and others who couldn't take the long separation, sued for divorce. It was a depressing situation, but eventually the war ended and Tim came home for a while anyway.

The Korean War did not enhance her attitude toward the army as Tim and she became separated a second time. This time, however, the separation was more bearable because they knew the period of time that he would be away. In June 1951, Tim volunteered to go to Korea with the Utah National Guard. He did not have to go because of his marital status, but felt it his duty to serve his country. She had persuaded him to stay out of the military for approximately five years, but she couldn't prevent him from going to Korea.

Tim served in Korea with the "Flash and Dash Battalion," the 653rd Field Artillery Observation Battalion with Lieutenant Colonel Reed H. Richards of Salt Lake City commanding. He had been in Korea for several months when she received a letter from him asking her if she would object if he extended his time in Korea three months. One of the reasons being that he was told he could get promoted to major if he did. She didn't want him to extend so she ignored his letter, and never mentioned the subject in any return letters. One night Tim telephoned from Korea. "You haven't answered my letter regarding my extending for three months," he said.

She hadn't wanted to make the decision and was under the impression the time had passed for a decision to be made so answered, "I'd rather be married to a live captain than a dead major."

There was a long wait and finally he said, "Okay, I won't put in for an extension. I'll come home when my time is up."

She didn't give him the answer he wanted, but he turned down the extension because of her. As it turned out though, he had to serve the extra three months anyway because there was not a replacement for him when his time was up, but he was not promoted to the higher rank at that time.

Doris Irons:
Communications Get Better

It takes two to make a conversation, a speaker and a listener. If one party doesn't listen, there can be no communication. This happened to Tim and Doris, but they found a solution.[1]

A separation of a man and a woman can in some cases improve their relationship. The letters they wrote during the one year separation while Tim was in Korea helped mature their marriage. Letters were so important that they longed for them and wrote to one another each day. In the course of one year they had a great deal to say and managed to get much said. Doris commented:

"While in a normal conversation we used to tune each other out. We couldn't do this with letters. We learned to listen to what the other said. I told him in my letters why I didn't like the military, and he couldn't butt in and say, 'yes, but you see...' and explain his point of view. He would read my letter all the way to the end. I also read his letters to the end, and I learned from reading his letters that he really loved the excitement of serving men and God in the capacity of a chaplain. I don't think he would have wanted to stay in the military in any other capacity, but he loved helping and serving others, and this was the type of work a chaplain performed. He told me over and over again that he wanted to make a career of being a military chaplain. He felt that this was his calling and he loved it, but needed my support. I, of course, found myself in a perplexing situation, having to make the decision whether or not he should make the military his career. It was a hard decision to make but at least I felt better making it since I understood Tim a lot better because I had read all those letters."

In addition to general letter writing, they made it a project to read the same book and discuss it by letters. One of the books they read and discussed was *A Marvelous Work and a Wonder* by LeGrand Richards. They would each read a chapter in the book, and then write to each other and tell what they thought about it

---

1. *Ibid.*

and compare notes. They read other books dealing with a variety
of subjects like psychology and sociology. This, too, aided them
in learning about one another and increased their appreciation of
each other and brought them very close. In fact, many times since
Korea, Tim has said, "Doris, let's do some letter writing. We are
not listening to each other."

Timothy H. Irons:
Chaplain Tim's Clothing Drive

*Americans have always been willing to help others in need by
giving and giving generously. During the Korean War, Americans
made contributions that saved the lives of many Korean children.
The following account tells how it happened.* [1]

During the fall of 1951, Chaplain Timothy Irons stopped at a
store in a small south Korean town to get some supplies. His driver
went into the store while he waited in the jeep. It was cold, very
cold, and he sat there shivering, though warmly dressed, when a
group of Korean children surrounded him and asked for a candy
bar. He noticed their scantily clad, dirty, shivering bodies. The
sight of them nearly broke Tim's heart. He is a very kind and
sensitive man, and thought to himself that many of these young
children of God would be dead by spring if nothing was done. He
decided to do something about it. He consulted with Major Jack
Adamson, a Mormon friend in the Air Force, and they decided to
write home to their families and have them send clothing. His
letter to Doris read:

"...go through all our children's clothing, and if they have
two pairs of pants, send me one; if they have two undershirts, send
me one; if they have two pairs of pajamas, send me one. I want you
to divide what our kids have with the Korean kids over here...."

It was a nice gesture on Tim's part, but being realistic, Doris
realized that if the situation was as bad as he described, many other
Korean children must be in a similar plight and she knew that the
meager articles of clothing from their children's wardrobe wouldn't
go very far. She talked with her bishop, Brent Goates, thinking that
he might be interested in turning the problem into a ward project.
That way many more articles of clothing could be sent. She went
to him and said, "Bishop, Tim wrote me describing the terrible
plight facing the Korean children this winter. Here is his letter."

---

1. *Ibid.*

She didn't know it at the time, but Brent Goates worked for the *Deseret News.* He read the letter very carefully and said, "I work for the *Deseret News,* and I feel that this is something that will be of great interest to the newspaper. I will see if we can get some sort of campaign going to help those children."

With the help of Brent Goates, the *Deseret News* sponsored a drive and called it "Chaplain Tim's Clothing Drive." People from the Utah area contributed to the drive. It became very successful, but was mostly a local drive until Lowell Thomas, the famous radio news broadcaster got involved. He stopped in Salt Lake City on his way to the coast and noticed a large van located in front of Walgreen's Drug Store on the corner of Main and South Temple, that had the words, "Chaplain Tim's Clothing Drive." Being a newscaster, he made inquiries and learned about the clothing drive for the Korean children. He felt it so news worthy that on his next broadcast (from Lake Tahoe) he mentioned the drive over the national radio hook-up. His comments caused the project to expand from a local project to a national one. After his broadcast, thousands of people from all over the United States forwarded new and used clothing to Chaplain Irons in Korea.

Because of the broadcast, Tim's friends in Harbor Springs, Michigan; Fort Sill, Oklahoma; and St. Johns, Arizona got involved. Tim worked as a lifeguard in Harbor Springs, Michigan during the summer of 1939 and 1940. He stayed at the home of Al and Dora Goodrich. When they learned that he headed up this drive, they helped to organize a group in Harbor Springs, Michigan. In addition, friends from Fort Sill, Oklahoma, and St. Johns, Arizona organized groups to get clothing to him. Further, *The Church News* pushed the project with more publicity by running articles explaining the need of the Koreans.

Tim received packages from nearly every state in the union. The project which started with a request to his wife to send some clothing grew until he received over 800,000 pounds of clothing during that winter of 1951-1952.

No one knows how many children are alive today because of the clothing sent by the thousands of people who cared enough to help children—children of God.

Doris Irons:
A Coupon Book

Often, a gift costing very little in monetary terms is highly cherished. One Christmas, Doris sent Tim just such a gift.[1]

1. *Ibid.*

Because of the clothing drive, Doris couldn't send Tim a personal package for Christmas. She feared that it would get mixed up with all the packages of clothing. She did want to send him something, naturally, and one day while reading a magazine she decided that she would make and send him a coupon book. She got the inspiration when she saw an advertisement for tires. The ad read, "...tires hug the curves like crazy." She took the words "hug the curves like crazy" and pasted them on a sheet of paper the size of an air mail envelope. She put at the top, "Redeemable on Demand." She looked and found others. She put a picture of an apple pie in the coupon book, and again headed it "Redeemable upon Demand." Another was a picture of a couple dancing. She placed the title "An evening of dancing" with that one. It was fun looking through the magazines finding pictures to put in the coupon book and it turned out to be a fantastic gift when finished. Doris commented that Tim enjoyed redeeming his coupons, especially the "hug the curves like crazy" one.

Doris Irons:
The Usual Devotional

A young woman from a small Mormon community becomes "the Chaplain's wife" and faces her first major task. The following is an account of that situation.[1]

Doris was proud of Tim and the fine job he did while serving in Korea. She was especially proud of the clothing drive, and had a feeling she, too, had been of service to someone. She got a taste of what he felt working as a chaplain. When he returned, they decided he was to stay in the military. She faced a great challenge when she became "the Chaplain's wife." In military circles, the chaplain's wife is a very prominent person and much is expected of her. Doris came from a small Mormon town and knew only Mormonism. She didn't know or understand anything of the Protestant religions. Nevertheless, she and Tim had confidence in her ability to adjust.

Her first major test came when she went to Germany in 1954. She was part of a group of ladies called the Protestant Women of the Chapel. It was a movement that got support from the administrative Protestant Chaplains during the 1950's. All army posts had the organization, and, of course, as a chaplain's wife, she

---

1. *Ibid.*

became a leader in the movement. She had never heard of it before, but there were to be meetings monthly, with set goals for the group. One day, Betty Cannon, Rose Penoyer (wives of Protestant chaplains), and Doris had a meeting about the organization and she suggested they have a devotional at the beginning of each meeting. They both felt it a good idea and said to her, "Doris, would you please conduct the meeting?"

This upset her, because she hadn't been reared Protestant, and didn't know exactly what a Protestant devotion consisted of. She asked Betty, "Now, just what do you want me to do in this devotional?"

Betty said, "Oh, the usual."

"Oh, the usual?" queried Doris.

Betty said, "Yes."

That was no help at all. "I presume you want a prayer with this devotional. Who should we ask to say the prayer?" Doris asked.

"Oh, you're conducting, you do that."

"The usual."

"Yes, the usual," Betty said.

"How long should we have the devotional? The usual time?" By this time Doris was convinced that maybe there was such a thing as "the usual."

"Oh yes, the usual time," was Betty's reply.

She thought to herself, I'm not getting anywhere with the conversation. She was answering her own questions instead of letting Betty answer them. Then it occurred to her that perhaps Betty didn't know any more about it than she did. Doris continued asking questions, "What should the devotional be like?"

"Oh, the usual."

"Yes, I understand, but what exactly is the usual?"

Betty replied, "I don't know. I suppose all churches are pretty much the same, just go ahead and do what you would do in the Mormon Church."

Doris went to Tim and explained her situation, "What is the 'usual'?" she asked of him.

He said, "Just read a scripture, give a thought and have a prayer."

She worked hard to put together a good devotional. She used the Relief Society magazine visiting teaching message for the thought with it's related scripture. She thought it very appropriate for the occasion, and the ladies were thrilled with her message, and it was suggested that all devotionals in the future follow the same pattern. She was asked to show other groups the way to present a good devotional. "I am thankful for those Relief Society magazines, because I got most of my material from them." Her reputation spread until it came to the attention of one of the administrative chaplains in the area. He invited her to attend a planning meeting at Berchtesgaden for the organization of the Protestant Women of the Chapel, and he specifically asked Doris to bring her Relief Society magazines.

Upon arrival at Berchtesgaden she sought out Chaplain Ed Curtley, a Disciple of Christ, who was in charge of the meeting. He said to her, "Mrs. Irons, I've been looking for you. Now, don't tell anyone that you are a Mormon. May I have your books?"

Doris felt funny because of what he said, and asked, "Why shouldn't I tell anyone I'm a Mormon?"

He explained that they hoped to use the magazines for much of the planning, and that it was against regulations to use denominational material. She understood, and then he told her to give him the books, but she said, "I go with my magazines."

He said, "No, just give them to me."

She said, "No."

"Okay, Mrs. Irons, you win. You can be on the planning board."

That is what she wanted all along. She helped in the organization of the Protestant Women of the Chapel. She prepared and conducted devotionals for the ladies on the committee to show them what an appropriate devotional could be like. The Relief Society Magazine kept her in ideas for all the years she served as a chaplain's wife. "It was a great aid to me, and it gave me a reputation of excellence for which I am indebted to the magazine."

Doris Irons:
Part of the Family

The Iron family experienced a full Sunday. They attended both Protestant and LDS services. Later lots of Mormon soldiers visited their home, causing Sunday to be one "hectic" day, too hectic for one member of the family.[1]

Tim saw to it that Protestant services and LDS services did not conflict so that the family could attend both. This made Sunday a long, hard, tiring day, especially for the children. Their

---

1. *Ibid.*

children loved to invite the Mormon servicemen over to their quarters for Sunday dinner after services, and sometimes they had as many as 35 soldiers in their small home. They sat on the floors, in the kitchen and in the living room. She often wonders how she provided food for the large gangs. She remembered the miracle of the loaves and fishes when He provided food for the multitudes, and it seemed they too never ran short. But Sunday was a hectic day with all the servicemen around. Sometimes she didn't know all of them. They made themselves at home, got into the cupboards, opened cans of food and cooked it, and sometimes there weren't enough pots and pans to cook with. She says, "It was fun and we loved it."

Because of this situation, one Sunday after the soldiers left, their daughter, Sanoma, complained, "I've had it. I'm sick and tired of having all these G.I.'s around here every Sunday. There is no privacy. I want a quiet day with *my* family. I want to be *alone* with *my* family."

Tim and Doris talked it over, and decided that on the next Sunday, they wouldn't invite anyone to Sunday dinner, they would have a family time. That became a problem because their two sons, Tim and Richard, loved to invite the servicemen home for dinner. They had to practically gag them on that particular Sunday, but they still managed to invite a few. Doris and Tim explained to the men and they understood so they had their family alone Sunday.

That Sunday was one of the most boring Sundays they had ever experienced. It was deathly quiet. Sunday evening Sanoma said, "I think we should have our soldiers over every Sunday. They are part of our family too."

Lawrence E. Reichmann:
Tim Preaches Mormonism

A military chaplain serves men of all faiths, not just members of his own particular denomination. It appears difficult for a Mormon to work in this capacity, but, for those who served, most found very little problem. A Mormon chaplain could skillfully quote Mormon scripture while giving a sermon. He wouldn't come out and say "Nephi said..." he would subtly remark, "An ancient prophet once said..." The following account deals with just such an event![1]

---

1. *Ibid.*

Tim and Doris had a wonderful friend in Germany by the name of (Lawrence E.) Reichmann. He is now a M.D. practicing in Salt Lake City. Just prior to leaving Germany he and his wife, Ruth, moved in with them. Larry often said he couldn't understand how Tim could preach in a Protestant church and feel comfortable. Larry worked at the post hospital, and one Sunday morning he decided he would take a few patients to Church and stay to hear Tim preach. He sat next to Doris. As the service proceeded, Larry began to constantly look around and appeared to be very uncomfortable. His behavior caused Doris some anxiety and she began to listen intently to every word that Tim said to see if he was saying words like "grace," etc. which aren't spoken often in the Mormon Church. She became very critical of his sermon and when he did use the word grace, she thought, how will I ever explain that to Larry? The service finally ended, and Larry said to her, "I've got to talk to you."

That evening at home. Larry said, "Can we talk somewhere alone?"

They went into another room, and he said, "I kept watching the commanding officer's face (Colonel Conrad). He listened so intently to every word Tim spoke. Do you think he will report Tim?"

She said, "What for?"

"For preaching Mormonism. He taught Mormon doctrine. Won't he get into trouble? I thought he had to teach Protestant doctrine."

"Oh Larry, that's funny. And all the time I worried because Tim used words like grace, and I felt that you might object."

"Does he always preach like that?"

"Yes, Larry, he preaches the Gospel of Jesus Christ."

Doris Irons:
All of Tim's Wives

Mormons gave up the practice of plural marriage late in the nineteenth century. It appears that all Americans are not aware of this. To the surprise of Doris Irons, she encountered a humorous situation regarding Tim and all his wives![1]

It is amazing how naive some people are about the religious beliefs of others. Tim and Doris attended a banquet for chaplains

1. *Ibid.*

and their wives at Kaiserslautern, Germany. Chaplain (Colonel) Mitchell Phillips conducted the meeting and sought to improve the Protestant Women of the Chapel organization by getting all the Protestant chaplains behind the movement. He said, "I want all you Protestant chaplains to make sure that your wives attend PWOC meetings."

One of the quick-witted chaplains jumped to his feet and said, "Chaplain Tim here wants to know if he can send all his wives."

That statement caused quite a stir, especially among those that didn't know Tim. Those who knew him kidded him about the statement. The word got around that Tim was a Mormon chaplain, and of course, everyone knew about "the Mormons and all their wives." Many in the audience thought Tim had more than one wife. Chaplain Phillips seemed embarrassed because of the commotion, and Doris felt that some response was needed. She stood up (with every eye in the hall on her) and said, "As Tim's first wife, I shall decide who shall attend." That took care of it and Chaplain Phillips went on to other business.

At the end of the evening as they were leaving the banquet, Doris noticed a couple of women making their way rapidly toward her, and they were gathering up other women on the way. They stopped her and said, "We would like to get acquainted with you Mrs. Irons. We want you to feel welcome."

At first she thought they had a job they wanted her to do but she wasn't interested in doing any job at that time. Then one of them in her syrupy voice asked, "Where do you live?"

Doris said, "We just moved to quarters, and I am very happy being there."

"Were you on the economy?"

"Yes, at first, then we lived in a two room BOQ (bachelor officers quarters), which seemed like the Waldorf Astoria. Now we are in regular quarters."

Then she asked Doris that special question, and she realized that the woman thought Tim was actually a polygamist, "How many of you are there?"

Doris thought she'd go along with her and play dumb. "Oh, there are six of us."

"That must have been awfully hard on all of you being in a two room BOQ."

"Yes, it was, but we managed quite well."

"How in the world did you all sleep there?"

"Well, we had three in one room and three in the other."

Doris almost laughed as she wondered what they pictured in their minds.

"What kind of quarters do you have now?"

"We have four bedrooms."

"Isn't that still crowded with six of you?"

"Oh, after living in a two room BOQ it's better than the Waldorf Astoria."

She had the time of her life toying with them.

"Are you the oldest?"

"No, Tim is."

"What are the ages of the others?"

"Sanoma is 12, Timothy is 7, Richard is 6, and Celeste is just a baby."

They looked shocked, and finally one said, "You must be talking about your children."

Doris answered, "Of course, who did you think I was talking about?" She knew very well who they were talking about, but it was quite a surprise to learn that in an enlightened society like ours, refined women still believed that the Mormons practiced polygamy.

Doris Irons:
The World Day of Prayer

Doris Irons had the privilege of being involved in the planning and implementation of a great program instituted for and behalf of women. The following is an account of her experience.[1]

Each year during the month of February, Doris recalls the wonderful experiences she had participating in the World Day of Prayer services while in the military. The Utah papers don't mention very much about the event, but it is an annual event sponsored by Christian women and the Protestant Women of the Chapel organization for the betterment of mankind, especially women. While stationed in Germany, the P.W.O.C. got involved with the first World Day of Prayer, and Doris was selected to lead the group in her area. The event was organized in such a way that for a solid twenty-four hours prayers were said around the world. Protestant groups around the earth had been given a certain time to pray so that for twenty-four consecutive hours the world would be with prayer. They prayed for the betterment of mankind, but espe-

---

1. *Ibid.*

cially for women. Many Protestant women felt that many Christian women lived exceedingly difficult lives and the group hoped to better their condition with this special day.

The Protestant women involved were extremely sincere in this endeavor. The World Day of Prayer was always an inspiration to Doris. She felt that the women sang the hymns with far greater fervor on the World Day of Prayer than at any other time. She recalls that on that First World Day of Prayer occasion when she led the group in prayer, she mentioned how bounteous was their repast and asked a blessing upon other less fortunates in the world. She asked that they might not suffer from lack of food or medical aid. She expressed a desire that the women open their hearts and purses and share with their brothers and sisters. After the devotional, one lady suggested that it would be wonderful if all fasted for one day and contributed the money they would have spent on food to some worthy cause in addition to the regular offering. As a group they couldn't contribute much, but decided to get other Protestant groups involved. As the movement expanded to many other Protestant organizations, a great deal of money was raised and donated to an international depository and distributed at their disgression. In the years following, the World Day of Prayer was designated as a day of fasting too.

It was exciting to be involved with such a fine group, and each February when Doris recalls the World Day of Prayer she finds a place where she can be alone and offer a prayer. It is a universal prayer, because she is interested in all of God's children and hopes that they will be blessed. She believes the concept of the World Day of Prayer does something for her—it stretches her feelings for humanity beyond what she ordinarily feels.

Doris Irons:
A Look Back

A hymn, a song, a name—all bring back memories. Doris Irons recalls the past. Did she enjoy being "the Chaplain's wife"? What does she remember as the best part?[1]

As Doris looks back she says, "I enjoyed being a chaplain's wife. We had a good life. I especially learned to appreciate and respect people of other persuasions. I learned that many are just as devoted to their religion as I am to mine, and they believe in

---

1. *Ibid.*

their way as I believe in mine. I learned that there are many wonderful people in God's world and I am grateful I could meet a few of them and count them as my friends and brothers and sisters."

VIII
A Wave Weds a Chaplain

Irene Hailes of Salt Lake City married Chaplain Eldin Ricks in the Salt Lake Temple June 9, 1949. Elder Harold B. Lee, a member of the Council of the Twelve Apostles performed the marriage. Irene had grown up in the Pioneer Stake in Salt Lake City and knew Brother and Sister Lee intimately. Sister Lee was her Gleaner teacher for many years, and both treated her like a daughter. All her life they advised her and helped her to make right decisions, including choosing a husband.

Elder Harold B. Lee served as the Chairman of the LDS Servicemen's Committee during World War II and, after the war, interviewed many of the returning LDS chaplains to evaluate the effectiveness of the Church's wartime servicemen's program. When he interviewed Chaplain Eldin Ricks, he evidently was sufficiently impressed with him that he felt that he and Irene would be a good match, and he put into motion a plan which brought them together. This chapter deals with Irene Hailes and her experiences with the military during the Second World War which led to her meeting and marrying a World War II Mormon chaplain.

Irene Hailes:
Doctrine and Covenants 9:7-9 Works

The scriptures teach and inspire, but, in order to get a testimony of them, one must apply the teaching in his life. Irene Hailes did and received the promised knowledge which is expressed in the following account.[1]

I came from a family that had salt water in its veins. My father and all his brothers served in the British Navy as did their father before them. I wanted to join the U.S. Navy when World War II began, but at that time, the navy had no program for women.

---

1. Irene (Hailes) Ricks interview.

I had no desire to join the Women's Army Corps, but soon after the United States' entry into the war, the navy started its WAVES program. I wanted to join badly, but for some reason, was afraid to enlist.

Each month Lieutenant Commander Symes came to Salt Lake City to recruit women into the WAVES, and each month I would go to his office and talk endlessly with him about enlisting. But, I never quite had the courage to take the step.

While visiting with my neighbors, Brother and Sister Lee, I mentioned to them that I would like to join the WAVES. Sister Lee said, "If I were young, I think I would like to join the WAVES also. It sounds so exciting."

Brother Lee, laughing at his wife's comment said, "Irene, I don't believe that the military is a good place for a nice young lady. There are all kinds of problems in the service."

I knew that many soldiers and sailors had a poor reputation and I appreciated his advice, but I couldn't get the idea out of my mind. The problem haunted me for several months. Then one day Brother Lee said, "How are you and the navy coming along?"

I said, "Brother Lee, I just can't make up my mind. I can't seem to reach a decision."

"Are you praying about it?"

"Yes, I am, but I can't seem to get an answer. I don't get a yes or a no answer."

"Then indecision must be your decision."

Feeling frustrated, I said, "Isn't there something I can do. This problem is driving me crazy. I really want to join the WAVES, but I want to do it only if it is the right thing to do."

I could tell that he felt bad for me, knowing the turmoil in my mind. He went to a book shelf and returned with two books. He handed one to me and said, "The Lord has given us direction in solving difficult problems like yours. Turn to Doctrine and Covenants 9, and we will read verses 7 to 9. Listen carefully as I read:

> "Behold you have not understood; you have supposed that I would give it unto you, when you took no thought save it was to ask me.
>
> But, behold, I say unto you, that you must study it out in your mind; then you must ask me if it be right, and if it is right, I will cause that your bosom shall burn within you; therefore, you shall feel it is right.

But if it be not right, you shall have no such feelings, but you shall have a stupor of thought that shall cause you to forget the thing which is wrong; therefore, you cannot write that which is sacred save it be given you from me."

He read the scriptures beautifully, and as word after word proceeded out of his mouth, I understood what the Lord meant and expected of me.

Brother Lee said, "Do you understand what I just read?"

I nodded that I did.

He said, "Follow the directions outlined, and if you pray hard enough, you will get a feeling that will let you know what to do, but you must pray hard."

"Thank you, Brother Lee, I am going home tonight and really pray hard, harder than I have ever done before."

"I know you will, and whatever you decide, I know that it will be right." I left his home feeling wonderful. He had given me the confidence to seek the answer from the Lord, and knowing that he would support me made me feel that much better. I believe the reason I couldn't come to a decision earlier was due to his feeling toward women serving in the military. That night I prayed harder than I had ever prayed in my life. I had the confidence that I would get an answer to my prayer. I wanted to have the right feeling if I were to join the WAVES. I awoke the next morning with my answer. I felt my bosom burning just like the scripture said it would and I knew that the Lord approved my joining the WAVES. Doctrine and Covenants 9:7-9 really worked. I could now join the WAVES with peace of mind.

Elder Lee must have thought that my prayers would lead to the opposite answer, because the very next day when I joined the WAVES, a young Mormon girl went into his office at the Church office building seeking his advice about joining the WAVES. Elder Lee said to her, "I have a very good friend who wanted to join the WAVES. Call her, and she will tell you."

The phone rang at my home, and a voice on the other end said, "Can you help me to decide whether or not to join the WAVES. Elder Lee felt you could help me."

"I joined the WAVES a couple of hours ago, and I feel great," was my response.

Elder Lee was astonished at my decision but he accepted it graciously. Sister Lee smiled when she heard it, just smiled. They had an open house for me in their home and invited all my friends to attend the afternoon of the day of my departure. I left for New York on Valentine's Day, February 14, 1943.

Irene Hailes:
A Little Bit of Heaven

Is the Church the same everywhere? Can a member go any-where and feel at home in a strange place? Irene Hailes answers those questions in the following account.[1]

I received one of the best assignments that the navy gave to women during World War II. Out of the several hundred girls finishing basic training at Hunter College, New York City, I was assigned to the Link Training School at Atlanta, Georgia. The Link Trainers were used to train pilots to fly by instruments under a variety of simulated conditions. The use of Link Trainers saved a great deal of actual flying time as cadets could learn to fly using instruments and never leave the ground. It was a choice assignment. and I spent approximately three months in training before being assigned to the Pasco Naval Air Station, Pasco, Washington. I had never heard of Pasco so I looked on the map and found that Pasco, Washington, was located in no man's land on a branch of the Snake and Columbia Rivers. I was very disappointed but not as disap-pointed as when I arrived. I thought Pasco, Washington, to be the most desolate place in the world, and said to myself, "Irene, why did you ever join the navy?" I learned from my experiences that first impressions can be deceptive.

I arrived at Pasco Naval Air Station with nine other WAVES. We were the contingent to operate the Link Trainers. Upon our arrival, we received a conducted tour of the naval air station. In the library we introduced ourselves to one another and gave our home towns. I said, "I'm Irene Hailes, and I come from Salt Lake City." I didn't notice, but a cadet who was reading a book in the library heard the magic word, "Salt Lake City," and came over to me and said, "Did you say that you were from Salt Lake City?"

"I did."

"Are you a Mormon?"

"I am."

"Oh, that's great." He shook my hand and said, "We have the most wonderful branch here in Pasco. Our Branch President, Lyal Stringham, is the most wonderful man. You'll love it here."

---

1. *Ibid.*

I felt better already. He was so enthusiastic about Pasco. Could it be that I had misjudged this place? "What are you going to be doing here at Pasco?"

"I'll be working with the Link Trainers."

"Lucky you. The man in charge of the Links is Eddie Blazer. He's a Mormon from Ephraim, Utah."

I could hardly believe what I was hearing. My first day in this desolate place, and I learn that the branch is fantastic, and my boss is a Mormon from Ephraim. That night I hardly slept because I was so excited about meeting the people of the branch and Eddie Blazer.

The next morning the bus picked us up at our quarters and took us to the Link Building. In the center of the building, we found our Links. There were ten of them lined up with five on each side. We all chose one and sat down at the table next to it ready to go to work when Eddie Blazer entered the area. He introduced himself to us collectively and then proceeded to take a few moments to introduce himself to each of us individually as we stood in line. I was the sixth girl, and when he approached me, I said, "I'm Irene Hailes. I understand you are from Ephraim, Utah. I am from Salt Lake City."

"Good heavens, are you a member of the Church?"

"Yes, I am."

He gave me a vigorous handshake and invited me into his office. He didn't even bother to talk to the other four WAVES. All nine looked at me wondering what I had said or done to rate being escorted to the office of the officer in charge. When we arrived in his office, he said, "There is another Mormon on the base. He instructs the cadets. I'll have him come over. He is a returned missionary. We have a great branch here. You'll just love Pasco." He picked up the phone and made a call and shortly a young naval officer came into the office. He introduced himself, "I'm Dave Cameron, I live in the Wasatch Ward in Salt Lake City."

"I'm Irene Hailes and I'm from the Cannon Ward."

I can't describe how excited I was. It felt so good to be among them. Never before had I felt such excitement in being a member of the Church. I felt as though I had known Dave and Eddie all my life and yet we had just met. I believe one must be a member of the Church to comprehend the special love you can feel for total strangers. This was my first experience with that feeling but not my last. After a moment or two, Dave Cameron said, "How would you like to go for a ride in an airplane?"

Would I? All the time I had trained at Atlanta with the Link Trainers and worked with all those instruments I had never flown. I often thought how nice it would be to see how the instruments actually worked in an airplane. I replied, "Oh, would I, I'd be the happiest girl in the world." I think I could honestly say I felt I was anyway.

"Let's go." Dave was an instructor and could take planes up when he wanted to so he called operations and got a clearance. As I walked by the girls, one asked, "Where are you going?"

I said, "I'm going for an airplane ride."

They looked green with envy and they followed us out to the flight line. Dave took me up, and I had a marvelous time looking at all those instruments and seeing how they worked in an airplane rather than a Link Trainer. We landed, and Eddie took me back to the Link Building. The girls came to me and said, "What did you do to get that ride? What did you say to him? What happened anyway?"

"I didn't say or do anything."

"Well how come you got such special treatment?"

"Well, they are both Mormons, and I am a Mormon."

"That doesn't mean anything," one girl said. "I'm a Catholic, and I meet other Catholics all the time, and it doesn't mean a thing to me or them.

Another girl said, "I'm a Methodist, and we don't do anything like that. Tell us, what really happened?"

"I told you. It is because we are Mormons."

They didn't believe me, but it was true. The only reason I was treated like a queen was because I was a Mormon, and Eddie and Dave were delighted to do anything to help me. When members of the Church are few and far between, one learns to appreciate them a lot more than where they are in the majority, and I found by being in the military and being in such a minority, we sought out each other more than we might have done had we been stationed in Salt Lake City.

I served at Pasco for a short time and then received a transfer to Oklahoma City Naval Training Station. I hated to leave Pasco because now I thought it was beautiful, and as the train departed the station, I burst into tears. I must have sobbed loudly, because a navy officer in the seat behind me said, "Is there something I can do to help?"

I said, "No. You can't help. No one can help. I've been transferred to Oklahoma City."

"Lady, Oklahoma City can't be that bad. I've heard it's a nice place."

"But I don't want to leave Pasco. I love it here."

He must have thought I was crazy. He said, "Everybody wants to leave Pasco."

"I don't. There are so many wonderful people here."

"I'm sure you will find lots of wonderful people at Oklahoma City."

"Do you really think so?"

"You bet I do. There are wonderful people everywhere you go."

He made me feel better, and I knew he was right. There are wonderful people everywhere, but I had so many great friends at Pasco that it was difficult to leave. But, much to my surprise, Oklahoma City was another Pasco.

I arrived at the Oklahoma Naval Training Station in a very depressed state of mind. I left my little bit of heaven on the shores of the Snake and Columbia Rivers and didn't know what to expect at my new assignment. My second night at the station, I went to do my wash in the laundry room. It was a large room with several washers, and also had an area for the WAVES to do their ironing.

One girl said, "Hi, you're new, aren't you?"

"Yes."

"What's your name?"

"I'm Irene Hailes," and I started to cry. I couldn't get the thought of Pasco out of my mind.

"What's the matter?"

"I just left Pasco, Washington and I just loved it there."

"You'll like it here. This is a good place to be stationed. Where are you from?"

"I come from Salt Lake City."

One of the girls doing her ironing heard "Salt Lake City" and came over. "Are you from Salt Lake City?" she asked.

"Yes."

"Are you a Mormon?"

"Yes."

"So am I." Without any thought we embraced and tears gushed from each of us. The other girls couldn't understand how two girls who had never met until that moment and didn't even know each others names could be so happy about meeting one another. She didn't understand Mormons.

The Mormon girl said, "I am Elizabeth Welker, and I come from Stafford, Arizona. What is your name?"

"I'm Irene Hailes, I'm so glad to meet you." I no longer felt
depressed. I found myself among friends.

Her next words sounded like music. "We have a great branch
here in Oklahoma City. Brother Cullimore is the branch president
and he's the greatest."

After Pasco and Oklahoma City, I came to the conclusion
that wherever Mormons meet, one could find "a little bit of
heaven."

Lyal Stringham:
A Branch President

*The branch president, like the bishop, is the father of the
ward. Irene Hailes encountered a very special "branch president"
in Pasco, Washington.* [1]

Thanks to Eddie Blazer, on my first night at Pasco, I received
permission to visit the home of Lyal Stringham, the branch president. Once again, the other WAVES were overwhelmed. They had
never seen nor heard of anyone receiving such special treatment,
and they couldn't believe it was simply due to my being a Mormon.

I had a wonderful evening. Brother and Sister Stringham
were the most gracious and hospitable people I had ever known.
They had lots of opportunity to display their hospitality as the
Pasco Branch held all its meetings at their home. In addition, Mormons visiting loved ones on the base stayed at the Stringham home
because Pasco didn't have a hotel. The house always had people
there.

The Stringhams not only provided a place for Mormons in the
area to meet but fed many of the Mormons on the base. Everybody loved them, and the way Sister Stringham stretched her food
reminded me of Jesus feeding the multitudes. During the war,
everyone used ration cards to obtain food, particularly butter and
sugar and I often wondered how she could feed so many people,
but her larder never seemed to run empty. It seemed that when she
was down to her last cup of sugar, a neighbor would give her a
coupon for an extra five pounds of sugar, and someone else would
give her some coupons for some other commodities. It was an
inspiration to all of us that she never ran out of food.

They aided the members in other ways also. Their unselfish-
ness was unbelievable. We started an MIA group and first met at

---

1. *Ibid.*

their home, but as the group grew bigger and between 50-75 people began to attend, we needed a larger place to meet. Our branch president, Lyal Stringham, rented the Methodist Church one night a week so that we could hold our MIA meetings. The cost was $10.00 per month, and he paid it out of his own pocket. That's the kind of people the Stringhams were. They set a fine example for us to follow.

Bryan Espenschied:
The Lord Provides a Group Leader

The key man to the LDS World War II Servicemen's Program was the Group Leader. He was set apart, and had the responsibility to organize meetings. Livermore Naval Air Station needed one. Irene Hailes went to the Lord and he answered her prayers. [1]

Unlike Pasco and Oklahoma City, Irene Hailes arrived at Livermore Naval Air Station in California, and didn't meet any Mormons. For a time she felt lonely but soon located a small branch near by. Brother Frank Webb, the branch president, told her that he couldn't get permission to hold LDS services on the base and that the cadets were restricted to the base and could not attend at the branch.

She needed help, and so she went to see one of the chaplains and related her problem. She asked for his assistance in getting a meeting started for Mormons. He said, "I don't know if there are any Mormons on the base or not. When new naval personnel arrive, they fill out a card which lists their religious preference, but there are only four choices: Catholic, Protestant, Jewish, or none."

"I'm sure there are Mormons on the base. What can we do to notify them that we will hold meetings?" she asked.

"We can advertise by placing notices on the bulletin boards around the base."

"Can we have some place to hold our meetings?"

"Yes, you can use the chapel Wednesday evenings, and I will see to it that an announcement is made over the loud-speakers and will also see that a notice is posted on the bulletin boards around the station."

"That sounds great."

"What do you want me to announce."

---

1. Irene (Hailes) Ricks interview. Bryan Espenschied tape.

She said, "Just say that an MIA meeting will be held in the chapel for LDS personnel at 1900 hours Wednesdays. That should do it."

On Wednesday, the loud-speakers blared all over the station, "Now hear this, attention all LDS personnel, LDS MIA will be held in the base chapel tonight at 1900 hours." It was repeated again. She could hear some servicemen saying, "Did you hear that, what was all that ABC, XYZ or LMQ all about." It dawned on her that Mormons have their own peculiar language and that the announcement could only be understood by a member of the Church.

That Wednesday evening, she went to the chapel and brought along her LDS hymn book and sat down at the organ. The chapel was located on the main street of the base and she opened the front door of the chapel so that the music could be heard as people passed by. It was a little after seven and she was playing "Come Come Ye Saints" when four young naval cadets came into the chapel. They seemed to enjoy the music, because they beamed. They came over to the organ and when she finished she said, "Hi, Cadets."

One replied, "Hi WAVE, are you a Mormon?"

"Yes, I am. I am Irene Hailes from Salt Lake City."

Once again Irene felt that bond of brotherhood and friendship come surging forth. It was the same that she had known at Pasco and Oklahoma City. What a wonderful feeling!

They held a meeting to decide the direction their program should take. They decided that they needed a group leader, a person who could organize, implement, and lead the programs of the Church. Because of the strict schedule accorded the cadets, they decided that no cadet could hold the position. It had to be filled by a regular navy man. The MIA meetings continued every Wednesday evening, and after a few short weeks, the group grew to 35 attending, all cadets, and Irene. No regular navy man attended. Irene became discouraged because she was in charge of the program, a program designed to have the leadership of the Priesthood. With that problem in mind, she took her problem to the Lord. She prayed for a group leader.

The Lord heard her prayer. Yes, He heard the prayer of a very faithful LDS WAVE, and He answered her prayers. He selected a young man 2,000 miles away attending Aircraft Maintenance

School in Chicago, Illinois. His name was Bryan Espenschied.[1] Bryan didn't know that he had been chosen by the Lord to go to Livermore, California. In fact, Bryan had never heard of it. He looked forward to his new assignment to the Ford plant at River Run, Michigan. The navy had a policy that the top men in the Aircraft Maintenance School had the opportunity to attend flight engineers school at the factory that produced the B-24's. He looked forward eagerly to that choice assignment because he wanted to become a flight engineer.

Just prior to graduating from school, however, the Lord worked upon the mind of Bryan Espenschied, and caused him to lose interest in attending the engineering school and he withdrew his name. He didn't know why, but he changed his mind. Because he was the top man in his class, the navy offered him a choice of serving at any navy air base in the United States. Again, he didn't know why, but he felt compelled to choose Livermore Naval Air Station, California.

Bryan arrived at Livermore on a Thursday, the day following the MIA meeting. Upon his arrival, he was assigned to work in the control towers. Those in the control towers worked a set number of hours and had certain days off each week. Bryan received Wednesdays off and he decided that on his first day off he would see the sights of San Francisco. On Tuesday evening he left Livermore for a date he had made with a young lady whom he knew that worked as a technician at the Oakland Hospital. He took her to a stage play and later to dinner. That evening he planned on getting a room and staying in town rather than going back to the base. He took her to her home in the Berkely Hills area after their date, and he headed for town to get a room for the night. He hoped to get an early start sightseeing the next day. It had been raining all evening, and by the time he arrived in downtown Berkely, he was soaked to the skin. He intended to stay at the YMCA and as he walked down the street of Berkely he could see the lights of the YMCA flashing on and off, but he elected to walk into the entrance hall of an office building where he stood up all night jumping up and down beating himself with his arms in an attempt to keep warm. All the while he could see the sign of the "Y" flashing on and off, and for a quarter he could have slept in a

---

1. Bryan Espenschied is presently vice president of Milne Transportation, Salt Lake City, Utah. He is serving on the General Melchizedek Priesthood Committee and recently served as president of the Western Canadian Mission.

warm bed and gotten out of his wet clothes. He seemed to have lost his senses as he became absolutely obsessed with the idea that he had to get back to Livermore Wednesday morning. He knew the "Liberty Boat," a bus, departed from Berkely at 6:00 a.m. taking servicemen to the base. He was fearful that he might fall asleep and miss the bus so he literally stood up all night to keep himself awake in order to catch the 6 o'clock bus. The bus arrived at the appointed time, and he boarded it and returned to Livermore, arriving there at approximately 7:45 a.m.

No sooner had Bryan arrived back at his barracks when he lost the obsession and literally chastized himself to think that on his day off, the day he had planned to see the sights of San Francisco, he found himself in his barracks with nothing to do.

Had Bryan's free agency been taken from him? Had the Lord made him do things that he hadn't wanted to do? Twice within a period of two weeks, he had made strange decisions—decisions that he hadn't intended to make. The answer is 'no,' because in Bryan Espenschied's daily prayers, he always invited the Lord into his life 'to give him guidance and direction in the things that he stood in need of each day.' The Lord was doing as Bryan had requested. Nevertheless, Bryan didn't understand what was happening to him, and he felt rather stupid and disgusted with himself for his apparent inability to control his thoughts.

Later that afternoon, he heard the announcement over the loud-speaker that the LDS MIA would be meeting at the base chapel at 1900 hours. He was bored with not having done anything all day and he changed into his best uniform, and headed over to the chapel for the meeting.

Irene Hailes was there, and she noticed him enter the chapel. He arrived a little late. She noticed his great big smile, and his easy manner as he walked over to everyone and shook their hands. She felt great. She knew he was the one. She knew that the Lord had answered her prayers. He sent a group leader to Livermore.

Bryan Espenschied:
The Mormons Excel at Livermore

Mormons are noted for their high achievement. Bryan Espenschied tells of an experience he had while stationed at Livermore, California. [1]

---

1. Bryan Espenschied tape.

The Lord placed his new group leader, Bryan Espenschied, in a position at Livermore where he could assist the Latter-day Saint cadets on the base. He arrived at Livermore on a Thursday with 20 other men. They filled out a variety of forms, one of which pertained to burial instructions in case of death. Bryan wrote that he wanted to be buried by an authority from the Mormon Church. Shortly after he filled out the forms, an officer came into the room and called, "Who is Espenschied?"

"I am." Bryan replied.

"You come with me. The rest of you remain where you are."

He took Bryan to the flight control tower and placed him in charge of scheduling the cadets and their instructors. He had the complete responsibility for mustering the cadets before the control tower, assigning them to the airplanes, assigning them instructors, check pilots, and any other activity that dealt with their flight training. The assignment amazed him because he hadn't been trained for control tower work. He was an aircraft mechanic. The assignment bothered him as to why he was chosen. One day he approached Captain Morgan, the officer in charge of the control tower and asked, "Why did you select me for this assignment? Are you aware that I had no training for such an assignment?"

The captain answered simply, "I know that you didn't have the training, but I needed a good reliable man in the tower. I noticed on your form that you were a Mormon, and I have found Mormons to be a highly responsible people. In fact, almost every class that goes through flight training here produces a Mormon as its "outstanding cadet" of the flight. I've learned to admire and respect them."

In addition to being outstanding cadets, Bryan learned from the Catholic chaplain at St. Mary's, California where the cadets received their pre-flight training that in each group, Mormons attained the highest scholastic grades. One day the Catholic chaplain said to Bryan, "What does your Church do to young men that make them so outstanding?"

"Chaplain, it must be the Church."

Jim Yardley:
Prayer and Fasting

How much is a man's life worth? The saints at Livermore, California placed a high value on the life of Cadet Jim Yardley. The following account relates their devotion. [1]

---

1. Irene (Hailes) Ricks interview. Bryan Espenschied tape.

The final part of flight training consisted of each cadet flying a specified number of hours at night. An LDS cadet, Jim Yardley, was engaged in that activity when another cadet became confused and forced Jim and his plane out of the traffic pattern as he was coming in for a landing, which caused Jim to power dive his airplane into the ground. The crash put a three foot hole in the landing field, and caused the base to close for a day while the runway was repaired. The broken body of Jim Yardley was rushed by ambulance to the nearby hospital at Camp Parks. He was only barely alive, and although the doctors gave him no chance to live, the Latter-day Saint servicemen at Livermore believed in a mightier power than medicine.

Bryan Espenschied arrived at the control tower the next morning, very much aware of the accident. He checked the duty roster to learn the name of the cadet who was in the accident. To his surprise he saw the name, Jim Yardley. He knew Jim was a member of the Church, and, being the group leader at Livermore, he took it upon himself to find out Jim's status. He made some inquiries and learned that Jim had been taken to the hospital at Camp Parks. He contacted the chaplain at Livermore who arranged transportation for him and a young cadet, Grant Stucki.

Upon their arrival at the hospital, Bryan announced that they were members of the Mormon Church. "We are authorized ministers of Christ's Church and have come to give Jim Yardley a religious blessing."

A group of doctors nearby overheard them, and informed them that they couldn't see Jim. One of the doctors said, "I'm sorry, you can't see him."

Bryan became insistent and said, "We must see him. He needs a religious blessing."

"What that boy needs is rest," the doctor answered.

Bryan became very much exercised at the doctor's attitude and replied, "Is Jim Yardley conscious?"

"Yes, he is."

Very forceably he said, "Then, Doctor, let him make the decision, not you."

The doctor felt he had better find out and went to Jim's room. He returned shortly and said, "Yes, he would like to see you."

The two elders of the Church entered his room only to be astonished with what they saw. Jim's head was twice the size of a normal head. His forehead had struck part of the aircraft when it crashed and it almost literally decapitated him. There was a scar across his forehead from temple to temple, though at that time they couldn't see it because of the bandages which almost entirely covered his face. The doctors later told Bryan that they had never seen a person live with a body so badly broken. In addition to the swelling of his head, he had severe internal injuries. His right arm was broken in two places, and both legs were broken with compound fractures. He wasn't a particularly pretty sight. Bryan said, "Jim, we have come to give you a blessing. Do you want one?"

"I do," he replied.

Jim had never lost consciousness and that in itself was a miracle. Bryan thought that if he had lost consciousness, he might not have been able to intervene between him and the doctors. Bryan continued, "Jim, do you want to live?"

"Yes."

"Grant and I will kneel by the bed and pray to unify us before we administer to you, and it will also give you an opportunity to have a prayer of your own. Jim, your life is in the hands of God."

After their prayer, the men arose and administered to the patient. They anointed him on the cheek, because the rest of his head was bandaged. Bryan blessed him to live on the condition that he live the rest of his life in a manner pleasing to the Lord.

Bryan wasn't satisfied that he had done all that he could. He felt Jim needed more than the blessing. He gathered all the available LDS servicemen and said, "If Jim is going to live, it will be because of our faith and our prayers that the Lord will preserve his life."

The men agreed to fast for 24 hours. After 24 hours, Jim was still alive, and they knew that the Lord had answered their prayers. They decided to pray and fast for an additional 24 hours to thank the Lord for sparing Jim.

Each day Bryan checked the duty roster and saw Jim's name thereon. One day Jim's name was missing, and everyone who had seen the list felt that he had died, but Bryan knew better. He had the peace of the spirit that had assured him all was well, and all was progressing well with Jim. He answered: "Jim is not dead." He wasn't dead. There had been an error in preparing the roster that day.

Church members visited Jim often at the hospital, and watched him progress toward getting well. About a week after the accident, Bryan and Irene visited him and saw him without the bandages on his head. It was unbelievable. A scar was across his entire forehead, but the scar looked as though the healing process had been going on for many weeks, and not just for a matter of days. It was clearly

evident to them that the Lord had intervened and had accelerated
the healing process.

Jim Yardley remained in the hospital only for a number of
weeks rather than the months that the doctors had anticipated
and as soon as he was well enough to travel home he received a
medical discharge. World War II was over for Jim Yardley.

The base chaplain spoke to Irene about their group and the
fasting and praying they did for the cadet. He said, "Young lady,
in all my years of serving in the ministry, I have never witnessed
greater devotion than your group demonstrated in behalf of that
boy. I honestly believe that your prayers and fasting saved that
cadet's life."

Several years later while serving on the MIA General Board,
Irene met the family of the young man whose life had been spared.
They came from southern Utah and she related the story of the
fasting and praying. Jim's parents broke down in tears of gratitude
to a handful of Latter-day Saints who fasted and prayed for 48
hours that their son might live.

Irene Hailes:
"I Didn't Think I Could Ever Face You Again
If You Saw Me Drinking"

*One doesn't like to disappoint a person he admires. Irene
Hailes helped many young cadets keep on the "straight and narrow." She relates the following account.* [1]

In the military many temptations were placed before young
Latter-day Saints. They faced loneliness and often faced pressure
from men of other faiths who didn't believe in our standards.
Some of our servicemen gave into these pressures, though many
did not. I found myself in a special place at Livermore in the hearts
of many men. They had a Mormon girl to speak to, and some of
them told me later that they even felt that my very presence at
Livermore had kept them on the straight and narrow.

Bryan and I would often go to the ship's store in the evening
for the purpose of finding some of our cadets. Once as I entered, I
noticed one of our Mormon cadets sitting at a table with a glass of
beer in front of him. I pretended that I didn't notice him or his
beer, but out of the corner of my eye, I saw him very slyly push
the glass to the far end of the table, get up and come over to our
table.

---

1. Irene (Hailes) Ricks interview.

Just prior to his leaving Livermore, he spoke to me saying, "Irene, one night I almost had a beer, but because you came into the ship's store that evening, I couldn't drink it. I didn't think I could ever face you again if you saw me drinking. I thought how much I would not only hurt you personally, but also hurt the other fine Mormons who live the standards and set the example that they do. That evening my entire attitude changed toward the Word of Wisdom. I decided from that moment on I would never break the Word of Wisdom. Thanks, Irene."

Another cadet at Livermore said to me, "I want to thank you for all you have done for me."

I said, "What did I do?"

"I used to drink coffee before I came to Livermore, but your presence at the ship's store caused me to reflect upon what I was doing. I knew I was doing something I shouldn't, and I knew that I would break your heart if you saw me drinking coffee. I haven't had a cup of coffee since I got here. Thanks, Irene."

Irene Hailes:
Have a Coke?

Mormons are observed by others much more than they would like to believe. Who would ever think that people noticed who drank Coca Cola and who didn't?[1]

While at work one hot summer afternoon, a young naval officer approached my desk and handed me a Coke, "Irene, here, have a drink."

The thought of having a nice cold refreshing drink appealed to me, but I replied, "No thanks, I don't drink Coke."

"Oh, come on, I bought it especially for you. It's a hot day and it will refresh you."

"No thanks."

"But it's already opened."

"I don't wish to be rude or ungrateful, but it's against my principles to drink Coke."

"What's wrong with drinking Coke?"

"It's not good for you. Coke contains caffeine."

He laughed and then pointed to another officer standing nearby and said, "My friend over there bet me that you would drink this Coke. I bet you wouldn't."

---

1. *Ibid.*

I didn't quite understand what was happening, but the other officer joined us, and said, "It looks as though I lost the bet." He then looked right at me and said, "Tell me why so many Mormons are inconsistent in their behavior?"

"What do you mean, inconsistent?"

"Well, I know quite a few Mormons, and they wouldn't drink a cup of coffee if their life depended upon it, but they drink Coke. They both contain caffeine, and I believe that Coke has even more caffeine than coffee. Tell me, how can Mormons justify that behavior?"

"I can't justify the behavior for all Mormons, but for myself, I don't drink Coke, and I know many others that don't." My answer didn't appear to satisfy him.

Are Mormons as inconsistent as he thought?

Harold B. Lee:
It's Hard to Obey When You Don't Agree

Samuel said to Saul, "...to obey is better than sacrifice...." *(I Samuel 15:22). Sometimes members of the Church do not agree with decisions made by Church leaders, and therefore, do not obey them. The first law of heaven is obedience, whether members like the decision or not, they must as good Latter-day Saints obey it. The following experience is just such a case.* [1]

Many Latter-day Saints found themselves stationed in the Oakland area during World War II, and due to the large numbers, the Church bought a very spacious and beautiful home for the servicemen. Shortly after its purchase, servicemen and women spent their weekends remodeling the home to make it suitable for both living and activities. It was hoped that there would be rooms available for servicemen to spend the night because hotels were expensive and many of their respective camps were quite a distance from the home. It was suggested that one wing of the home be used for service women to stay. It would consist of approximately three bedrooms. Apparently the word got back to Church leaders in Salt Lake City that men and women would be staying under the same roof in the servicemen's home in Oakland, and shortly thereafter, Elder Harold B. Lee, chairman of the LDS Servicemen's Committee, came to Oakland to review the plans. After meeting

---

1. *Ibid.*

with local Church officials he said, "We cannot allow women to stay here. We will have to find other accommodations for them."

One of the local leaders said, "They will be disappointed, they worked so hard getting this home ready."

"That may be so, but we must avoid the very appearance of impropriety."

A second man said, "Brother Lee, there is a WAVE here that I think will convince you that women should be permitted to stay."

Another said, "I agree. Wait until you meet her. She will change your mind."

Good naturedly he inquired, "Who is this WAVE who will convince me that I should allow women to stay here?"

"Her name is Irene Hailes, and she has a way of getting around problems."

"Irene Hailes? I'm glad to know that it is Irene Hailes. She is like a daughter to me. Where can I find her?"

He found me and said, "Now Irene, I understand from these gentlemen that you are going to convince me that women should be allowed to stay in this home where men also will be staying, is that right?"

His words surprised me. I didn't know or even suspect a problem existed, but I could tell by the tone of his voice that women were not going to stay in that home, but I asked anyway, "Why can't women stay here?"

"It's very simple—it doesn't look right. We have high standards to live up to, and we want to eliminate as many temptations from the paths of our young people as possible. Understand?"

I said, "I do," but I really disagreed with him but accepted his decision. I didn't realize until a few years later that Elder Lee had read my mind as well as he did. I traveled with he and Sister Lee to a stake conference in Canada. He presided and during the Sunday conference he asked me to speak to the congregation about my experiences in the military. After I spoke, he approached the podium and told the audience that he would speak on the subject of obedience. He then proceeded to relate the story of the servicemen's home in Oakland, and said, "I knew the decision I made was correct, but I knew that Irene did not agree with me. I knew that she had worked very hard to fix up that home anticipating that women would be able to stay there. It's easy to obey authority when you agree with it, but it's very hard to obey when you don't agree with the decision. Irene disagreed with me, but accepted my decision without complaining or sulking. She learned to live with it and that is what all Latter-day Saints should do when decisions are made by the brethren. We don't make decisions without great thought and much prayer. We can't guarantee that you will be pleased with every decision we make, but after it is made, a good Latter-day Saint should obey."

Irene Hailes:
Harold B. Lee Plays Cupid

Elder Harold B. Lee thought of Irene Hailes as an "adopted daughter." After the war, he interviewed a young Mormon chaplain that he felt would be ideal for her, and he put a plan in motion. [1]

The June MIA conference in 1946 contained a special program welcoming home the LDS servicemen and women. Elder Lee, who was serving as an advisor to the MIA, recommended that a committee be appointed to supervise the program. One evening Sister Lee confided in me, "Irene, Harold wants you to serve on a committee for the servicemen's program, and he told me that there is a special young man on the committee he wants you to meet. Harold says he is outstanding."

I was excited, but several days passed and I hadn't been told by Brother Lee that I was assigned to a committee. Then one day I received a call that he wanted to see me in his office. I went over and he told me that he would like me to serve on the committee.

I said, "I'd love to."

"Good, by the way, there will be a young man assigned to the committee that I think a great deal of. His name is Eldin Ricks, and I want you to meet him. You won't be able to find anything wrong with him. He was one of our outstanding chaplains during the war, and I think you two will get along very well."

I looked forward to that first meeting of the servicemen's committee. I was the only girl on the committee, and there were several men. As I looked them over, I wondered which one was Eldin Ricks. We started our meeting by introducing ourselves, and then I saw him. The meeting lasted a few hours, and after the meeting Eldin came over to me and said, "I'm Eldin Ricks. Would you care to go somewhere with me to get a bite to eat?"

I said, "I'd love to."

I didn't know it at the time, but Elder Lee had told Eldin to be on the lookout for Irene Hailes and even said some very nice

---

1. *Ibid.*

things about me. Somehow I knew I had met Mr. Right and to make a long story short, we later married in the Salt Lake Temple, and Elder Harold B. Lee sealed us for time and eternity.

I have often thought the reason that I didn't get married as young as many of my girl friends was because the Lord saved Eldin just for me and I had to wait until the war was over to find him. Now, after twenty-five years of married life, I still believe that it was nothing short of divine inspiration that prompted Elder Lee to conclude that the two of us were meant for each other.

Irene Hailes:
Speaking in the Tabernacle

Irene Hailes felt honored to be asked to speak in the taber-nacle, but, later realized how frightened she was. [1]

During the 1946 MIA conference, one serviceman and one servicewoman were chosen to speak at the tabernacle. I was the woman chosen. It was an honor, but one I didn't seek because I was afraid to speak before so many people. To make matters worse, on the day I was to speak, a railroad executive spoke in the after-noon session and said, "I have been in this historical tabernacle many times. I love the special spirit that surrounds it, the reverence of the place, but I am almost overcome emotionally just to have the experience of speaking here from the pulpit."

When he said that I thought, "How can I ever speak up there tonight if this executive has trouble?" I was afraid that I would not measure up and I went home feeling terrible. I cried off and on all afternoon, but knew what I had to do and went to the tabernacle for the final session. I was very nervous waiting for my time to speak, but finally it came, and as I approached the pulpit I surprised myself because I felt composed. I told the story of Pasco, Washington, and Eddie Blazer and Dave Cameron and how they treated me like a queen. I told how no one could understand just because I was a Mormon that I would receive such special treatment. When I told how Eddie Blazer invited me into his office and how envious the girls were of me, the audience broke out in laughter. I turned and saw President George Albert Smith sitting behind me stretch out his legs and roar. I felt comfortable. The war was over, and I was at home with the people that I loved.

---

1. *Ibid.*

IX
Thirty Years Later

Where are these chaplains of World War II 30 years later? This chapter not only answers that question, but considers their growth, using the following criteria as the measurement for success: marriage, career, and service to the Church. It should be noted, however, that information on all forty-five is unavailable, because some could not be found and others are dead.

How did they succeed in marriage? Of the thirty-four chaplains measured, none had a divorce, and all became fathers with a total of 161 children. The following interesting table is submitted showing how many children each chaplain had.

Number of Children	Number of Chaplains
13	1
9	1
8	2
7	3
5	7
4	11
3	6
2	3

What post war occupational choices did they make? A study of thirty-five shows them holding or having held the following positions:

Position	Number of Chaplains
Business Executive	9
College Professors	7
Educational Administrators	4
Government Services	4
Seminary and Institute Directors	3
Professional Chaplains	3
Lawyers	2
Doctor (M.D.)	1
Tabernacle Organist	1
University President	1

Did they remain active in the Church? The following table is a breakdown of the many callings that they have received or positions that they presently hold:

Position	Number of Chaplains
Members of the Stake High Council	16
Bishops	13
Counselors in the Bishopric	7
Stake Presidents	4
Members of the Stake Presidency	4
Members of the various General Boards	4
Mission Presidents	3
Patriarchs	2
Regional Representatives	1

From studying the above three tables, it can be concluded that the men who represented The Church of Jesus Christ of Latter-day Saints as chaplains during World War II are, as a group, an elite company of men.

The following alphabetical list gives a brief account of where each of the forty-five Second World War chaplains are today:

Badger, Brian Garr resides in Salt Lake City with his wife, Wanda (West), and five of their nine children, David, William, Mary Jane, Rob, and John. Their four other children are married. Stephen lives in Salt Lake City and is employed as the Business Manager of the Park City School District; Barbara (Badger) McKeown also resides in Salt Lake City; Becky (Badger) Harding lives in Highland, Utah; and Brian T. Badger attends the University of Utah and is majoring in pre-dentistry.

The former chaplain has held many Church positions, including service as a bishop, a member of the stake high council, and a member of the Monument Park Stake presidency.

Brother Badger works in the education field and presently is the Business Manager and Treasurer for the Granite School District.

Badger, Howard C. is involved in the real estate business, a field in which he has been working since 1940. He is self-employed and owns the Badger Reality Company of Salt Lake City.

Mr. Badger and his wife, Eleanor (Ashton), and their daughter, Lisa, abide in Salt Lake City. Their other three children, H. Dennis, Julie (Badger) Jensen, and Carla (Badger) Belnap, are all married, and make Salt Lake City their home.

Brother Badger has served in many Church positions including that of a member of the Parleys Stake high council, the Mission President of the South African Mission, a member of the MIA General Board, and is presently a Regional Representative to the Twelve.

Barney, Delbert is retired and lives in Provo, Utah.

Berrett, Lyman C. lives in Salt Lake City with his wife, Louise (Lockman) Berrett. They have three married children, Lanette (Berrett) Brown, Denney L. Berrett, and Vicki Lynn (Berrett) Alexander, Both daughters live in Chicago, and their son, Denny, teaches in the elementary school in Riverton, Utah.

Brother Berrett has previously served as a bishop, as a member of the stake high council, and now is the patriarch of the Salt Lake Cutler West Stake.

Mr. Berrett is employed by the LDS Church Education Department. He is the District Coordinator of the Salt Lake Valley South Seminary District.

Boud, John W. is the co-founder and former president of one of Utah's largest retail stores, Fashion Fabrics, Inc. He and his wife, Sharon, live in Salt Lake City with their family which consists of thirteen children, John, David, James, Joseph, Stephen, Richard, Rebecca, Barbara, Mark, Elizabeth, Thomas, Michael, and Robert. Six of the boys have served or are presently serving on missions for the LDS Church.

The former chaplain has served in the capacity of a bishop for eight years, a member of the Salt Lake Cottonwood Stake presidency, and is presently the Harrisburg-Pennsylvania Mission President.

Braithwaite, Royden C. is the president of Southern Utah State College at Cedar City, Utah. He and his wife, Alice (Todd), live in that city. They have four children, three boys and one girl. Their three sons are married. Robert attends the University of Utah Law School; Karl works in Washington, D.C. on the environmental subcommittee for U.S. Senator Edward Muskie; and Douglas is enrolled in the MBA program at Harvard University. Their only daughter, Elaine, attends the University of Utah.

Mr. Braithwaite has held many Church positions including serving as a member of the Provo Stake high council, and the Cedar City West Stake high council.

Campbell, Eugene E. lives and works in Provo, Utah. He is a professor of history at the Brigham Young University, and is the author of several books including *Life of Hugh B. Brown* and *History of Fort Bridger.* He is presently writing Volume 6 of the New Comprehensive History of the LDS Church.

Mr. Campbell is the father of five married children, Bruce, Mary Ann, Jean, Sharon, and Edward.

Professor Campbell has held several Church positions, including institute director, bishop's counselor, a member of the stake high council, and has authored many Church manuals.

Christensen, Jay B. (Deceased).

Christensen, Rex L. (Whereabouts unknown).

Cooley, Vernon A. and his wife, Kay, make their home in Salt Lake City, Utah. They are the parents of three married children. Vernon E. Cooley is a real estate broker in Salt Lake City, Craig H. Cooley is an engineer with Hewlett-Packard in Loveland, Colorado, and Susan (Cooley) Johnson resides in Bountiful, Utah with her husband.

The former chaplain has served twice as a bishop, and also served as a member of the Parleys Stake high council in addition to many other callings in the Church. He has also worked as a guide on Temple Square for twenty years.

Mr. Cooley is self employed as a broker-dealer working with investments and insurance.

Curtis, Reuben Emerson resides in Salt Lake City with his wife. He is the father of five children, all married, and has 21 grandchildren.

After World War II, Mr. Curtis served as the chaplain at the Veterans Hospital in Salt Lake City until his retirement in 1969. He is enjoying his retirement, and travels extensively.

He has held many Church positions including that of a bishop for six years.

Curtis, Theodore E., Jr. lives in Santa Clara, California with his wife, Violet (Taylor). Mr. and Mrs. Curtis have two children. Theodore lives in Flint Michigan. He is a professor of sociology at the University of Michigan at Flint. Dorothy (Curtis) Wilkinson and her family live in Saratoga, California.

The former chaplain made the military a career. He served as a chaplain, obtaining the rank of full colonel in the United States Army. He retired in 1958 after serving in a variety of assignments both overseas and in the United States. Like his brother, Reuben, he enjoys his retirement.

Brother Curtis served as the bishop of the Forest Dale Ward in the Granite Stake of Salt Lake City, as a member of the San Francisco Stake high council, as the patriarch of the San Jose, California West Stake, and is presently the patriarch of the Santa Clara, California Stake.

Darley, Roy M. resides in Salt Lake City with his wife, Kathleen (Latham). They are the parents of five married children. Margaret (Darley) Kirkman lives in Bountiful, Utah; Janice (Darley) Quinn makes Salt Lake City her home; David L. Darley also resides in Salt Lake City; Elizabeth (Darley) Gessel lives with her family in New York City; and Philip E. Darley calls Fairbanks, Alaska home. Brother Darley has nine grandchildren.

Mr. Darley served on the General Board of the MIA for over 25 years, and has been a former member of the General Music Committee of the Church. For the past 29 years, Roy M. Darley has worked as a tabernacle organist.

Dalebout, Lee W. lives in Salt Lake City with his second family. His first wife passed away, and he remarried Marion Lorene Petersen and is the stepfather to her six children. He had one daughter, Bonnie K., by his first marriage.

The former chaplain has served as a bishop and also as a member of the stake high council.

He has recently retired as the Executive Director of the Nursing Home Association, and is presently self-employed as a psychologist. In addition, he is the chaplain at the Utah State Hospital at Provo, Utah.

Durham, L. Marsden (Deceased)—Chaplain Durham died on September 25, 1945 from a fall at Hilo, Hawaii while recuperating from wounds received during the battle for Okinawa. He lived in Salt Lake City, and, as a chaplain, won the Bronze Star and the Purple Heart.

Ericksen, Gerald L. presently resides in Salt Lake City with his wife, Erna (Sconberg), and their son, Robert. They have four other children, Mrs. Karen (Ericksen) Fuhriman who resides in Salt Lake City; Mrs. Mimi (Ericksen) Chappell of San Francisco, California; David who lives in Salt Lake City; and Eric who is presently serving a two year mission for the Church in the Boston, Massachusetts Mission.

Brother Ericksen has been active in community affairs. He has served as president of the Fullerton, California Rotary Club from 1956-1957, a member of the Salt Lake City Chamber of

Commerce, chairman of the Great Salt Lake Boy Scouts Council of 72 Stake Presidents in 1969, vice-chairman Board of Governors to the Latter-day Saint Hospital in Salt Lake City, vice-chairman LDS Hospital Board Executive Committee, 1971-73, and is presently a member of the LDS Hospital Research Committee.

Some of his Church callings are as a member of the high council in three separate stakes, as a member of the Orange County, California Stake presidency and as the stake president of the Emigration Stake from 1963 to 1973.

Mr. Ericksen is the manager of the Utah General Office for New York Life Insurance Company, and is the president of the All Insurance Industry Association. In addition, he has won several awards as a General Agent.

Ellsworth, S. George is a professor of history at Utah State University, and has written two books, *Utah's Heritage* which is used by the public schools throughout the state to teach the students Utah history, and *Dear Ellen—Two Mormon Women and Their Letters.*

Professor Ellsworth lives in Logan, Utah with his wife, Maria (Smith). They have two children, both sons. One is attending the University of Minnesota doing graduate work in the field of physics, and the other son is serving the Lord in the Pennsylvania-Pittsburg Mission.

Brother Ellsworth has held many Church positions including being called to serve as a member of the Utah State University Stake high council.

Evans, Howard C. (Whereabouts unknown).

Fitzgerald, John W. chose to work in the education field as his career. He received an Ed.D. degree in School Administration from Stanford University. He worked as principal of several schools in the Granite School District. The last seventeen years he spent as principal of the Morningside Elementary School in Salt Lake City.

Chaplain Fitzgerald served as a chaplain with the Utah National Guard for over 20 years. When he retired recently, the National Guard honored him with "The Minute Man Award" for outstanding service.

Mr. Fitzgerald is retired and lives in the Holiday section of Salt Lake City with his wife, Mary Elsie (Barr). They are the parents of three married daughters, Marilynne (Fitzgerald) Lima; Suzanne (Fitzgerald) Burke; and Kathleen (Fitzgerald) Thomas.

Flint, Leon H. lives in Salt Lake City with his wife, Ruth (Hickenlope), and their son, Robert. They also have three daughters, Ruth (Flint) White who lives with her family in Danville, Kentucky; Nancy (Flint) Fletcher who resides with her family in Glendale, Arizona, and Marilee who is a co-ed at Brigham Young University.

Chaplain Flint recently retired after 20 years of service as the chaplain for the Utah National Guard. He has served in several Church positions, and is the general sales manager for the O.C. Tanner Company of Salt Lake City, Utah.

Freeman, Leo F. (Deceased).

Gibbons, Robert G. (Deceased). Brother Gibbons remained active in the Mormon Church throughout his life. Prior to World War II, he worked as a seminary teacher. Following the war, he worked for the state of Utah as a veterans' coordinator. He later worked for Logan City until he retired in 1969. In addition, he remained an active chaplain by serving in the U.S. Army Reserve until his retirement in 1961. He is survived by his widow, Ruth, and two children, Marianne G. (Gibbons) Poulsen, and Robert B. Gibbons.

Hendrickson, Hyrum A. and his wife, Ida (Smith), make Scottsdale, Arizona their home. They are the parents of seven married children. Ruel is a motel operator in Snowflake, Arizona; Anthony is the department chairman, Department of Commerce, at Mesa High School, Mesa, Arizona; Carole sells real estate in the Scottsdale area; Sharon (Hendrickson) Cassady is a housewife in Salt Lake City; Brian W. is a lawyer in Mesa; Lilly (Hendrickson) Shulte and her family reside in Tempe; and Charles lives in Tempe and is an engineer for the Arizona Public Service.

Mr. Hendrickson has served as a bishop, a member of the stake high council, and as the president of the Snowflake Stake. He has been employed as the principal of Snowflake High School, superintendent of the Snowflake District and presently is the Executive Secretary of the Arizona Inter-Scholastic Association.

Hess, Milton J. presently practices law in Clearfield, Utah. He resides in Farmington, Utah with his wife, Fern (Gregory), and four of their six children, Stephen, Paul, Christine and Anne. Stephen and Paul recently returned from missions. Two other sons are married, Todd G. who works as an institute director in the Church education program in California and Gerald Hess who is a practicing attorney in Salt Lake City.

The former naval chaplain has held several positions in the Church including that of a bishop of the Farmington Ward, president of the Davis Stake, Mission President of the West Australia Mission, and is presently a patriarch.

Irons, Timothy H. retired from the U.S. Army in 1969 after serving as a military chaplain for approximately 20 years. He served in the Italian and European campaigns during World War II. He also served in Korea. He and his wife call Nephi, Utah home. They have four children, Sanoma, Timothy, Richard and Celeste.

Jackson, A. Gifford resides in San Leandro, California with his wife, Verna. He has served as the president of the San Leandro California Stake for the past ten years. Prior to his present calling, he has served as counselor in the stake presidency, as a bishop, and as a member of the stake high council. He is the father of three sons, E. William, who lives in Ojai, California; Clark C., who makes his home in Sacramento, California; and Rod W., who resides in San Francisco. President Jackson is presently a municipal employee working in the City Attorney's office for the city of Oakland, California.

Jones, Ray L. lives in Northridge, California with his wife Sibyl (Nelson) and their son, David. One unmarried daughter, Mary, attends Brigham Young University. They have six married children, LaRein (Jones) Marx lives in Northridge, California; Lorin works as a carpenter and lives in Spanish Fork, Utah; James lives in Santa Rosa, California and is a scientist employed by Hewitt Packard; Eugene is enrolled in the Graduate School at Brigham Young University; Ivan is a C.P.A. employed by the Arthur M. Anderson Company of Los Angeles, California; and Marla lives in Lacresenta, California.

Brother Jones is active in the Church and has served in the branch presidency and also has been a member of the high council of the Los Angeles Chatworth Stake.

He presently trains students to work with the deaf, and is employed by California University at Northridge.

Mann, Grant E. resides in Bountiful, Utah with his wife, Mirian (Sconberg), and three of their four children, Annette, Richard, and Lawrence who is attending BYU. They have a married daughter, Margie (Mann) Madsen, who lives with her family in Fruit Heights, Utah.

The former World War II chaplain was recalled to active duty in 1948, and became the first LDS U.S. Air Force chaplain. He remained in the military for ten years and served in Korea. He has served in the bishopric and also in the high council of the Bountiful East Stake. Brother Mann is self-employed as an Insurance Agent in Bountiful, Utah.

McBride, Orlando S. (Deceased). Died at the age of 39 of a heart ailment in July 1947.

Mitchell, Albert O. presently resides in Provo, Utah with his wife, Jeanette. His first wife, Margaret, died in 1965. He retired from Brigham Young University having been employed as a professor of Speech and Dramatic Arts. He has eight children by his deceased wife, Marjorie. They are Douglass, a lawyer in Salt Lake City; Carl an engineer in Palo Alto, California; a daughter, Margaret, who works as a secretary at Stanford, University; Albert O. Jr., a lawyer practicing in Los Angeles, California; Nancy is married and resides in Scottsdale, Arizona, and Scott, the youngest, is a student at the University of Utah.

Brother Mitchell has served in several Church positions including being a member of the MIA General Board from 1948 to 1970. He is presently an assistant leader of the High Priests Quorum in the Oak Hills First Ward in Provo.

Nelson, Robert A. lives in San Jose, California with his wife, Marion (Smith) Nelson. They have four children, all married, Saundra (Nelson) Aker who lives in Seattle, Washington; Leland R. Hamilton, resides in Montana; Susan (Nelson) Ford lives in Los Altos, California; and Margaret (Nelson) Pnell makes LaFayette, California her home.

Brother Nelson has been actively involved in community affairs, serving as the former mayor of Walnut Creek, California; past chairman, past president and board member of the San Jose Kiwanis Club; and vice-president, Finance, of the San Jose Chamber of Commerce.

He has worked in the bishopric of the Laurel Crest Ward, Salt Lake City, and has served on the Walnut Creek Stake high council.

Mr. Nelson is presently the president of the R.A.N. Corporation, a management corporation which manages approximately 3,000 condominium projects which include a country club and a restaurant.

Nelson, Warren Richard (Whereabouts unknown).

Neslen, C. Clarence (Deceased). Brother Neslen was involved with politics throughout his life. He served as the mayor of Salt

Lake City from 1920-1928 and held many other government positions. He served as the bishop of the 20th Ward in Salt Lake City for 26 years and also was a member of the high council of the Pioneer and Ensign Stakes.

Peterson, Vadal W. presently resides in Salt Lake City with his wife, Gertrude (Tody), and one daughter, Anne. Their four other children are married. Robert is an electrical engineer living in Salt Lake City; Kathy (Peterson) Wright also resides in Salt Lake City; Patricia (Peterson) Hoff lives in Denver; and Margo (Peterson) Boyer resides in San Ramon, California.

Brother Peterson has held many Church positions. He is presently employed as an assistant principal at East High School in Salt Lake City. He has previously been the principal of South East Junior High School.

Probst, Reed (Deceased) served in the Pacific for approximately three years where he contracted recurring malaria which led to his unfortunate death. He won the Silver Star and was cited by the Chief of Chaplains as being "an outstanding chaplain."

Rich, Wendell O. resides in Salt Lake City with his wife, Pearl. They have five children, all married. Carl lives in San Diego, California; Kenneth resides in Walnut Creek, California; David W. lives in Roy, Utah; Ralph J. lives in Tucson, Arizona; and Joanne (Rich) Duncan in Provo, Utah.

Wendell is presently retired from the Church Department of Education. He had been the director of LDS Institute at Logan, Utah and the executive vice president of the LDSSA.

Brother Rich has held a number of Church callings including serving as the first counselor in the stake presidency at the Utah State University Stake at Logan, Utah. In addition, he has written three books, *Our Living Gospel*, *Distinctive Teachings of the Restoration*, and *Oil For Their Lamps* which he co-authored with William E. Berrett.

Richards, Glen Y. (Deceased) was a navy veteran of both World War I and World War II. He remained active in the Church throughout his life. He worked as an attorney in Salt Lake City, and also served as an assistant to the Salt Lake County Attorney.

Ricks, Eldin is presently living in Provo, Utah with his wife, Irene. They have four children, Harold Lee, Marjorie, Dennis, and Stanford. Eldin teaches religion at BYU, and has served in a variety of positions in the Church. He presently is a member of the U.S. Army Reserve holding the rank of a full colonel.

Rowley, George R. (Whereabouts unknown).

Sessions, Marc resides in Los Angeles, California. Brother Sessions resides with his wife, Doris (Huck). They have four children. Two are married. Doris Ann (Sessions) Tharp lives in Granada Hills, California; Jay lives in Alhambra and is employed as an accountant; Jim, a graduate of the Church College of Hawaii, resides in Toluca Lake and is presently employed as a security guard; and Don attends Loyola School of Law.

Brother Sessions has served in the bishopric and presently owns his own manufacturing corporation in Hollywood, California. The firm specializes in making custom soap for finer hotels. In addition to serving in World War II, he also served during the Korean War.

Simmons, Elbert resides in Provo with his wife, Vivian (Olsen). They have four children. Janet lives at home with her parents; Daniel is on a mission; Rulon is a scientist working for Kodak in Rochester, New York; and Elaine (Simmons) Cornish lives in Baltimore, Maryland.

Brother Simmons has served as a 2nd counselor in the bishopric and as a high councilman. He is presently Associate Professor of Zoology at Brigham Young University.

Smith, Wilford E. resides in Provo, Utah with his wife, Ruth (Christensen). They have five children. Charlotte is married and lives in Provo; Emery, a CPA resides in Salt Lake City; Sherman is a medical student at the University of Utah; Ronald is an artillery officer in the U.S. Army; and Jeffrey, the youngest, is presently serving on a mission in Japan.

Brother Smith has served in a variety of Church assignments including serving on the stake high council and is presently the bishop of the Oak Hills First Ward in Provo, Utah.

Bishop Smith works as Professor of Sociology at Brigham Young University, and is also a chaplain in the U.S. Army Reserve holding the rank of a full colonel.

Watkins, Jack resides in Salt Lake City with his wife, Vanja (L. Yorgason). They are the parents of five children, David, Linda, Janet, Janell, and Emily. Brother Watkins is a practicing M.D. in the Salt Lake City area. He has held many Church positions including being called as the first counselor in the bishopric.

Widdison, Milton resides in Salt Lake City with his wife, Ruth (Slieght) and his son, Rick. He has three other children. Lynn (Widdison) Frolich who also lives in Salt Lake City; Lelan (Widdison) Rigby who lives in Manhattan, New York; and Gary who is on a mission.

Brother Widdison has served in the bishopric of the Highland View Second Ward and is presently employed as a social worker at the VA Hospital in Salt Lake City.

Woolley, George R. lives in Salt Lake City with his wife, Louise (Berber). They are the parents of three children, Dr. LeGrand H., Dr. Bruce H., and Mrs. Lavon L. (Janice Woolley) Warner. Brother Woolley is retired. Prior to his retirement, he served as the director of the Institute of Religion at the LDS Business College in Salt Lake City.

X

The Korean and Vietnam Wars

World War II ended shortly after the United States Army Air Corps dropped atomic bombs on Hiroshima and Nagasaki in August 1945. The world literally shouted with joy as the war was finally concluded, and the soldiers, sailors and marines returned home to their families. The world hoped for an everlasting peace. For that purpose, government leaders of many nations met in San Francisco on April 25, 1945 and on June 26, 1945 adopted a United Nations Charter. As 1946 approached, the peoples of the world held a very optimistic view about the future.

After the war, Church leaders interviewed many of the returning LDS chaplains to learn how the LDS Servicemen's Program of World War II worked, especially overseas where no formal Church organization existed. The chaplains had played a major role in its program, and the leaders sought insights from them, because of their experience. One chaplain, Eugene Campbell of Tooele, Utah, recalled saying to Elder Mark E. Petersen, "Brother Petersen, I hope all this information is not necessary. Hopefully, we won't have any more wars after this one."

Elder Petersen shook his head and said, "Rest assured that there'll be wars and we'll have chaplains in wars."[1]

Chaplain Campbell commented, "He seemed very sure of himself."

How right the apostle was. In less than five years, the United States once again found itself involved in a foreign war. North Korea invaded South Korea, and under the sanction of the United Nations, the United States entered the conflict which lasted three years, from June 25, 1950 to July 27, 1953.

Among those called to serve in the Korean War were LDS chaplains, including four veterans of World War II, Theodore E. Curtis, Jr., Timothy H. Irons, Grant E. Mann, and Marc Sessions. Others that served during this period are contained in the following list.[2]

---

1. Eugene Campbell interview.

2. Joseph F. Boone, "The Roles of The Church of Jesus Christ of Latter-day Saints in Relation to the U.S. Military 1900-1975," 2 volumes. (Unpublished Ph.D. Dissertation, Brigham Young University, 1975).

MORMON CHAPLAINS THAT SERVED
DURING THE KOREAN WAR ERA (1950-1960)

U.S. Air Force Chaplains

Reed A. Benson
Calvin C. Cook
Joel R. Garrett
Leo W. Goates
Darrel A. Harper
Howard F. Hatch
Grant E. Mann
James R. Palmer

Morris W. Parker
Jack R. Pearson
Raynal Pearson
Keith B. Romney
James K. Seastrand
Marc H. Sessions
James W. Sirles
Robert W. Smith

Melvin E. Tietjen

U.S. Army Chaplains

Lell O. Bagley
Earl S. Beecher
Leland H. Campbell
John R. Connell, Jr.
Ross L. Covington
Theodore E. Curtis, Jr.
Marvin R. Green
William H. Green, Jr.
Harlan Y. Hammond
Darrel A. Harper
Richard H. Henstrom

Timothy H. Irons
Spencer D. Madsen
Mark L. Money
Benjamin F. Mortensen
Spencer J. Palmer
Robert E. Parsons
Lawrence R. Rast
Russell C. Robertson
Kay A. Schwendimen
William C. Tanner, Jr.
Elmer W. Wahlstrom

U.S. Navy Chaplains

Paul R. Cheesman
Robert F. Gwilliam

Edward R. Gwynn
Herbert J. Marsh

Cornelius W. Nielsen

The LDS chaplains that served during this period had many personal experiences. The following accounts are only a few of them.

Danny Roberts:
A Memorable Group Leader

Sometimes a person enters one's life and leaves an unforgettable impression. Danny Roberts was just such a young man according to Chaplain Timothy Irons, who said, "Danny should be praised to the high heavens."[1]

Chaplain Timothy Irons spent one year in Korea with the 7th Infantry Division. In that division was a Mormon group leader by the name of Danny Roberts. Many group leaders served the Church in Korea, but Danny did things that set him apart from the others. For example, each Sunday, under all kinds of circumstances, he held LDS services. That doesn't sound unusual, but because of military tactical situations, sometimes no other Latter-day Saint attended. What did Danny do? Did he cancel the service? No, he didn't. He called the meeting to order precisely at the proper time. He presided and conducted. He sang the opening song, gave the opening prayer, and conducted the business as usual. During the sacrament he sang, blessed and passed. He concluded the service with a song and a benediction. He even submitted a report showing that one person attended. That's the type of person he was.

Tim described Danny as "just a really sweet kid." He loved everyone, and because of this, got deeply involved with the Koreans, and organized a group of them and held services for them. Nothing was too good for a service he conducted. Once, he called upon the chaplain of the 7th Division, a colonel, to come and speak to the Koreans. Imagine a private asking a colonel to speak. The chaplain came. Chaplains don't mind. They are ministers of God first and officers second. Shortly after he spoke, the commanding chaplain said to Chaplain Irons, "That Danny's quite a guy."

Tim agreed, "Chaplain, Danny is quite a guy."

Grant E. Mann:
Five Memorable Days with an Apostle

After World War II, an apostle went to Europe to aid the Saints and organize the European Mission. After the Korean War ended, another apostle, Harold B. Lee, traveled to the Far East to establish the Far East Mission. He stopped at Korea where he met with several LDS chaplains, including Grant E. Mann, who described some of the highlights of that meeting.[2]

During Elder Harold B. Lee's trip to Asia to organize the Far East Mission, he stopped in Korea and met with several LDS

---

1. Timothy H. Irons interview.
2. Personal interview with Grant E. Mann.

chaplains, Grant E. Mann, J. Spencer Palmer, Mark Money, and Richard Hendstrom. Those four Mormon chaplains had the opportunity to travel with the apostle for five days—a memorable experience.

Included on Elder Lee's agenda was an invitation to attend an LDS Conference at the 38th Parallel. However, a hitch developed in getting Elder Lee to the conference. Mother nature played havoc with the weather at an area known as K55 where the small group was located. No aircraft could get in or out. Time began to run out. They had to leave within two hours or Elder Lee would miss the conference. They prayed. Each and every one prayed that the weather would clear, and then something strange occurred. The weather cleared. The men boarded the aircraft, and made it to the conference. Chaplain Mann has had many choice experiences in his life, but that one must rank high on the list, an opportunity to pray with an apostle and see the prayer answered.

In addition to the chaplains' having some memorable experiences, Elder Lee had one when he flew in a helicopter. It was his first ride, and when he returned, he said, "That was great."

Brother Lee had a great sense of humor, and an ability of putting people at ease. He told the chaplains of a meeting he had with General Maxwell D. Taylor, the Far East Commander and Commander of the United Nations Forces. As they greeted one another, the General asked, "Mr. Lee, would you like a cup of coffee?"

"No thank you, General, Latter-day Saints don't drink coffee."

"Well, would you like a drink?"

"Mormons don't drink either."

Elder Lee noticed General Taylor getting a little uncomfortable. He didn't know what to say or offer him as his small courtesies had been refused. To put him at ease, Elder Lee said, "General, I'd like to tell you a little story about a young Mormon missionary from hay country in Idaho. This young man had hayed all his life and loved it. The Church sent him on a mission to the southern part of the United States, and during the hay season, he and his companion were walking down a road in a rural area when he spotted a farmer haying and pitching the hay into a truck. The elder said to his companion, 'I think we should help that farmer.'

"They went over and asked him if they might help. The farmer was grateful for their help and after an afternoon of hard work, the farmer turned to the young men and said, 'Come to the house, and I'll make you a nice brew.'

"One of the elders replied, 'We are Mormon missionaries and we don't drink.'

" 'How about a cup of coffee?' asked the farmer.

" 'We don't drink coffee either.'

"Puzzled, the farmer said in desperation, 'Then, what can I do for you?"

"The boy from Idaho said smiling, 'Can't we just suck some eggs together?' "

The General understood, and they struck up a fine relationship and discussed the Latter-day Saints serving in the Far East.

Each evening when the five of them gathered together, Elder Lee allowed them to ask him any questions they wished. They asked many, and he answered every one. He answered them very clearly using the scriptures to justify his answers. He urged them to do the same: "Men, use the scriptures. That is where you will find the answers to your questions."

One of the questions that Elder Lee answered was about the building of temples. He replied, "The Church would someday build temples in places all over the world so that they would be available to all the members of the Church. In some cases they will be small, but nevertheless, they will dot the earth wherever members of the Church are found.

That's the way it was for five days—five memorable days.

Timothy H. Irons:
Missionary Work in Korea

The Church of Jesus Christ of Latter-day Saints is a missionary Church. Its members are taught and encouraged to be missionaries. Its young men serve two years of a full time mission converting the peoples of the world. This missionary zeal extended to the military. Chaplain Timothy Irons recalls a group of military missionaries. [1]

During the Korean War, many young Latter-day Saint servicemen struck up fine relationships with the Koreans. The Koreans wanted to learn to speak English very badly, and a group of Mormons thought this would be a fine way to do missionary work. Chaplain Irons noticed the novel way they went about teaching the Koreans the gospel.

The men decided that they would use two text books to teach the Koreans to speak English. They chose *Principles of the Gospel*

---

1. Timothy H. Irons interview.

and *The Book of Mormon.* While other Koreans being taught to speak English were learning of George Washington, Thomas Jefferson, and Abraham Lincoln, the group being taught by the Mormons learned of Nephi, Alma and Moroni. They found that their innovative approach was an effective method of teaching the gospel and English also.

Sergeant Stewart:
A Very Courageous Latter-day Saint

Benjamin F. Mortensen, who served in Korea from 1952 to 1953, wrote the following true account. It appeared in The Instructor, March 1969. While serving in Korea, Chaplain (First Lieutenant) Mortensen received the Silver Star for gallantry, and, in addition, also received from the Republic of Korea the Chung Mu Medal for gallantry and meritorious service. The former chaplain presently works as a clinical psychologist at the Utah State Hospital in Provo, and also resides in Provo with his wife, Rene, and their six children. He is an active member of the LDS Church and currently serves as a member of the BYU 7th Stake high council.

I met him just once—at a sacrament meeting held with the LDS servicemen of the 15th Regiment, 3rd Infantry Division, during the Korean War. There were about 15 of us crowded into a front-line bunker. Using our own canteen cups and C-ration crackers, we blessed and partook of the sacrament; and since it was the first Sunday of the month, we then turned the time over to the bearing of testimonies.

He introduced himself simply as Sergeant Stewart from Idaho, and proceeded to tell us how the Lord had blessed him during the previous month. I noted that he was short—about 5' 5'' tall—and weighed around 160 pounds, with strong arms and shoulders. He mentioned that his great ambition since childhood had been to become a good athlete. Coaches had considered him small for team sports, so he had concentrated on individual competition and had gained some success as a wrestler and distance runner. He had arrived in Korea with the rank of private. Some ten months later he was wearing sergeant's stripes—and they were well-deserved, as we would soon discover.

As he bore his testimony, Sergeant Stewart was moved to tell us about his comapny commander, whom he described as a giant of a man named Lieutenant Jackson. He was 6' 7'' tall, weighed a hulking 245 pounds, and had been an outstanding college athlete.

The sergeant spoke of him in glowing, somewhat biased terms, as the bravest, sharpest, and greatest company commander in the entire U.S. Infantry—one who would not ask his men to do anything he would not first be willing to do himself. With noticeable pride he further depicted him as a man's man, a tremendous officer, and a Christian gentleman, inspiring those who were fortunate enough to serve under his command.

A few days prior to our church service Sergeant Stewart had been assigned to a patrol. Leading and at the point of the patrol was Lieutenant Jackson. Bringing up the rear, as they moved down the steep hill in diamond formation, was the sergeant. As they neared the base of the hill, they were ambushed by enemy snipers. The lieutenant, being out in front, was riddled up one side by automatic small-arms fire. As he fell he managed to drag himself to the shelter of a nearby rock and tree, while the rest of the patrol scrambled up the hill to regroup.

Since he was next in command, the responsibility of the patrol now fell upon the shoulders of Sergeant Stewart. He immediately formed his men into a half-moon perimeter defense and then assigned his largest and seemingly strongest man the mission of going down the hill to rescue the lieutenant. The others would provide him with cover.

The man was gone for approximately half an hour, only to return and report that he could not budge the wounded officer—he was too heavy. It was like trying to lift a dead horse. The men started grumbling about getting out of there before someone else got hit. Someone was heard to say, "Let's forget about the lieutenant; after all, he's just a nigger!" At this point Sergeant Stewart turned to his men, and pulling himself up to his full 65-inch stature he spoke in very matter-of-fact tones: "I don't care if he's black or green or any other color. We're not leaving without him. He wouldn't leave any of us in similar circumstances. Besides, he's our commanding officer and I love him like my own brother."

There was a moment of silence, and then the sergeant approached one of the corporals and said quietly but with great authority, "You take charge—and wait for us, I will bring him back."

Carefully, and as noiselessly as possible, he inched his way among sporadic sniper fire toward the lieutenant. When he finally reached him, Lieutenant Jackson was weak from loss of blood, and he assured the sergeant that it was a hopeless cause—there would be no way to get him back to the aid station in time. It was then that Sergeant Stewart's great faith in his Heavenly Father came to his assistance. He took off his helmet, knelt beside his fallen leader and said, "Pray with me, Lieutenant."

We were held spellbound in that meeting. It was as though we were witnessing one of the great human dramas of our day. A spiritual drama of love and brotherhood, so lacking in today's world, was unfolding before our very eyes. Tears rolled down the sergeant's cheeks as he spoke—and we wept silently with him. He couldn't remember all he had said in his prayer, but he recalled reminding the Lord that never in his life had he smoked a cigarette. Not once had he tasted alcohol in any of its forms.

At this point he digressed for a moment to explain that he had abstained from liquor and tobacco not only because it was his religious belief, but also because of his great motivation to develop a strong, healthy body in order to achieve his athletic aspirations. That day, however, as he communed with his Father in heaven, he knew without doubt why he had lived the Word of Wisdom so conscientiously throughout his young life.

"Dear Lord," he pleaded, "I need strength—far beyond the capacity of my physical body. This great man, thy son, who lies critically wounded here beside me, must have medical attention soon. I need the power to carry him up this hill to an aid station where he can receive the treatment he needs to preserve his life. I know, Father, that thou hast promised the strength of ten to him whose heart and hands are clean and pure. I feel I can qualify. Please, Dear Lord, grant me this blessing."

"Brethren," he continued, "as I prayed I could feel my muscles bulge with energy, and I knew at that moment, as I had never known before, that God truly hears and answers the prayers of his faithful children. I humbly thanked him, said amen, put on my helmet, reached down and gently picked up my company commander and cradled him over my shoulder. We then started slowly our ascent up the hill—Lieutenant Jackson crying softly as he whispered to me words of gratitude and encouragement."

I met Sergeant Stewart just once. For less than two hours it was our privilege to be in his company. I could feel the presence of greatness as I sat in that bunker listening to that choice young man. His spirit touched my spirit, and my faith was kindled because of his Christlike attitude and his soul-stirring testimony regarding the Fatherhood of God and the brotherhood of all men.

Timothy H. Irons:
The First Berchtesgaden Conference

One of the great events in Europe for LDS servicemen is the Berchtesgaden Conference, a conference where all the Mormons from all over Europe meet with one another. The following account by Timothy H. Irons explains how the conference began.

Chaplain Ed Curtley, one of the leading army chaplains in Europe, and a member of the Disciples of Christ, wanted to provide religious retreats for those Protestants in Europe who wished to attend. He asked Chaplain Timothy Irons, a member of the LDS Church, if the Mormon Church would be interested in participating. Chaplain Irons had the vision to see it as a great opportunity for all the Mormon servicemen in Europe to meet and partake of each other's spirits. "I think it's a fabulous idea, but I can't speak for my Church. I have to get approval from the Mission President. I will check with him and let you know.

The Mormon chaplain paid a visit to Kenneth Dyer, the European Mission President, to discuss the matter. President Dyer agreed with him that it would be a very worthwhile venture to bring together the Latter-day Saint servicemen scattered throughout Europe.

Chaplain Irons contacted Chaplain Curtley and said, "Chaplain, It's been approved. The Mission President is behind the program and we'd like to know when we can get started so we can begin planning."

"You can start right away. By the way, how many men do you think will attend?"

"I think we will have about 2,000 men and women in attendance."

"That figure sounds unrealistic, but if any group can get that many to participate, it's you Mormons."

"I don't think we'll have any problem. Mormons love to attend meetings like these. Believe me, just about every Mormon serviceman in Europe will be there."

"O.K., Chaplain, but with that large of a group we'll have to find an area that can hold that many people."

The resort town of Berchtesgaden, Germany was chosen. The time selected was during their off season. Berchtesgaden was a great summer and winter resort area located in the Bavarian Alps of southern Germany, and, in the Fall of 1954, the first conference was held. Even Chaplain Irons was surprised at the great number of members in attendance. The military cooperated by providing transportation to bring Church members to the conference from all over Europe. In a very short time, all available housing was taken by the Latter-day Saints.

In the meantime, the army which ran the hotels knew that a group of 2,000 American servicemen were coming to town for a few days and they loaded up with cases and cases of beer. But when the Saints arrived they were quite surprised to learn that no one drank beer or any other alcoholic beverage. The Mormons requested milk and hundreds of gallons was needed to satisfy their demands. This caused the army some upheaval—they had to scour the area for enough milk. That was one of the highlights of the first European conferences at Berchtesgaden.

The army never again stocked up on beer when the Mormons moved in for their conference. They did insure, however, that enough milk was available.

The conference has become one of the highlights of Mormon servicemen stationed in Europe. The conference continues to be a source of great fellowshipping and one of inspiration.

*   *   *   *

The Korean War ended and peace prevailed once again, but not for long. Within a decade, the United States became involved in another war, in southeast Asia, in a small country known as Vietnam.

Most of the Mormon chaplains that had served during the Korean War had been released from the military, and during the period of peace, the Chief of Chaplains in Washington, D.C. changed the eligibility requirements, which eliminated most Mormons from being appointed to the chaplaincy, because of the Church's lay priesthood approach to Church positions. Few, if any, could meet the requirements, and during the years 1958-1965, not a single member of The Church of Jesus Christ of Latter-day Saints was appointed. This situation caused concern within the Church and its Military Relations Committee. After all, many Latter-day Saints served in the military, and Church leaders felt it only fair that the Church have a proportional number of Latter-day Saints serving as chaplains. But it was not to be, as the position of the Chief of Chaplains remained rigid.

The Military Relations Committee took another approach. In 1965, a group of Mormon Congressmen approached the president of the United States, Lyndon Baines Johnson. When President Johnson asked how President David O. McKay was, one of the members of the group responded that President McKay would like nothing better than to have Mormons serve their country in the capacity of chaplains. The president of the U.S. was informed of the rigid requirements that prevented this, and asked if he could do something to alter the requirements of members of a lay church. Because of that request, President Lyndon Baines Johnson interceded in behalf of the Mormons, and within a very short period, members of the Mormon Church were able to meet the eligibility requirements. Incidently, this happened just in time for the Vietnam War.

As in previous wars World War I, World War II, and the Korean War—the new group of Mormon chaplains once again served their country valiantly in Vietnam, and other parts of the world. The members of the Mormon Church who served as a military during the Southeast Asia period are contained in the following list.[1]

Mormon Chaplains

That Served During the

South East Asia Period (1960-1976)

U.S. Air Force Chaplains

Joseph F. Boone	Richard J. Hawkins
Barry H. Bright	J. Kent Larkin
Adam S. Brown	J. Kent Millington
Dale R. Carver	Jan H. Nelson
Robert L. Christiansen	Val J. Neuenswander
Robert R. Cordner	G. Barry Nielsen
Philliph M. Eyring	Ralph R. Nielsen
Crozier K. Fitzgerald	Russell L. Osmund
Leo W. Goates	James R. Palmer
David E. Goff	Morris W. Parker
Peter M. Hansen	John B. Probst
Darrel A. Harper	Alexander Roberts
Howard F. Hatch	James W. Sirles

Farrell M. Smith

---

1. Joseph F. Boone's Ph.D. dissertation.

U.S. Army Chaplains

D. Brent Anderson	Donald G. Hanchett
Terry R. Baker	Don G. Hess
Mark F. Breinholt	Brent H. Holmes
Norman K. Bryner	Timothy H. Irons
Cline G. Campbell	Wayne E. Kuehne
A Marius Christensen	Calvin S. Kunz
Douglas C. Christensen	Spencer D. Madsen
John H. Cooper	Joseph F. McConkie
Michael G. Curzon	Claude D. Newby
Arnold T. Ellsworth	Frederic G. Peterson
H. Lynn Galbraith	Lawrence R. Rast
Garry B. Green	Frank D. Richardson
Marvin R. Green	Kenneth S. Smith
William H. Green, Jr.	George B. Young
Blaine D. Hall	Richard H. Whaley

U.S. Navy Chaplains

Earl L. Cardon	Preston N. Kearsley
Merlin H. Cluff	Thomas R. Pocock
Joel R. Fletcher	David E. Smith
N. Vernon Griffeth	Lloyd M Taggart

Richard F. Wood

During the year 1976, the United States celebrates its Bi-Centennial and finds itself at peace, but for how long? Will the words of Mark E. Peterson continue to ring true: "Rest assured that there'll be wars and we'll have chaplains in wars." Let's hope not, but if we do, one thing that the military can be assured of and that is the Mormon Church will provide a group of Latter-day Saints who will pick up the gauntlet and serve their country and their God once again, the Mormon Chaplains.

Appendix

Table III

Mormon Chaplains That Served
During World War II (1941-1946)

Name	Date of Appointment	Branch of Service
C. Clarence Neslen	5-11-26	U.S. Army
Theodore E. Curtis	7-1-28	U.S. Army
George R. Woolley	12-13-28	U.S. Army
Reuben E. Curtis	4-9-29	U.S. Army
Reed G. Probst	4-26-34	U.S. Army
Robert G. Gibbons	6-4-36	U.S. Army
Howard C. Evans	5-3-40	U.S. Army
Orlando S. McBride	8-31-40	U.S. Army
Milton G. Widdison	4-14-41	U.S. Army
Leo F. Freeman	5-16-41	U.S. Army
John W. Boud	7-6-41	U.S.N.R.
Milton John Hess	3-10-42	U.S.N.R.
Glen Young Richards	9-10-42	U.S.N.R.
Anthon Gifford Jackson	10-23-42	U.S.N.R.
Vernon A. Cooley	2-9-43	U.S. Army
Eldin Ricks	2-23-43	U.S. Army
Gerald L. Ericksen	3-43	U.S. Army
Rex L. Christensen	6-9-43	U.S.N.R.
Marc H. Sessions	8-7-43	U.S. Army
Hyrum A Hendrickson	8-9-43	U.S. Army
Marsden Durham	10-13-43	U.S. Army
Lee W. Dalebout	10-28-43	U.S. Army
Grant E. Mann	2-19-44	U.S. Army
Jack B. Watkins	3-6-44	U.S.N.R.
Howard C. Badger	3-22-44	U.S. Army
John W. Fitzgerald	3-22-44	U.S. Army
John B. Christensen	4-10-44	U.S. Army
Samuel G. Ellsworth	4-14-44	U.S. Army
Ray L. Jones	5-1-44	U.S. Army
Lyman C. Berrett	5-10-44	U.S. Army
Wilford E. Smith	6-28-44	U.S. Army
Eugene E. Campbell	7-6-44	U.S. Army

Name	Date of Appointment	Branch of Service
Timothy H. Irons	7-6-44	U.S. Army
Leon H. Flint	7-21-44	U.S. Army
Roy M. Darley	10-21-44	U.S. Army
Elbert R. Simmons	11-20-44	U.S.N.R.
Vadal W. Peterson	12-26-44	U.S. Army
Warren R. Nelson	2-1-45	U.S. Army
Albert O Mitchell	2-8-45	U.S. Army
Geroge R. Rowley	3-7-45	U.S. Army
Briant G. Badger	3-20-45	U.S.N.R.
Royden C. Braithwaite	4-6-45	U.S. Army
Wendall O. Rich	4-30-45	U.S. Army
Robert A. Nelson	7-30-45	U.S. Army
Delbert Barney	8-23-46	U.S. Army

Index

F

G